CATCH FISH NOW!

on

Florida's West Coast

by
Mike Babbidge

Disclaimer

The Florida and Federal fishing regulations summarized in the Appendix are subject to change at any time. Currently applicable bag limits are particularly dynamic in nature. Accordingly, the reader should stay tuned to developments to ensure full compliance with the law.

The LORAN coordinates contained in this book are uncorrected for plotting on navigational charts. Also, due to the varying reporting approaches used by local artificial reef programs, there is no guarantee that the numbers provided correspond to the center of the deployed material. Finally, latitude and longitude coordinates are listed in degrees/minutes/hundredths of minutes. These numbers were provided for the most part by local sources. In some cases, conversions to 'hundredth of a minute' were converted from reported degrees/minutes/seconds as nautical charts depict latitude/longitude or 'hundredths of a second' format provided by local GPS users. If latitude and/or longitude are followed by a "c," the coordinate(s) are for the geographic center of the permitted site.

Most of the pictures in Chapters 2-5 were either taken by the author or downloaded from the Internet from sources that were verifiably in the public domain. The few remaining photos were obtained from miscellaneous second and third hand sources. Conscientious efforts were made to determine the origin and/or proprietary status of each of these. Although a conclusive determination was not possible in every case, selected pictures in this category were used -- but only if they reflected favorably on the area being described.

Published by

BABBIDGE & CO.
FISHING, WRITING, & PUBLISHING

MIKE BABBIDGE   *Ph 850-302-0630*
848 Tropic Avenue   *Fax 850-302-0631*
Ft. Walton Beach, FL 32548 *E-mail BABBCO@gnt.net*

Design Layout and Pre-publication Preparation by

Old South Books
Vivian Wandling, Owner
Shalimar, FL
850-651-0709

Printed in the United States of America

CATCH FISH NOW!
on
Florida's West Coast

Table of Contents

List of Figures

If you wish to be happy
for one hour
get intoxicated.

If you wish to be happy
for three days,
get married.

If you wish to be happy
for eight days,
kill your pig and eat it.

If you wish to be happy
forever,
learn to fish.

Ancient Chinese Proverb

CHAPTER 1

ANGLING OVERVIEW
OF FLORIDA'S WEST COAST

This is the second in a planned five book series of geographically oriented "how-to" books on Florida saltwater sportfishing. Book 1 covers the Panhandle of Florida. Books 3 - 5 address the 10,000 Islands/Keys, the Southeast, and the Northeast parts of the state.

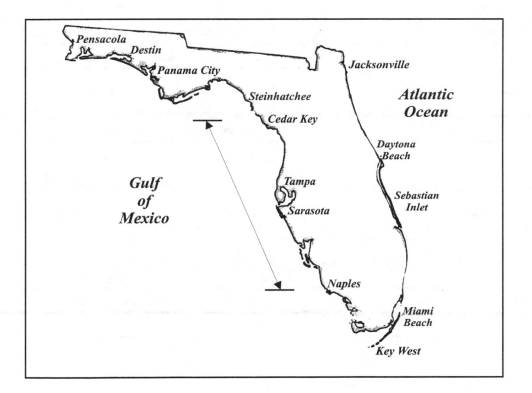

Figure 1.0 - CATCH FISH NOW! *on Florida's West Coast*

CATCH FISH NOW! *on Florida's West Coast* covers the 300 mile stretch of coastline highlighted above. The book is designed to give you the information you need for immediate fishing success in West Coast waters. In the process, it answers the following questions:

• When, where, and what kinds of fish are biting?
• How do I rig up and what kind of bait do I use to catch them?

As you'll see, **CATCH FISH NOW!** provides an abundance of "how-to" information and "hot tips" that will give you an edge - - on the catching part of fishing. The book is easy to use. Read Chapters 2 - 5 to decide when and where you want to fish. Then, read Chapter 6 to find out how to **CATCH FISH NOW!** And that's all there is to it.

Possibilities	Best Time To Try
Amberjack	Available year round
Barracuda	Available year round - Spring/Summer
Black Drum	Available year round - Summer/Early Fall
Black Sea Bass	Available year round
Blackfin Tuna	Available year round - Summer
Bluefish	Available year round
Blue Marlin	Late Summer/Early Fall
Bonito	Available year round
Cobia	Migratory - Spring/Summer/Fall
Dolphin	Late Spring through early Fall
Flounder	Available year round - Late Summer/Fall
Grouper	Available year round
Jack Cravalle	Available year round
King Mackerel	Migratory - Spring and Fall
Permit	Available year round - Spring/Summer
Pompano	Available year round - Spring/Summer
Redfish	Available year round
Sailfish	Summer/Fall
Sheepshead	Available year round - Winter
Snapper	Available year round
Snook*	Available year round
Spanish Mackerel	Migratory - Spring/Summer/Fall
Swordfish	Late Summer
Tarpon	Migratory - Spring/Summer
Triggerfish	Available year round
Tripletail	Available year round - Summer/Fall
Trout*	Available year round

Possibilities	Best Time To Try
Wahoo	Probably available year round - Summer
White Marlin	Summer
Whiting	Available year round
Yellowfin Tuna	Spring/Fall
* Subject to closed season. Catch and release OK. Please see Appendix for dates.	

Figure 1.1 - West Coast Gamefish Availability Summary

Figure 1.1 begins to put this story in perspective. Saltwater sportfishing on Florida's West Coast is a big deal. There really are over 30 gamefish or families of gamefish available. And many or most of these can be caught year round somewhere in West Coast waters.

The data in the summary were synthesized from the fishing reports published in West Coast newspapers and other publications over the last several years. The information in the reports usually comes from area bait and tackle stores, marinas, lodges and landings. But it is historical in nature. And although it provides useful long-range planning insights, it cannot tell you what happened yesterday or what might happen today. Fortunately, there are a number of other sources of current fishing information readily available to West Coast fishermen. Here are some of the best.

- **Area Newspapers**. Most of the regional and local papers have regular fishing reports. Some of these also publish superb weekly fishing features by noted outdoors experts.
- **Area Bait and Tackle Stores**. All of these are usually excellent sources of current fishing information.
- **Fishing Boat Docks**. Another way to find out what's biting is to visit the docks where the party and charter boats come in from their daily trips. Return times vary for these boats, but the half-day trips usually start returning to port between 11 a.m. and noon and all-day trips between 4 and 5 p.m.
- **VHF Radio**. A final very timely way to determine local fishing activity is to monitor a VHF radio. Almost all boats now rely on VHF radio for boat-to-boat and boat-to-shore communication, so listening to the almost continuous traffic can provide very current information. A number of different frequencies are usually in use, but channel 68 is a good place to start your monitoring. According to the Federal Communications Commission, other channels of interest might include: Emergency - #16; other recreational boater channels - #'s 9, 69, 71, 72, and 78; working channels for commercial boats only - #'s 1, 7, 8, 9, 10, 11, 18, 19, 63, 67, 79, 80, and 88; and marine operator - #'s 24-28, 84, 85, 86, and 87.

So, OK, so much for what's happening. Now the question is - - where's the action?

Clearwater to Palmetto

Bradenton to Englewood

Cedar Key to Dunedin

Port Charlotte to Sarasota

Florida's West Coast

Bays	Surf	Piers	Inshore	Offshore
Black Drum	Bluefish	Black Drum	Barracuda	Amberjack
Black Sea Bass	Flounder	Bluefish	Black Drum	Blackfin Tuna
Bluefish	Jack Cravalle	Bonito	Black Sea Bass	Blue Marlin
Cobia	Pompano	Cobia	Blackfin Tuna	Bonito
Flounder	Redfish	Flounder	Bluefish	Cobia
Grouper	Sheepshead	Grouper	Bonito	Dolphin
Jack Cravalle	Snook	Jack Cravalle	Cobia	Grouper
King Mackerel	Spanish Mackerel	Permit	Flounder	King Mackerel
Permit	Tarpon	Pompano	Grouper	Sailfish
Pompano	Trout	Redfish	Jack Cravalle	Sheepshead
Redfish	Whiting	Snapper	King Mackerel	Snapper
Sheepshead		Snook	Permit	Swordfish
Snapper		Spanish Mackerel	Redfish	Triggerfish
Snook		Tarpon	Sheepshead	Wahoo
Spanish Mackerel		Tripletail	Snapper	White Marlin
Tarpon		Trout	Snook	Yellowfin Tuna
Tripletail		Whiting	Spanish Mackerel	
Trout			Tarpon	
Whiting			Triggerfish	
			Tripletail	
			Trout	
			Whiting	

Figure 1.2 - Where the West Coast Fish Are

The diversity of fishing opportunities in West Coast waters is equally impressive. Figure 1.2 highlights the point. In fact, there are only a few species that can't be caught in more than one place, fishing in more than one way. For example, King Mackerel can be caught off area piers and in some area bays, if it's too rough to get out in the Gulf for some small boat, Inshore trolling. Flounder provide another good example. At several times during the year, these fish may be caught Inshore by bottom fishing on structure, drifting or anchored in a bay, off one of the area's piers, and more often than not, in the surf. Keep in mind, however, that the matrix is a generalization. The fish shown for each venue are only the most commonly caught species. Now and then, other species show up for surprise visits. Sailfish have been hooked and landed from area piers. Cobia and King Mackerel are both caught in some of the bays in the area. And Grouper can be caught with some consistency in all area bays if you know where to fish. But, in every case, these can be exceptions to what a fisherman should expect. Another important point is that both Figure 1.1 and 1.2 only address what are usually considered gamefish. There are other species available that are fun to catch and, in some cases, good to eat, too. Sharks, Sailcats, Ladyfish, Pinfish, Grunts, and a variety of Jacks fall into this category. They, too, can be caught with regularity in West Coast waters.

Now, with the generalities out of the way, it's time to get serious. The fish are out there waiting - - for you! So, if things go according to plan, this book will help you - - **CATCH FISH NOW!**

Presentation Format	Florida's West Coast			
	Cedar Key to Dunedin	Clearwater to Palmetto	Bradenton to Englewood	Port Charlotte to Naples
Annual Fishing Summary	✔	✔	✔	✔
Monthly Catch Data	✔	✔	✔	✔
Bays	COMBINED	✔	✔	✔
Surf		✔	✔	✔
Piers		✔	✔	✔
Inshore		✔	✔	✔
Offshore	✔	✔	✔	✔
-----CATCH FISH NOW!-----				
*Rigging *Proven Tactics *Your Winning Edge		*Natural Baits *Artificial Lures *Tackle Suggestions		

Figure 1.3 Overview - CATCH FISH NOW! *on Florida's West Coast*

Chapters 2 - 5 will present a geographically oriented trip down the West Coast, starting in Cedar Key and finishing up in Naples. The only break in our standard presentation format will be in Chapter 2 because, as you'll see, it describes a very unique stretch of coastline. After we've talked about when and where to fish, we'll finish up in Chapter 6 with how to get the job done. A summary of relevant state and federal fishing regulations closes out our discussion. Let's go fishing! Next stop - - when and where to do it.

-- PERSONAL NOTES --

CHAPTER 2

CEDAR KEY TO DUNEDIN

The northernmost portion of the Florida West Coast is unique in several respects. For one, it is almost estuarial in nature - - even many miles Offshore. As a result, it includes a significant number of shallow bays, keys, passes, islands, and lots of rivers and creeks. For another, and with only a few notable exceptions, it essentially has no surf in the traditional sense. What much of it does have, however, is endless salt marsh woven with miles of tidal creeks, emptying into shallow grass flats laced with limestone outcroppings and oyster bars. Near shore, waters deepen very gradually, only about two feet per mile as you move farther Offshore. By any standard, the result is some very interesting fishing and boating challenges.

Figure 2.0 - Cedar Key to Dunedin

Two specific topographical features characterize this stretch of coastline. First, the Hudson area is a major habitat break on the Gulf shoreline. South of Hudson, there are white sand beaches like much of the rest of Florida. To the north, however, the shoreline becomes almost a continuous, broad, shallow area of marsh. Just Offshore, shallow grass flats extend from the Anclote Keys more than 100 miles north. Second, and unlike the mostly sandy bottom to the south, a shallow water rock bottom stretches from the same Keys all the way north to Chassahowitzka Pt. Obviously, the combination of all this marsh, grass, and rock makes this whole area very fishy indeed.

As noted in Chapter 1's overview, we're going to talk about this segment of the coast just a tad differently than subsequent segments. Instead of individual Bay, Surf, Pier, and Inshore coverages, they'll be lumped together - - because they're really one and the same topographically. We're basically talking small boat fishing - - whether it's up an area river or up to 10 miles or so Offshore. To get things started, let's review the kinds of fish available to be caught and when the best time to get them is . . .

Possibilities	Best Time To Try
Amberjack	Available year round - August/September
Barracuda	Summer months
Black Drum	Available year round - Summer
Black Sea Bass	Available year round - January/February
Bluefish	Available year round - Summer/Fall
Bonito	Available year round
Cobia	Migratory - Late Spring/Summer/Early Fall
Dolphin	Summer
Flounder	Available year round - Fall
Grouper	Available year round - Fall/Winter
Jack Cravalle	Available year round
King Mackerel	Migratory - Late Spring through Fall
Permit	Winter - Power plant discharge channels
Pompano	Winter - Power plant discharge channels
Redfish	Available year round
Sheepshead	Available year round - Winter
Snapper	Available year round - Summer
Snook*	Spring/Summer/Fall
Spanish Mackerel	Migratory - Spring/Summer/Fall
Tarpon	Migratory - Late Spring/early Summer
Triggerfish	Available year round
Tripletail	Late Spring through early Fall
Trout*	Available year round
Whiting	Winter

* Subject to closed season. Catch and release OK. Please see Appendix for dates.

Figure 2.1 - Gamefish Availability

Only a couple of words of explanation are needed about figure 2.1. Specifically, if there isn't a qualifier after a "Best Time to Try" recommendation, that means the whole period is good. Redfish are an example of this. On the other hand, if there is a qualifier, it simply indicates the very best time within a particular period. Mr. Amberjack can help us here. You can catch him every month of the year. But he seems to be the most hungry and aggressive in August and September.

OK, with that top level summary in mind, let's take a look at fishing action on a month-to-month basis. The following narrative is only supposed to give you a feel for what typically goes on between Cedar Key and Dunedin. It is certainly not all inclusive.

January
- Bonito, Triggerfish, Black Sea Bass, and Amberjack available on and over Offshore structure as close as 4 - 9 miles out.
- Almost all Speckled Trout and Reds are in the creeks and rivers. Black Drum too.
- Whiting biting well in Inshore deep cuts.
- Sheepshead are everywhere around artificial reefs and Offshore channel markers.
- Some Trout in the Suwannee's East and West Passes.
- Great sight fishing for Reds in the St. Martins Keys area off Homosassa.
- Small Snappers widely scattered in area rivers and canals north of the Anclote River.
- Trout, Pompano, Permit, Bluefish, and Jack Cravalle in the Anclote power plant outfall canal.
- Grouper off Weeki Wachee in 50 feet of water and on patch reefs off Tarpon Springs.

February
- Rocky tidal creeks are full of Reds and Sheepshead.
- Grouper, Triggerfish, and Sea Bass in deep water (85') on structure.
- Bonito are scattered Offshore.
- Spawning Sheepshead on Offshore reefs and around navigation markers. They're also active in the Anclote River.
- Some Trout still way up area rivers.
- Spanish Mackerel starting to show off Crystal River and Homosassa.
- Anclote Power Plant hot water producing big Specs, Pompano, Permit, and Bluefish.
- Reds on flats with natural springs and around the Crystal Beach spoil banks. Pompano also around these banks.
- Homosassa flats loaded with Specs.

March
- Spanish starting to show off Weeki Wachee in 35 feet and off the Seahorse Reef farther north.
- Trout moving on the grassbeds around markers two and four of the Homosassa channel and at White Shell Bar at Suwannee.

- Grouper starting to get active in 50 - 60 feet of water.
- A few Kings entering the area from the south off Dunedin.
- Sheepshead still thick on Offshore artificial reefs out from Crystal River and Cedar Key. Sea Bass and Triggers, too.
- Bluefish in the "muds" off Homosassa along with Trout, Jack Cravalle, and Ladyfish.
- Cobia riding the backs of stingrays on New Port Richey flats.
- Trout either in tidal creeks or cuts in bars depending on the weather.
- Scattered Snook and legal Snapper cooperating in Gulf Harbor's canals.
- Big Specs still possible around Anclote Power Plant.
- Around New Port Richey, Snook getting active in creeks, canals, channels, springs and dredge holes.

April
- Spanish on Seahorse Reef off Cedar Key and Spotty Bottom off Suwannee.
- Trout, Reds, and Spanish at the "Seven Brothers" and #4 marker off Homosassa.
- Bluefish thick around Hedemon Reef.
- Kings and Jack Cravalle over deep grass beds and hard bottom areas.
- Reds, Black Drum, Flounder, and Sheepshead still in area creeks.
- Grouper on relatively close-in rocks off Tarpon Springs in 30 - 40 feet.
- Cobia starting to show at Offshore spots like the Whistle Buoy and Steel Tower.
- Big Snook, Reds, and Specs showing well in Pasco County creeks and rivers.
- AJ's and big Groupers in 85 feet of water off Port Richey.
- Kings in 35 feet of water off Anclote Key.
- Snook on the flats near the same key.
- Homosassa flats filling with early arriving Tarpon.

May
- Kings in the Kingfish Hole north of Seahorse Reef.
- Big Cobia on Offshore channel markers and on the flats farther south.
- Tripletail on the Inshore channel markers in the Waccasassa Bombing Range.
- Sand Trout thick in the Suwannee, Cedar Key, and Steinhatchee areas.
- Reds and Specs on area grass flats and particularly good between Suwannee and Horseshoe.
- Tarpon in Waccasassa Bay, northwest channel of Cedar Key off North Key, Suwannee's Ranch Bar Gap, and the river's East Pass.
- AJ's and Barracuda on the White City Bridge Offshore.
- Kings off Tarpon Springs on spoons and planers in 35 - 50 feet of water.
- Snook are starting to cooperate around the mouth of the Anclote River.
- Grouper and bigger Kings in 50 feet of water off Weeki Wachee.

June

- Reds and Trout on the grass flats and feeding heavily.
- Cobia off Crystal River and Homosassa and on Pasco County flats.
- Groupers on rocky reefs in 35 - 50 feet of water in the north and 65 - 70 feet farther south.
- AJ's on the White City Bridge reef off Suwannee.
- Spanish on the Spotty Bottom area off Suwannee.
- Tripletail on area channel markers.
- A few Dolphin, Barracuda, and isolated Sailfish available Offshore from Bayonet Point.
- Black Sea Bass and King Mackerel around the Kingfish Hole.
- Jack Cravalle and Cobia around the Steel Tower off Cedar Key.
- Tarpon in the deepwater of the Suwannee River's Alligator Pass and on the flats off Weeki Wachee.
- Sailfish and Wahoo in 100+ feet of water Offshore.
- Snook still active in Weeki Wachee Inshore waters.

July

- Specs on deep grass beds (8 - 20 feet) and shallow grass flats and oyster bars.
- A few smoker Kings well Offshore (85 feet of water off Tarpon Springs).
- Tarpon widely scattered.
- Spanish on the Offshore reefs, particularly Seahorse off Cedar Key.
- Cobia and Tripletail on many channel markers.
- Grouper, Triggerfish, and Black Sea Bass on Offshore reefs.
- Giant Black Drum at Cedar Key (Pelican Reef off #4 channel marker) and the area between Lone Cabbage Reef and Suwannee Reef.
- Reds on oyster bars.
- Snook around the spoils islands off the Anclote River channel, along adjacent beaches, and in the passes around Anclote Key.
- Barracuda abundant on Pasco County Offshore reefs and wrecks.
- Flounder in the channel off the north end of Anclote Key, and schools of Reds on the flats on both sides of the mouth of the Anclote River.

August

- Kings starting to show well on their way south in 50 - 65 feet of water.
- Offshore Reds on Spotty Bottom.
- Trout on Offshore deep (20 feet) grass beds. Seahorse Reef very productive for Specs.
- Grouper well Offshore. Anchored boats draw Cobia, AJ's and Barracuda.
- Spanish thick off both ends of Anclote Key and 1 - 2 miles off its beaches.
- Some Triggerfish in 40 feet of water.
- Dolphin, Barracuda, and AJ's on the White City Bridge.
- Flounder and Snapper around the mouths of channels and in area canals.

September
- Kings reappearing in the Kingfish Hole, Spotty Bottom, and the Bombing Range.
- Cobia and Tripletail still on channel markers and other navigational aids.
- Grouper on deep water structure.
- Dolphin on patches of floating grass Offshore.
- Spanish and Kings off Anclote Key.
- Grouper off Hudson in 35 - 40 feet of water.
- Snook fishing great in Pasco County deep water holes and channels.
- Redfish on area shallow flats and along mangrove lines.
- Trout fishing steady over grass flats in 3 - 4 feet of water.

October
- Kings and big Spanish still cooperating across the area in 30 - 45 feet of water.
- Reds widely scattered and hungry.
- Big Cobia on Tarpon Reef south of Tarpon Springs.
- At the mouth of the Anclote River, Snook, Trout, and Jack Cravalle are eager.
- Grouper very active in 30 - 35 feet of water off Tarpon Springs.
- Trout and schools of Jack Cravalle on the flats at the mouth of the Anclote River.
- Snook working up the Anclote River.
- Grouper getting serious in 20 feet of water off Weeki Wachee.

November
- Kings in the Kingfish Hole off Cedar Key and south off Pasco County.
- Trout and Reds working up creeks and rivers.
- Grouper in shallow water (20 - 30 feet) on the rocks southwest of Big Bend Marker 12 and Old Barge Canal markers out from Crystal River.
- Schools of Bonito Offshore chasing bait.
- Jumbo Spanish still thick in the Tarpon Springs area on deep flats.
- Pompano, Permit, Specs, Reds, and Snook cooperating in the Anclote Power Plant outfall canal.
- Pasco County canals producing some big Trout, Reds, Snapper, Sheepshead, and a few Snook.

December
- Reds thick south of Steinhatchee River in Porpoise and Rocky Creeks and rocky bars at creek mouths.
- Specs loaded up in the Suwannee River's McGriff Channel, Alligator and East Passes, and connecting waterways.
- Grouper, Triggers and Black Sea Bass on the Old Grouper Grounds northwest of Cedar Key in 30 - 45 feet of water.

- Big Sheepshead off Cedar Key on channel markers and reefs and Crystal River on rocks in 10 - 15 feet of water.
- Redfish and Trout on shallow oyster bars in the Anclote River and in Signal Cove canals.
- Snook are up Pasco County rivers around warm water springs.

About five years of data were synthesized to compile this monthly narrative. Again, it's not a current fishing report. But it does provide some useful insights into year round fishing action between Cedar Key and Dunedin. Now we'll focus on more specific spots and areas that have a demonstrated record of producing fish. We will begin with a look at Inshore opportunities, including area rivers and power plants. After finishing that up, we'll head Offshore.

INSHORE

To get this discussion going, Figure 2.2 highlights those area parks, boat ramps, and piers of interest to the fisherman. Public, rather than commercial, facilities have been emphasized to the extent possible.

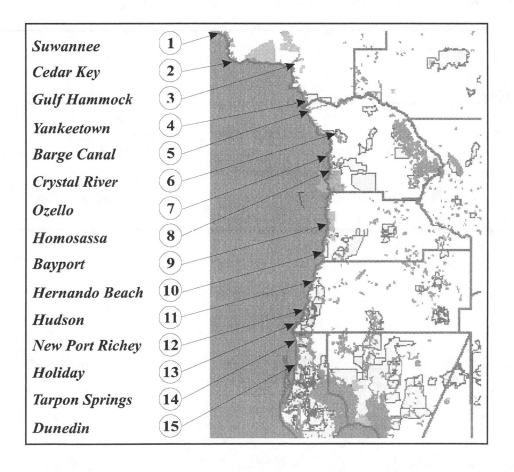

Figure 2.2 - Parks/Boat Ramps/Piers - Cedar Key to Dunedin

(1) Suwannee - There are several boat ramps and/or marinas in town.

(2) Cedar Key - City park, boat ramps ($5 honor system), and fishable seawall/dock downtown. Fishing pier and boat ramp SW side of Hwy 24 bridge into town.

(3) Gulf Hammock - Go west of town to the end of Hwy 326. There's a boat ramp on the Waccasassa River that permits access to Waccasassa Bay.

(4) Yankeetown - There are several boat ramps along the Withlacoochee River and at the end of Hwy 40.

(5) Barge Canal - Boat ramp at the Hwy 19 bridge over the canal. Access to the canal and the Gulf.

(6) Crystal River Area off Hwy 19: 1) Pete's Pier - West on SE Kings Bay Dr to SW1 Place. Boat ramps and docks. Access to Kings Bay, Crystal River, and the Gulf; 2) Ft. Island Gulf Beach - End of Hwy 44. Boat ramp and docks. Shore fishing. Access to the Gulf and Crystal River; and 3) Ft. Island Trail Park - Also on Hwy 44. Boat ramps, docks, and superb fishing pier. Shore fishing. Access to Crystal and Salt Rivers and the Gulf.

(7) Ozello Community Park - End of Hwy 494. Boat ramp and shore fishing. Gulf access. Fishing pier close by.

(8) Homosassa Area: 1) Public boat ramps at the end of Hwy 490; 2) MacRae's - West on Yulee Dr, 3.2 miles from Hwy 19. End of Cherokee Way. Boat ramp with access to Homosassa and Chassahowitzka Rivers and the Gulf; and 3) Chassahowitzka River Campground - End of Hwy 480 off Hwy 19. Boat ramp. Access to the river and Gulf.

(9) Bayport - Good boat ramp and nice park and fishing pier at the west end of Hwy 550, off Hwy 19.

(10) Hernando Beach Area: 1) Rogers Park - Boat ramp ($2); and 2) Jenkins Creek - Fishing pier and boat ramp.

(11) Hudson - The Hudson Beach Park is on the Gulf at 6345 Clark St. Nice facilities and a boat ramp. Shore fishing opportunities.

(12) New Port Richey - Boat ramp at the end of Green Key Rd west off Hwy 19.

(13) Holiday - Anclote River Park and Anclote Gulf Park. Both are located on Bailey's Bluff Rd. Nice facilities, shore fishing opportunities, and a boat ramp.

(14) Tarpon Springs: 1) Fred Howard Park at the end of Sunset Dr west of town; 2) There are also boat ramps at the other end of Sunset on the Anclote River; 3) Sunset Beach Park and boat ramp at the end of Gulf Rd; 4) Anclote Key State Preserve - The Reserve is located three miles off Tarpon Springs and is only accessible by private boat. Its four mile long beach is spectacular; and 5) Anclote River Park and boat ramp at the river's mouth.

(15) Dunedin: 1) Honeymoon Island State Recreation Area is located at the extreme west end of Hwy 586 north of the town; and 2) Caladesi Island State Park just Offshore from Dunedin. It is only accessible by private boat or via ferry from Honeymoon Island or the city of Clearwater. The Honeymoon Island ferry runs seven days a week, weather permitting. The first boat leaves at 10 a.m. and then hourly thereafter.

Now let's look at some specific spots and areas, beginning with Cedar Key.

Waterfront

(1) Airport Oyster Bars - Bars just off the town airstrip are usually thick with schools of big Reds in June.

(2) Grass Flats - The entire area west of town is particularly productive for gator Trout during their April - June spawning season.

(3) Town Docks - Great for Sheepshead and Redfish year round. Jack Cravalle and Spanish Mackerel schools wander by in the warmer months. Flounder are always a possibility, too.

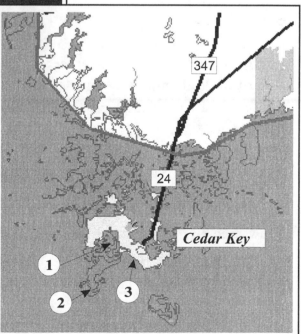

Figure 2.3 Cedar Key

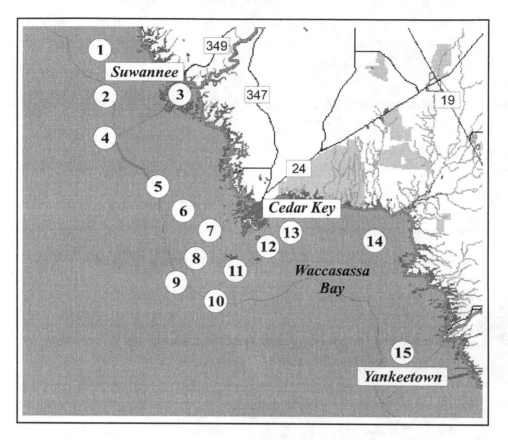

Figure 2.4 - Cedar Key Area

(1) Seven Brothers - North of Suwannee and southeast of Horseshoe. Two miles Offshore of Shired Island. At least seven bars, grass flats, and finger channels. LORAN: 14440.1/45689.3. Spanish, Specs, Sand Trout, Reds, Jack Cravalle, Blues, and Pompano. Closest boat ramp at Shired Island Park on SR 357.

(2) Red Bank and Hedemon Reef - Zone of reefs and grassy areas. Reds, Specs, and Cobia (April). Red Bank LORAN: 14429.6/45662.1. Hedemon LORAN: 14423.3/45646.0

(3) Suwannee River - Good wintertime area. Town has marinas and boat rentals but no shore fishing. River delta with two passes and five significant creeks that hold big Specs, Reds, Sheepshead, Mangrove Snapper, Black Drum, and Whiting.

(4) Spotty Bottom - Starts in the vicinity of LORAN: 14416.5/45665.1, GPS 29-16.510 and 83-18.603. Area extends seaward and may be up to 15 square miles. Great for many things, including big Spanish.

(5) Three - Ten Hole - Large area of flat, rocky, swiss-cheese bottom in 30 - 35 feet of water. LORAN: 14378.4/45553.3; GPS: 29-03.460/83-18.190. Grouper, King Mackerel, Sea Bass, and Spanish.

(6) Big Bend Offshore Marker 12 - Four miles north of Cedar Key northwest channel entrance. It's a large lighted navigation marker. Cobia (May - Oct), Sheepshead (Jan - Apr).

(7) Cedar Key Grass Flats - According to the experts, the most productive flats are located around Snake Key, outside Seahorse Key, and outside North Key.

(8) Kingfish Hole - Large area of flat, rocky, swiss cheese bottom in 20 - 24 feet of water. LORAN: 14388.7/45486.4; GPS: 29-02.697/83-10.473. Grouper, Kings, Spanish, Black Sea Bass, and Gray Grunts (Cedar Key Snapper).

(9) Grouper Grounds south of the Whistle Buoy - Very large area of flat, rocky, swiss cheese bottom in 30 - 35 feet of water. About 15 miles SSW from main ship channel entrance. LORAN: 14348.0/45386.0. Grouper, Cobia, Kings, Spanish, Mangrove Snapper, Sea Bass, and Grunts.

(10) Steel Tower - Lighted, 30 foot tall tower that marks SW end of Seahorse Reef. LORAN: 14378.5/45442.3; GPS: 28-58.525/83-09.241. Cobia (May - Oct), Sheepshead (Jan - Apr).

(11) Hook of Seahorse Reef - A 10 mile long sandbar between Seahorse Key and the Steel Tower. Extensive grass flats in 8 - 12 feet of water; LORAN: 14386.3/45448.0; GPS: 28-59.930/83-08.180. The "Hook" is a great spot for jumbo Spanish, Specs, and Bluefish.

(12) Snake Key - Northward running finger channels up to 16 feet deep that run through grass flats SE of the key. Specs, Blues, Ladyfish, Spanish, Cobia, Sharks, and Redfish.

(13) Corrigan's Reef - A half-mile long, sandy reef running N-S two miles east of Cedar Key. Specs, Reds, Flounder, and Sheepshead are all possibilities in cuts in the reef.

(14) Waccasassa Bay - River empties into NE corner. Grass flats at the river's mouth are good Spec fishing. Northern perimeter of the bay has significant rocks, oyster bars and Redfish. Waccasassa Reef is in the middle of the bay and sometimes holds gator Trout. Oyster bars and rock in up to 25 feet of water. Wooden frame targets from an old Air Force bombing range come out from the NE and attract Tripletail, Cobia, and Sheepshead.

(15) Yankeetown/Withlacoochee River - Check marker 1 on the Yankeetown navigation channel. LORAN: 14407.5/45282.7. Wide variety of possibilities including giant Sheepshead. The river itself is great for winter Reds, Specs, Mangrove Snapper, and more Sheepshead.

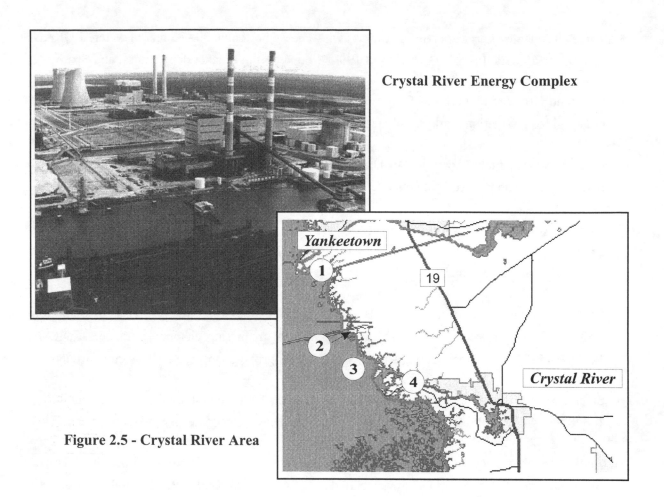

Crystal River Energy Complex

Figure 2.5 - Crystal River Area

(1) Cross Florida Barge Canal - In the spring, look for cruising Cobia around channel markers 7 and 18. In the winter, schools of Specs work their way inland as far as the Hwy 19 bridge. Sheepshead and Mangrove Snapper are also possibilities.

(2) Crystal River Energy Complex - The warm water discharge canal on the south side of the site is a mecca for fishermen in the winter. Most everything that lives in the area is there and cooperative.

(3) Crystal Bay - Lots of possibilities here. Big Reds in the fall along channel edges. The islands about due south of the mouth of Crystal River are usually productive for Specs and Reds. The grass flats around Gomez Rocks are also a favorite area for Specs. And the spoil islands between the Energy Complex and the barge canal are usually well populated with Specs, Reds, and Jack Cravalle.

(4) Crystal River - A beautiful river famous for its spring-fed clarity. Winter Spec and Red fishing in its headwaters is legendary. Tarpon can also be caught in the river in the summertime. Check coastal range markers for Cobia and Reds in the mangrove cuts.

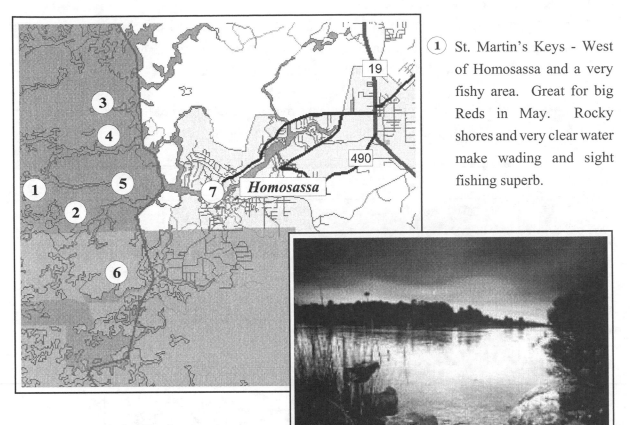

Figure 2.6 - Homosassa Area

① St. Martin's Keys - West of Homosassa and a very fishy area. Great for big Reds in May. Rocky shores and very clear water make wading and sight fishing superb.

The Homosassa River

② Homosassa Bay - Grass flats drifting for spring Specs is usually productive. Bars and channel edges can also produce Cobia and Reds in season.

③ Little Homosassa River - Just north of the big river. Look for Specs, Mangrove Snapper, and Reds in deeper holes year round.

④ Homosassa Flats - Very large schools of Tarpon present from May to July. World class Tarpon fly fishing. Five world records caught here and the 12 and 16 pound class Tarpon records are still held here.

⑤ Mason's Creek - Southwest of town, this creek is a local favorite for big Trout in the spring and fall. Small, shallow draft boats are mandatory.

⑥ Chassahowitzka National Wildlife Refuge - 30,500 acres of creeks, marshes, flats, and the Chassahowitzka River. A very shallow draft boat is required. All year: Sheepshead, Flounder, Sharks, Mangrove Snapper, Black Drum, Reds, and Specs. Seasonally: Tarpon, Bluefish, Snook, and

Cobia. Tarpon fishing is worthy of special mention. It's world-class! Really, really big fish populate the grass flats three to eight miles out in five to 14 feet of water. They're there from April through June. Fish above 160 pounds are not uncommon.

(7) Homosassa River - Something for everyone in the river at various times of the year. Tarpon (Aug - Oct). Specs, Reds, Sheepshead, and Snapper (winter). A few Snook (summer).

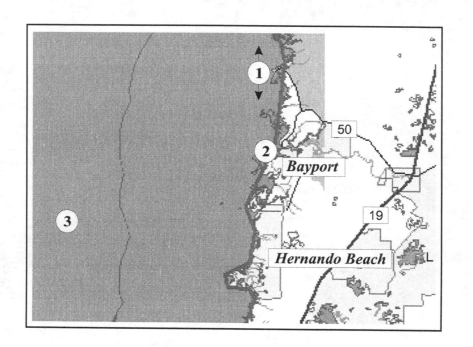

Figure 2.7 - Weeki Wachee Area

(1) Bayport to Chassahowitzka Flats - This several mile stretch of shoreline is typical of most of the "Nature Coast." It combines sandy bottom, grass beds, grass islands, limerock ledges and oyster bars to produce a very fertile fishery. Depth averages three feet and holds large numbers of Reds, Specs and Cobia in season. Top water is the way to maximize the excitement.

(2) Weeki Wachee River - At the river's mouth, the oyster bars around North Point, Fiddlers Point, and Cedar Point are all good for Redfish (Aug - Oct). At the end of the river channel markers, drift the grass flats for big Trout in the spring and fall.

(3) Off Weeki Wachee - Shallow water Gag Grouper. Going north of town 8-10 feet of water 10 miles out. Same depth 5 miles out going south. Lots of rock piles in either direction. Chum with live bait or troll lures.

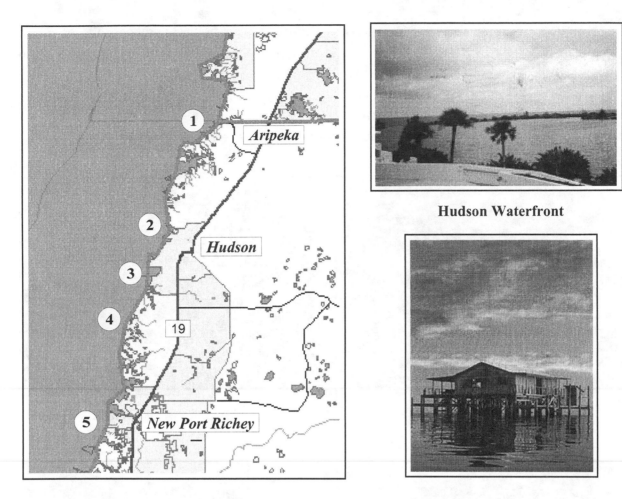

Figure 2.8 - Hudson Area

Hudson Waterfront

New Port Richey Fish Camp

(1) Aripeka - Rocky bars and cuts, grass points, and holes along mangrove shorelines are good for Snook. Knowledgeable local anglers say Aripeka is about the northern boundary of the most productive Snook territory.

(2) Hudson - Area residential canals good for winter Reds, Specs, and Snook. Visitor access to the area is via a boat ramp on Hudson Creek just West of Hwy 19.

(3) Fillman's Bayou Area - Great for Snook and gator Trout on live Sardines (May). Trout and Cobia are also possible.

(4) Pithlachascotee River - Grass flats extend in all directions from the river's mouth. Trout seem to consistently hang out in spotty bottom areas. Working east up the river, rocky bars often hold Snook and Redfish. Creek mouths can often be productive, too. There's a park and boat ramp adjacent to the Hwy 19 bridge over the river in Port Richey. Going the other way, don't overlook the relatively shallow boat channels into and along the Gulf. Snook start stacking up in them in early April and stay till June.

(5) New Port Richey Area - Lots of possibilities. Mid-late summer brings big schools of even bigger Redfish to Sand Bay and Green Key grass flats. Cobia roam under the Offshore stilt houses. Also check the numerous boat channels from the Gulf into this area's residential developments. Look for Snook in the slightly deeper holes in these channels and adjacent to dredge spoil on the bank.

Anclote Power Plant

Tarpon Springs Docks

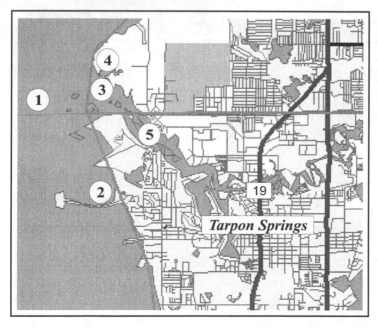

Fred Howard Park

Figure 2.9 Tarpon Springs Area

(1) Anclote Key State Preserve - There is deep water (12 - 20 feet) on both the north and south ends of the main island (Anclote Key). Snook fishing is superb (Jun - Aug). Both cuts can also be productive for Specs, Cobia, Spanish, and Flounder at various times of the year. The shallow flats east of the island produce Reds, Snook, and an occasional Shark.

② Fred Howard and Sunset Beach Parks - Each park provides shore and wading access to the relatively shallow waters of Anclote Anchorage, the bay between the mainland and the Keys. Specs and Reds are possibilities.

③ Anclote River Mouth - There are spoil bars south of the main river channel that can produce Specs, Reds, Snook, and Flounder.

④ Anclote Power Plant - The plant's warm water discharge canal is noteworthy to say the least. It is 200 feet wide, 4,600 feet long, seven feet deep, and particularly fishy during the winter. Most of the West Coast's full cast of fish can be caught in the canal.

⑤ Anclote River - Snook around docks on the lower stretches of the river (spring - fall) and inland above the Hwy 19 bridge (winter).

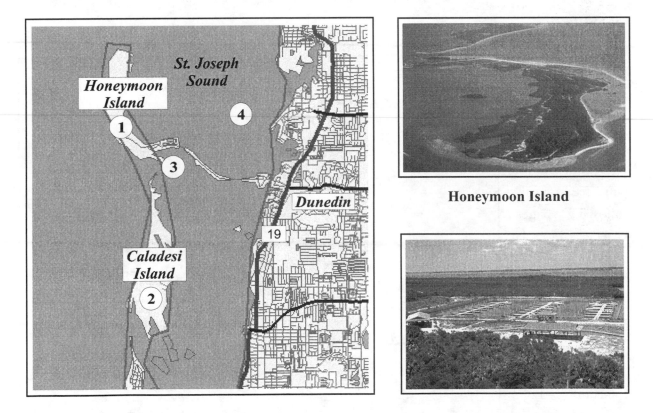

Figure 2.10 Dunedin Area

Honeymoon Island

Caladesi Island Marina

① Honeymoon Island State Recreation Area - Located at the end of SR 586 (Dunedin Causeway). Outside shoal is superior Tarpon water (May - July). The NW sand spit is equally superior water for Snook. Other possibilities around the island include: Flounder, Trout, Reds, Snapper, Whiting, and Sheepshead. Hurricane Pass between Honeymoon and Caladesi Islands another productive area to try. One of the best spots to launch a boat is Duke's Fish Camp on the Anclote River. For shore fishing, park at the last bath house and fish an incoming tide if possible.

(2) Caladesi Island State Park - The island is accessible by private boat or ferries from Honeymoon Island or the city of Clearwater. The Honeymoon Island ferry runs seven days a week, weather permitting. First boat leaves at 10 a.m. and then hourly thereafter. Great way for several hours of superb shore/surf fishing for Tarpon and Snook. Tarpon particularly good along the outer edge of the Caladesi shoal (May - July).

(3) Fish Hwy 586 bridge onto the island over the Intercoastal Waterway - - and the flats on the south side of the causeway. Snook, Specs, Reds, and Flounder.

(4) St. Joseph Sound - Good area for Trout, particularly around the spoil islands on the east side of the ICW.

OFFSHORE

So much for area river, bay, sound, and Inshore fishing opportunities. It's time to go a little farther out. As you will see on the following pages, there is an abundance of very fishy Offshore natural and artificial bottom structure between Cedar Key and Dunedin. Let's take a look.

Figure 2.11 - Offshore - Cedar Key to Dunedin

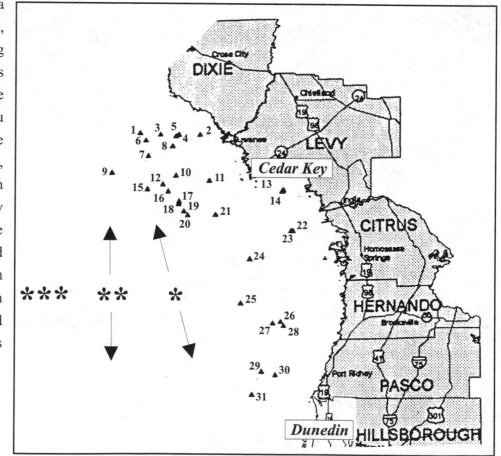

Spot #	Name	LORAN Coordinates	Latitude	Longitude	Depth (ft)	Structure
1	Suwannee Regional Reef 1	14408.65/45805.15	29/20.867	83/31.703	40	Center of 6 patches, 16 cement cubes per patch
2	Fish Haven, NW Red Banks Reef	14428.3/45668.1	29/19.46C	83/15.70C	13	Car bodies, refrigerators, scrap metal
3	Horseshoe Reef	14414.2/45753.1	29/19.90	83/26.08	25	Concrete culverts, modules, reef balls, rubble
4	Horseshoe Reef - Reef Balls	14414.9/45752.5	29/19.87	83/26.15	23	Concrete reef balls
5	Dixie Co. Big Bend Reefs	14422.0/45714.0	29/19.78	83/21.28	18	120 prefab cubes
6	Suwannee Regional Reef H	14403.2/45771.7	29/18.313	83/30.162	40	Center of 6 patches, 16 cement cubes per patch
7	Suwannee Regional Reef G	14393.95/45740.7	29/15.149	83/29.604	40	Center of 6 patches, 4 cement cubes per patch
8	Betty Castor Reef	14410.4/45699.9	29/16.50C	83/23.00C	22	Concrete/poly drum modules
9	White City Bridge Reef	14359.1/45770.2	29/09.998C	83/38.995C	55	Steel and concrete bridge rubble
10	Cedar Key Reef #4	14388.0/45630.0	29/08.966C	83/22.083C	26	Unknown
11	Cedar Key Reef #1	14398.3/45548.2 14398.5/45550.0 14398.4/45549.5 14398.5/45549.9 14398.6/45550.1 14398.8/45549.2 14398.7/45548.7 14398.8/45548.3 14398.9/45548.4 14398.9/45548.9	29/07.637 29/07.594 29/07.57 29/07.64 29/07.64 29/07.65 29/07.60 29/07.61 29/07.63 29/07.66	83/13.236 83/13.327 83/13.38 83/13.36 83/13.38 83/13.26 83/13.24 83/13.19 83/13.18 83/13.22	23	Patches of concrete culvert

Spot #	Name	LORAN Coordinates	Latitude	Longitude	Depth (ft)	Structure
12	Cedar Key Reef #3	14374.9/45640.7	29/06.852	83/25.656	40	Concrete culverts, lines run 20 - 200 degrees
		14374.8/45641.2	29/06.862	83/25.735		
		14375.0/45641.3	29/06.852	83/25.682		
		14375.1/45639.9	29/06.687	83/25.57		
		14374.9/45639.6	29/06.820	83/25.59		
		14375.4/45639.8	29/06.920	83/25.50		
		14375.1/45639.4	29/06.850	83/25.53		
		14375.6/45639.6	29/06.940	83/25.46		
		14375.3/45639.4	29/06.870	83/25.50		
13	Levy Co Big Bend Reef #1	14418.8/45378.6	29/04.930C	82/54.681C	21	Center of 6 patches, 4 concrete cubes per patch
14	Levy Co Big Bend Reef #2	14417.6/45378.2	29/04.629C	82/54.977C	18	Center of 6 patches, 16 concrete cubes per patch
15	Suwannee Regional Reef F	14373.15/45624.6	29/05.763	83/29.774	40	Center of 6 patches, 16 cement cubes per patch
16	Suwannee Regional Reef E	14372.0/45614.4	29/05.073	83/24.188	40	Center of 6 patches, 4 cement cubes per patch
17	Suwannee Regional Reef D	14369.6/45570.4	29/02.558	83/21.245	40	Center of 6 patches, 4 cement cubes per patch
18	Suwannee Regional Reef C	14367.25/45566.2	29/01.897	83/21.419	40	Center of 6 patches, 16 cement cubes per patch
19	Suwannee Regional Reef B	14363.8/45539.9	28/59.997	83/20.060	40	Center of 6 patches, 16 cement cubes per patch
20	Suwannee Regional Reef A	14362.7/45525.4	28/59.062	83/19.063	40	Center of 6 patches, 16 cement cubes per patch
21	Cedar Key Reef #2	14375.4/45466.4	28/58.93	83/11.910	26	Four patches of concrete culverts, slabs, manhole covers, boulders
		14375.1/45467.0	28/58.973	83/11.852		
		14375.2/45466.9	28/59.013	83/11.817		
		14375.3/45467.4	28/58.950	83/11.880		
22	Citrus Co. Big Bend Reef #3	14395.6/45281.5	28/55.3	82/52.5	26	96 prefab cubes

Spot #	Name	LORAN Coordinates	Latitude	Longitude	Depth (ft)	Structure
23	Citrus Fish Haven 2 - Big Bend Reef	14396.2/45278.1	28/54.9	82/52.3	23	96 concrete modules
24	Citrus Fish Haven 1	14356.2/45305.5	28/47.477	83/03.480	30	Boat molds, bridge rubble, concrete pipes
25	Jim Champion Reef	14337/45160 14336.9/45160.4	28/36.07 28/36.07C	82/56.06 82/56.06C	20 20	Concrete culverts, still barge, 956 cu. yds. concrete culvert
26	Bendickson Reef	14319/45140	28/31.118C	82/58.115C	26	10 M60 Army tanks
27	A.H. Richardson Reef	14325.8/45109.5	28/30.75C	82/55.33C	15-20	Skyway concrete rubble
28	Reef Ball Reef	14327/45131	28/30.016C	82/58.70C	25	Concrete reef balls
29	Pasco Reef No. 2	14274.9/45048.6	28/17.63	83/01.09	40	200' barge, concrete pipes, 10 M60 tanks
30	Pasco Reef No. 1	14275.5/44999.8	28/16.75 82/57.45		25	Concrete rubble, 4 barges, 4 hulls, steel tank
31	Pasco Reef No.3	14249.4/45022.6	28/11.5	83/03.56	40	2 PVC modules

*	Sand Patches - A huge area stretching from Port Richey in the south to Suwannee in the north in 8-20 feet of water. Look for white patches on the bottom. They are submerged islands of limerock. Grouper live on and around them.
**	10 Fathom Line - Roughly 20-30 miles Offshore. Spots along the line frequently hold good Red and Black Grouper, White Grunts, and Black Sea Bass. The following spots may be of interest: LORAN: 14314.3/45426.7, 14313.7/45421.9, 14307.3/45429.2, 14312.6/45425.3, and 14312.3/45422.7.
***	Florida Middle Grounds - This area is roughly 100 miles Offshore in 80-130 feet of water. It's comprised of underwater peaks, valleys, and ledges that cover several hundred square miles of bottom. The entire area runs SE/NW in direction and is approximately 50 miles off Bayport and 70 miles out from John's Pass. Amberjack, Dolphin, Red and Black Grouper, and Mango Snapper are seasonally available. The following spots may be of interest: LORAN: 14095.3/45669.3, 14158.7/45698.6, 14112.5/45686.3, and 14107.1/45626.6.

Legend - Figure 2.11

The following are expansions of the Suwannee Regional Reef data (Spots 15-20) in Figure 2.11. Each array consists of six patch reefs arranged in a hexagon. Each patch has either four or 16 concrete cubes. The distance between patches is either 80 or 740 feet.

Name	LORAN Coordinates	Latitude	Longitude
Array A			
N	14363.1/45525.4	28-59.181'	83-19.063'
NE	14363.2/45524.0	28-59.110'	83-18.957'
NW	14362.7/45525.8	28-59.109'	83-19.205'
S	14362.4/45523.4	28-58.943'	83-19.063'
SE	14362.8/45523.0	28-58.991'	83-18.948'
SW	14362.4/45524.9	28-59.007'	83-19-205'
Array B			
N	14363.9/45540.0	29-00.011'	83-20.060'
NE	14363.9/45539.9	29-00.004'	83-20.046'
NW	14363.9/45540.0	29-00.004'	83-20.073'
S	14363.8/45539.8	29-59.984'	83-20.060'
SE	14363.8/45539.7	29-59.991'	83-20.046'
SW	14363.8/45539.9	28-59.991'	83-20.073'
Array C			
N	14367.3/45566.3	29-01.910'	83-21.419'
NE	14367.3/45566.2	29-01.904'	83-21.405'
NW	14367.3/45566.4	29-01.904'	83-21.432'
S	14367.2/45566.1	29-01.884'	83-21.419'
SE	14367.2/45566.1	29-01.890'	83-21.405'
SW	14367.2/45566.2	29-01.890'	83-21.432'
Array D			
N	14370.0/45571.4	29-02.684'	83-21.250'
NE	14370.1/45570.2	29-02.632'	83-21.125'
NW	14369.7/45571.9	29-02.641'	83-21.350'
S	14369.2/45569.4	29-02.432'	83-21.240'
SE	14369.6/45569.0	29-02.486'	83-21.117'
SW	14369.2/45570.9	29-02.504'	83-21.378'
Array E			
N	14372.4/45615.4	29-05.194'	83-24.191'
NE	14372.4/45613.9	29-05.134'	83-24.068'
NW	14371.9/45615.5	29-05.095'	83-24.300'
S	14371.6/45613.4	29-04.952'	83-24.185'
SE	14372.1/45612.8	29-05.012'	83-24.050'
SW	14371.6/45614.6	29-05.987'	83-24.285'

Name	LORAN Coordinates	Latitude	Longitude
Array F			
N	14373.2/45624.7	29-05.776'	83-24.774'
NE	14373.1/45624.6	29-05.770'	83-24.760'
NW	14373.1/45624.7	29-05.770'	83-24.787'
S	14373.1/45624.5	29-05.750'	83-24.774'
SE	14373.1/45624.5	29-05.756'	83-24.760'
SW	14373.1/45624.6	29-05.756'	83-24.787'
Array G			
N	14394.0/45740.8	29-15.162'	83-29.604'
NE	14394.1/45740.7	29-15.156'	83-29.590'
NW	14394.0/45740.9	29-15.156'	83-29.617'
S	14393.9/45740.6	29-15.136'	83-29.604'
SE	14394.0/45740.5	29-15.142'	83-29.590'
SW	14393.9/45740.7	29-15.142'	83-29.617'
Array H			
N	14403.6/45772.7	29-18.436'	83-30.160'
NE	14403.6/45771.2	29-18.388'	83-30.026'
NW	14403.1/45773.0	29-18.368'	83-30.291'
S	14402.8/45770.7	29-18.190'	83-30.165'
SE	14403.2/45770.2	29-18.264'	83-30.025'
SW	14402.8/45772.1	29-18.243'	83-30.270'
Array I			
N	14408.7/45805.3	29-20.880'	83-31.703'
NE	14408.6/45805.1	29-20.874'	83-31.689'
NW	14408.6/45805.3	29-20.874'	83-31.716'
S	14408.6/45805.0	29-20.854'	83-31.703'
SE	14408.6/45805.1	29-15.860'	83-31.689'
SW	14408.6/45805.2	29-20.860'	83-31.716'

Figure 2.12 - Suwannee Regional Reef Arrays

Enough numbers. Try some of the spots that they represent. Many are only lightly fished, so quantity and quality should be impressive. Here are some other things to try as well:

- Trolling Tactics for Grouper - According to one expert on the subject, have two marker jugs onboard when trolling off the Nature Coast. When you get a hit, throw one jug out and note the compass heading. After landing the fish, reverse your compass heading and return to the first jug. If you get hit again, toss the second jug. You've now identified a good area between the jugs - - that can be fished more intensely while anchored-up. Don't forget to record relevant LORAN/GPS numbers.

- One approach to an Inshore Grand Slam - Start on an oyster bar NW of Hudson (Snook, Reds). Then move to the residential canals in the Gulf Harbors area (Tarpon). Finish on the grass flats off Aripeka (Specs). Congratulations!

- Tarpon on the Beach - From Hudson south, sight fish in swash channels that parallel the beach about 200 yards out.

- Port Richey Grass Flats - There are many square miles of them north of town. They begin in four feet of water close to shore and extend out 10-12 miles, where the water may be only 15 feet deep. Superior spring and fall Trout fishing in the shallows. In the summer, head further Offshore for consistently good fishing.

And that's Cedar Key to Dunedin. There are lots of fish - - and not all that many fishermen. Spectacular scenery, plenty of solitude and, most of the year, great fishing diversity. It's tough to leave - - except our next segment to the south has lots to offer, too.

-PERSONAL NOTES-

CHAPTER 3

CLEARWATER TO PALMETTO

The section of coast between Clearwater and Palmetto has an obvious but distinctive characteristic - - Tampa Bay - - Florida's largest open-water estuary. But it has other features of interest to a fisherman, too. Within its 40+ mile length, you'll also find 25 miles of very fishy surf and Intercoastal Waterway (ICW), five passes into the Gulf of Mexico, and four significant rivers with associated creek systems. And by virtue of the temperate climate and ideal habitat, there are quality fish ready and willing to bite year round.

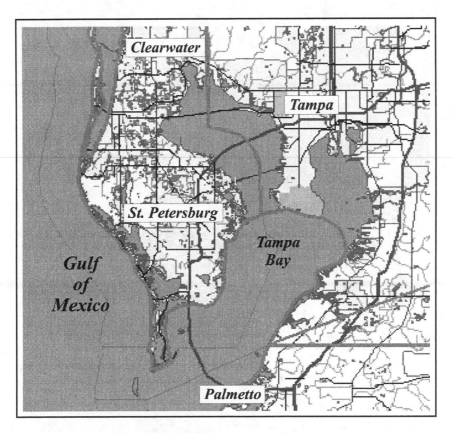

Figure 3.0 - Clearwater to Palmetto

Tampa Bay is a whole fishing story in and of itself. With the exception of the blue water gamefish, all other Gulf of Mexico species can be caught within the confines of the bay. Its 398 square miles are immensely fertile. Experts estimate that more than 70% of this part of Florida's fish, shellfish, and crustaceans spend some part of their lives in Tampa Bay. Figure 3.1 highlights the area's fishing possibilities.

Possibilities	Best Time To Try
Amberjack	Available year round
Barracuda	Available year round - Spring/Summer
Black Drum	Available year round - Summer/Early Fall
Black Sea Bass	Available year round
Blackfin Tuna	Available year round - Summer
Bluefish	Available year round
Blue Marlin	Late Summer/Early Fall
Bonito	Available year round
Cobia	Migratory - Spring/Summer/Fall
Dolphin	Late Spring through early Fall
Flounder	Available year round - Late Summer/Fall
Grouper	Available year round
Jack Cravalle	Available year round
King Mackerel	Migratory - Spring and Fall
Permit	Available year round - Spring/Summer
Pompano	Available year round - Spring/Summer
Redfish	Available year round
Sailfish	Summer/Fall
Sheepshead	Available year round - Winter
Snapper	Available year round
Snook*	Available year round
Spanish Mackerel	Migratory - Spring/Summer/Fall
Swordfish	Late Summer
Tarpon	Migratory - Spring/Summer
Triggerfish	Available year round
Tripletail	Available year round - Summer/Fall
Trout*	Available year round
Wahoo	Probably available year round - Summer
White Marlin	Summer
Whiting	Available year round
Yellowfin Tuna	Spring/Fall

* Subject to closed season. Catch and release OK. Please see Appendix for dates.

Figure 3.1 - Gamefish Availability

As was true of Figure 2.1, only a couple of words of explanation are needed about Figure 3.1. Specifically, if there isn't a qualifier after a "Best Time to Try" recommendation, that means the whole period is good. Redfish are an example of this. On the other hand, if there is a qualifier, it simply indicates the very best time within a particular period. Mr. Barracuda can help us here. You can catch him every month of the year. But he seems to be the most hungry and aggressive in the spring and summer.

OK, with that top level summary in mind, let's take a look at fishing action on a month-to-month basis. The following narrative is only supposed to give you a feel for what typically goes on between Clearwater and Palmetto. It is certainly not all inclusive.

January
- Snook in protected creeks and rivers like the Little Manatee and around residential docks along the Intercoastal Waterway.
- Reds both on the flats and on the bottom of deep protected channels.
- Grouper, Amberjack, and Snapper active on Offshore reefs in 30 - 50 feet of water to the south and 80 - 90 feet off Clearwater.
- Specs a good choice in holes on flats at low tide and along the edges of the Intercoastal Waterway.
- Sheepshead widely scattered, including on many flats.
- Residential docks very productive for Specs, Reds, Snook, and Sheepshead.
- Tampa Bay area power plants holding nice Cobia. Power plant by Davis Island is also producing good action for Permit and Pompano.

February
- Sheepshead on every bridge, pier, jetty, and piling in the area.
- Grouper, Snapper, and Black Sea Bass on Inshore structure.
- Specs starting to school in areas with mud bottoms.
- Snook active in the Manatee, Little Manatee and Alafia rivers.
- Oyster bars next to flats good first stop for Reds.
- Snook, Redfish, and Cobia can be found around Harbor Island, at the Big Bend and Gannon power plants, and up the Alafia River.
- Specs holding near outflow water from area power plants and in deep sections of feeder streams and creeks.
- Offshore reefs near warm water springs in 40 - 50 feet of water producing Blackfin Tuna, Grouper, Snapper, Bull Reds, Sea Bass, and Amberjacks.
- Stray King Mackerel wandering around Grouper spots.
- Specs active in the Picnic Island area.
- Tarpon cooperating in the Davis Island and downtown areas.

March
- Kings from the beach to 20 miles out from Sarasota to Hudson.
- Cobia, Bonito, Blackfin Tuna, Sailfish, and Wahoo Offshore chasing bait in 60 - 90 feet of water.
- Spanish are thick two miles off Clearwater beaches.
- A few early Tarpon and Cobia, Reds, Specks, and Snook on the shallow flats from Sarasota Bay to Crystal River.

- The Estuary, Palm River, McKay Bay and the Kitchen area north of the Alafia River all good for Reds, Snook, and Cobia.
- Area piers and bridges hot for Tarpon, Kings, Spanish, Snapper, Pompano and Snook.
- "Shrimp Muds" six to eight miles Offshore hold Mackerel, Specs, Bluefish, and Jack Cravalle.
- Grouper starting to cooperate in 60 feet of water and Spanish within two miles of the beach off Clearwater.

April

- Migrating schools of Kings and Spanish close-in crashing bait - - and well Offshore.
- Blackfin Tuna in 65 - 100 feet of water off Clearwater.
- Offshore reefs and wrecks loaded with Snapper and Grouper.
- Snook everywhere - - bridges, piers, under residential docks, and around mouths of rivers.
- Schooling Reds in swash channels on the downside of Gulf islands.
- A few Tarpon are starting to show on the Skyway Bridge.
- Cobia migrating both Inshore and Offshore.

May

- Kings in main Tampa ship channel east of the Whistler and on Pinellas County artificial reefs.
- Gag Grouper and Cobia in same areas.
- Snook outside barrier islands.
- Redfish on the bar north of Bishop's Harbor and Cockroach Bay off the east tip of East Beach at DeSoto Park, and all over Weedon Island area.
- Grouper, Wahoo, Sailfish, Blackfin Tuna, AJ's and Barracuda possible on bottom structure from 40 feet on out.
- Pompano and Permit cooperating off Tierra Verde bridges.
- Barracuda have infested Clearwater Offshore reefs.

June

- AJ's on Offshore wrecks, and Dolphin and Wahoo in 70 feet of water around weed lines.
- Trout cooperating on the flats at both ends of the Skyway.
- Cobia widespread, especially on Gulf flats.
- Reds in bay shallows and Gulf flats.
- Snook along the beaches, in the passes, and around docks at night.
- Grouper and Blackfin Tuna well Offshore in 110-120 feet of water.
- Offshore wrecks and reefs also hold good quantities of Snapper and an occasional Sailfish.
- Kings and Spanish plentiful closer in.
- Tripletail on crab trap buoys and navigation aids.

July

- Tarpon thick along area beaches.

- Grouper, Amberjack and Snapper Offshore in 75+ feet of water.
- Sailfish, Blackfin Tuna, Wahoo, Barracuda, and Dolphin also biting well Offshore.
- Deeper edges of major bays good for Reds.
- Some Cobia and very big Jack Cravalle on area flats.
- Night fishing on coastal bridges producing Specs, Reds, Snook, Tarpon, Snapper, Black Drum and Cobia.
- Monster Redfish (50"+) 20 miles off Clearwater.
- Bull Sharks in the 300 - 500 pound range hungry off the Gandy Bridge.
- Clearwater Pass producing some of everything.

August
- Blackfin Tuna, Sailfish, Barracuda, and Wahoo Offshore (30 miles). Dolphin, too.
- Grouper forty miles out.
- Early arriving Kings closer in.
- Tarpon in the bays and in some area rivers.
- Spanish, Snook, and Tarpon available on the Redington Long Pier.
- Big Snook also in area passes.
- Redfish and Specs on the flats early and late and at night. Also along the beach on high tides.
- Grouper and Snapper in the channels east of the Skyway Bridge.
- Black Drum and Tarpon off the John's Pass, Skyway, and Gandy bridges at night.
- Black Drum also off the Howard Franklin and the SR 60 bridges.

September
- Early Kings wandering in around major structure in 60 - 90 feet of water.
- Sailfish, Wahoo, Blackfin Tuna, and schoolie Dolphin in 80 feet of water between Clearwater and Tarpon Springs.
- Grouper still deep but biting well.
- Widely scattered schooling Redfish and Cobia on bars between bays and mangrove islands.
- Spanish and Jack Cravalle active over deeper grass flats.
- Redington Pier producing Cobia, Spanish, Snook and Tarpon.
- Big Snook terrorizing Clearwater Pass bridge.
- Jumbo Reds within a mile of the beach and in Clearwater Pass.

October
- Giant Spanish roam the bay and Inshore waters.
- Snook widely scattered around docks and piers across the area.
- Reds and Specs schooling on most area flats.
- Grouper coming into 60 feet off Anna Maria Island and 40 - 50 feet further north.
- Sailfish, Dolphin, and Wahoo a distinct possibility well Offshore in 70 - 90 feet of water.

- Triggerfish, Spanish, and Grouper three miles north of Tampa Bay ship channel markers 1 and 2.
- A few Cobia cooperating in 20 - 30 feet of water on artificial reefs.

November
- Prime time Permit in deep channels under the Skyway Bridge and Egmont and Southwest Passes adjacent to Egmont Key.
- Big Spanish Mackerel and Cobia at the mouth of Tampa Bay.
- Grouper also in Tampa Bay along main ship channel from Egmont Key to Port Manatee.
- Snook, small Tarpon, Reds, and Jack Cravalle near mouths of rivers and Intercoastal Waterway docks and bridges.
- Kings thick and active Offshore in 90 feet of water 20 miles west of Sarasota.
- Tarpon in the Garrison and Seddon ship channels and in residential canals.
- Barracuda eager on area artificial reefs and Bluefish cooperating on the top.
- Bluefish, Reds, Specs, and Flounder active in Clearwater Bay.
- Great Snapper fishing on the Skyway rock piles.

December
- Flounder, Specs, Reds, and Snook in deep potholes close to mouths of creeks, rivers, and warm water powerplant outflows.
- Grouper in shallow water (10 - 18 feet) off the beaches and within two miles of the Skyway main span on rocks.
- Kings chasing mullet around Southwest, Egmont, Pass-A-Grille, John's, Clearwater, and Hurricane Passes.
- Area powerplant's (Big Bend, Gandy, Oldsmar and Gannon) warm water good for Specs, Reds, Snook, Flounder, and Jack Cravalle.
- A few big Kings around the mouths of area passes.
- Grouper coming in closer (30 - 40 feet).
- Sheepshead on docks, piers, jetties, and mangrove roots.
- Big Cobia working Skyway Bridge and Offshore reefs.
- Whiting biting well off the Redington Long Pier. Sheepshead, Black Drum, and Silver Trout also cooperating.

About five years of data were synthesized to compile this monthly narrative. Again, it's not a current fishing report. But it does provide some useful insights into year round fishing action between Clearwater and Palmetto. Now we'll focus on more specific spots and areas that have a demonstrated record of producing fish.

BAYS

As we noted earlier, Tampa Bay is one big body of water. To do justice to it in terms of where to fish, we need to approach it in a systematic way. Figure 3.2 highlights the process. First, we'll talk areas and their proven spots - - as they relate to the shore and adjacent structure. We'll start on the west with the Intercoastal Waterway and Ft. DeSoto. The St. Petersburg Shore, Old Tampa Bay, Hillsborough Bay, and the Southeast Shore will follow. We'll look specifically at flats, holes, depressions, visible points, dropoffs, stickups, and even a few old trees.

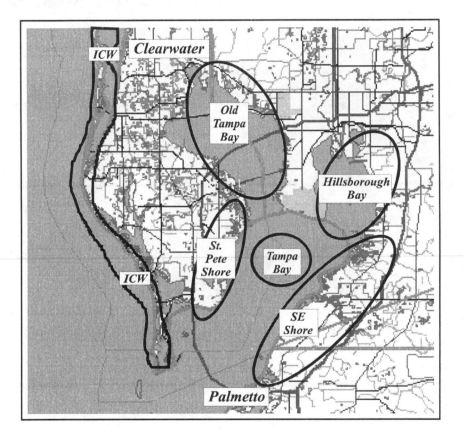

Figure 3.2 - Tampa Bay Fishing Areas

After we've talked about the periphery, we'll head out to deeper water. As you may know, Tampa Bay offers a tremendous diversity of underwater topography. There are over 55 miles of ship channels dredged out of solid limestone to a controlling depth of 48 feet. Great natural bottom structure is the result. But the story doesn't stop there. There are also additional deep water channels that have been cut by the Hillsborough, Palm, Alafia, and Little Manatee Rivers. And man has been busy, too. Yes, there are also 10+ artificial reefs within Tampa Bay waters. We'll talk about all this, and the big fish you can catch - - without even going out into the Gulf of Mexico. Let's get started.

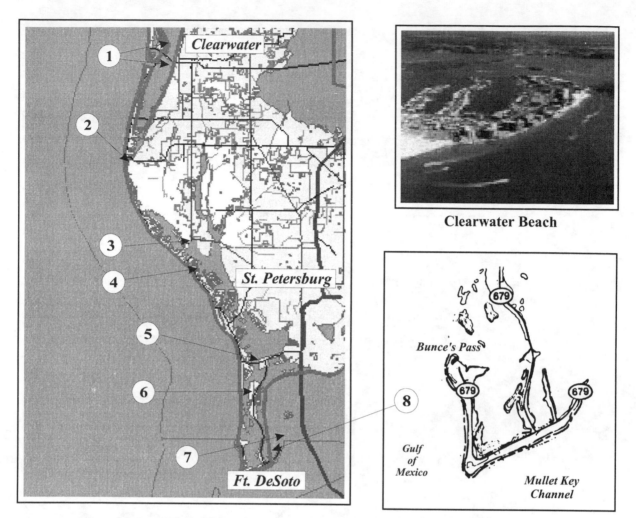

Clearwater Beach

Figure 3.3 - ICW and Ft. DeSoto   **Ft. DeSoto Park**

Before we get specific, it's important to note that the entire length of the ICW - - from Clearwater to the Tampa Bay ship channel south of Ft. DeSoto - - is very fishy. Every dock, canal, seawall, pass, and channel marker probably holds fish sometime during the year. So, if in doubt about a particular spot or area, try it. You'll probably be glad you did! OK, here are some specifics.

1 Clearwater Harbor - Specs, Cobia, Snook and Flounder on the flats. Spanish off the little bridges in the Clearwater and Bellaire areas. Check under the Bellaire Causeway bridge for great summer Mangrove Snapper action. The rocks at Clearwater Pass are a good spot for September Snook, Snapper, and Specs.

2 Narrows - Good early spring Trout fishing near Walsingham Road and close-by ICW drop offs (March - April).

3 Bay Pines Area - Snook, Specs, and Reds on the flats. Snook around the Bay Pines Bridge (April). Always Specs around the hospital.

④ Treasure Island - Keeper Grouper in the old Tarpon Hole near the Bluenose Hotel.

⑤ Isle del Sol - Keeper Grouper in the canals. The bridges along the Pinellas Skyway provide unbelievable Pompano fishing in mid to late Summer - - along with much more.

⑥ Tierra Verde Area - Usually something for everyone! Pompano and Spanish off the bridges while Snook, Specs, and Flounder cooperate on the flats. During the summer, Snapper, Cobia, and Sharks join the fun. Plenty of Sheepshead year round. Please see the Piers Section later in this chapter for the area around the Merry Pier in Pass-A-Grille.

⑦ Tarpon Key - Spring Cobia and big Reds on the flats.

⑧ Ft. DeSoto - Right on par with the Skyway piers as an incredible place to fish. Almost limitless flats, channels, and cuts accessible to waders and shore fishermen. (Specs, Reds, Flounder, Pompano, Permit, and you name it). Surrounded to the north and south by the deeper waters of Bunce's Pass and the Mullet Key (ship) channel. Big fish like Cobia, Tarpon, Shark, etc., are the result. The park's huge boat ramps on Bunces Pass are infinitely convenient to everything lower Tampa Bay and the Gulf have to offer.

Bartow Power Plant

Figure 3.4 - St. Petersburg Shore

① Pinellas Point Area - South of the airport, there's a combination of flats, a north/south bar, and relatively deep water between Big and Little Bayous. Reds, Specs, and Snook are all possibilities. Off Pinellas Pt proper, there is a large area of grass ideal for drifting for Trout. Wade fishing for the same guys is possible from the bar that parallels the shore.

(2) Whitted Airport - Dredge holes just off the shore are over 20 feet deep and good for winter Specs and a mixed bag the rest of the year.

(3) The Pier - Please see the Piers Section later in this chapter.

(4) Smack's Bayou, Coffeepot Bayou, and Snell Island Harbor - Relatively deep water (10 - 18 feet). Snook, Trout, Flounder, and Sheepshead almost year round.

(5) Weedon Island Wildlife Refuge - (County Park) 1,000 acres - 600 dry, 400 submerged. Open from 7 a.m. to sunset. Outboard motors are prohibited within the refuge boundaries. Absolutely superb wade, drift, or shore fishing opportunities. Reds, Specs, and Snook big and smart (spring - fall). Bayou Grande and Riviera Bay are adjacent to the park and are fishy themselves. The area around the Bartow Power Plant just north of the Refuge is also productive, particularly during the colder winter months for Snook. Deep water around the fuel docks is also good for Snook, Specs, and Sheepshead.

Double Branch Creek Area

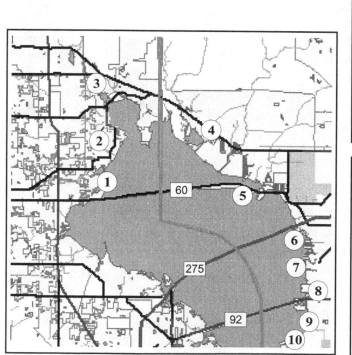

Figure 3.5 - Old Tampa Bay

Courtney Campbell Causeway

(1) Cooper Point - Snook and Reds inside the point in the springtime.

(2) Safety Harbor - Deep water in the mouth of the harbor holds Specs in the winter. Philippe Point, just a bit north of Safety Harbor, has a great ledge which produces Specs and Snook.

(3) Lake Tarpon Outflow - Winter Snook possible.

(4) Double Branch Creek Area - Flats can produce Specs year round. Snook in area creeks in the fall and winter. Big Reds on the flats in the fall. Upper Tampa Bay Park is a good spot to launch a very shallow draft boat.

(5) Courtney Campbell Causeway - Sand patches along the causeway good for Flounder in the fall. Legal Reds in the same area and in marshy areas around the east end. Ben T. Davis Park flats along the causeway are good wade fishing for Specs and Reds (spring - fall). Snook off the bridges at sunup and sundown. Boat ramp area good for Specs and Reds (Feb) on pumpkin seed jigs. Another consistently good area is around the Red Lobster. In August and September, Cobia cruise the bridge structure and channel markers.

(6) Frankland Bridge - Summer night fishing under the lights consistently produces Tarpon and Snook. In the fall, Cobia also a nighttime possibility. Black Drum to 50# on Blue Crab halves are sporting. Blacktip and Sand Sharks (Oct) are also fun. In August, scrape barnacles off the pilings, toss in a fiddler crab, and enjoy Pompano and Permit action.

(7) Between the Gandy and the Frankland - Grass flats between the bridges provide good top water Spec fishing in all but the coldest months. Residential canals ashore (east side) usually hold big Trout and Snook during the winter.

(8) Gandy Bridge - Giant Black Drum around bridge pilings (night). Pompano and Permit are there also (June - Sep). During the summer, Tarpon and Snook are a real possibility under the bridge lights. Seasonally, channel markers from the Gandy to the Skyway hold Tripletail and Cobia. West end dredge holes good for winter Snook and Trout. There are tackle shops on both ends of the bridge.

(9) Port Tampa - Just north of Picnic Island Park, big fish live in the area. Giant Snook and big Specs and Jack Cravalle are all possibilities. Rock piles scattered through the area hold Mangrove Snappers.

(10) Picnic Island Area - Holes just south of the island including "the" hole can produce Cobia, Specs, Reds, and an occasional Snook. The creek of the same name, which is also just south of the park, produces good Trout and Snook in the winter. Fall Reds and Specs can be found on the American Legion flats. Late summer Flounder fishing from the sandy areas around the island can produce big (3 - 6 lbs) results.

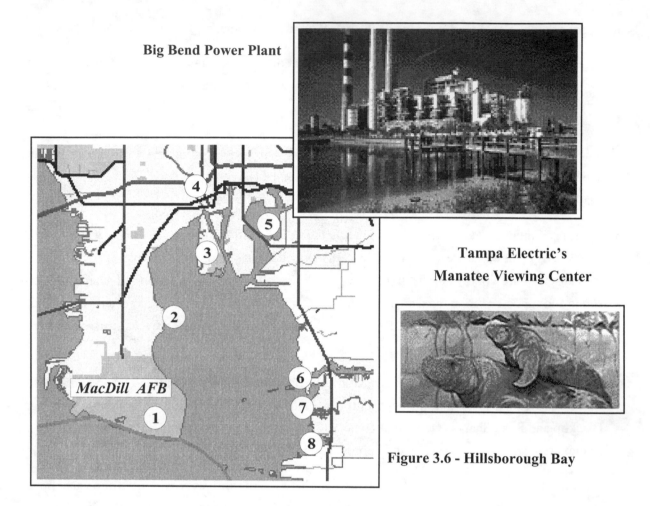

Big Bend Power Plant

**Tampa Electric's
Manatee Viewing Center**

MacDill AFB

Figure 3.6 - Hillsborough Bay

(**1**) Coon's Creek Recreation Area—This facility on <u>MacDill Air Force Base</u> offers a range of opportunities. First, it's situated on Coon Hammock and Broad Creeks, which are both excellent fishing areas. Trout, Reds, Snook, Sheepshead and Spadefish are all available almost year round. Second, it rents well equipped center console boats that may be taken the 19 miles to the Skyway Bridge to fish. Finally, live and frozen bait, tackle, and fuel are all available 12 hours a day, seven days a week. Adjacent areas are good, too. Fall Redfishing is very productive on MacDill flats.

(**2**) Ballast Point Pier - Please see the Piers Section later in this chapter.

(**3**) Davis Island Area -

- Snook, Reds, Specs, Jack Cravalle, Sheepshead, Snapper, Tarpon, Flounder, Cobia, Tripletail and Sharks are all present at one time or another.
- Year round, fish structure (pilings).
- Shore fishing: Try the half mile stretch of seawall on the east side of the island. Ample parking for fishing Seddon Channel. Also try the seawall that circles the seaplane basin on the eastern tip of Davis Island.

- Boat ramps for downtown: Davis Island next to Peter O. Knight airport and at Marjorie Park on Bering St.
- Cobia are around channel markers during full moon in June, July, and August.
- Another downtown spot: Go east of Hooker's Pt beyond 22nd St Causeway to McKay Bay. Ninety percent of shoreline mangroves will hold Reds on rising tides. Also Snook. No wading because there is a mucky bottom. Shallow draft boats are required.

(4) Hillsborough River - Winter Snook possible around river docks, bridges, and other deep water structure. Try under all the bridges from Platt St northward past Sulphur Springs. Upriver, check under the Columbus, Buffalo, Sligh, and Nebraska bridges.

(5) McKay Bay/Palm River - Reds, Sheepshead, and some Snook on structure in the bay and Snook up the river (Nov - March). In April, try from the flood control structure at Adams Dr to the mouth of McKay Bay.

(6) Alafia River - Good winter fishery for Snook upriver. Specs on the grass flats at the river's mouth in the spring. Reds also at the river's mouth. Big Cobia possible there, too (fall). Check the East Bay channel markers. Other possibilities include Black Drum near the phosphate plant, and Reds, Black Drum, Sheepshead, Specs, and Ladyfish off the Hwy 41 bridge (Aug).

(7) Bullfrog Creek - Just south of the Alafia River. Spring Trout fishing on the grass at the creek's mouth is usually great. In late summer - early fall, check the shallows of the Whiskey Stump and the Kitchen area for keeper Reds. Large Cobia hang out around the buoys in the same time frame. Big Snook off the Hwy 41 bridge are always a late summer possibility.

(8) Big Bend Power Plant - This Tampa Electric facility, which is just north of Apollo Beach, may be reached by boat or via car off I-75. Off exit 47, turn west on Big Bend Road and continue till it ends. The entire area in and around the plant is fishy year round. Trout, Reds, Snook, Sheepshead, Pompano, Cobia, and Snapper are possible. Winter fishing for all these guys would be spectacular in the plant's warm water discharge canal (south side) - - except it's closed to boat traffic. Tampa Electric sponsors a Manatee Viewing Center in that area that's open to the public every winter.

Little Manatee River

Piney Point Area

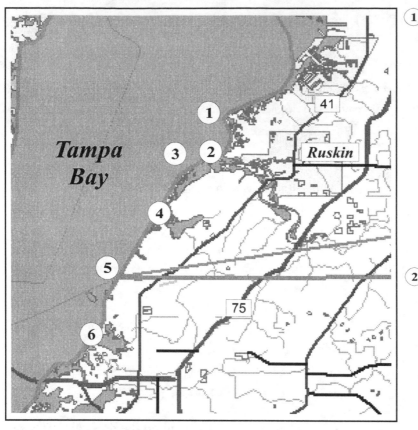

Figure 3.7 - Southeast Shore

(1) E. G. Simmons Park - On the north side of the Little Manatee's mouth, the park offers good year round fishing opportunities. There's a boat ramp, piers, good shore fishing, and access for the wade fisherman. Flounder, Black Drum, Specs, and Redfish are available, even in the winter.

(2) Little Manatee River - A beautiful river that can provide fine Red, Spec, and Snook fishing in the wintertime (Nov - Mar) and during much of the rest of the year, too. Flats at the mouth of the river are a great area to drift for Trout. In the summer, don't be surprised by Tarpon in the river's deeper holes. In the fall, look for Snook along mangrove shorelines and East Bay beaches.

(3) Barrier Sandbar - It protects the southeastern shore of Tampa Bay. It begins at Emerson Point in Manatee County and parallels the shore eastward past the Sunshine Skyway approach, past Port Manatee, then the hook at Ruskin, and all the way up the eastern shore to Pendola Point. There are numerous access points for flats fishing in one to four feet of water. Snook, Reds, Trout, and their friends will usually oblige. Hotspots: Both sides of the Skyway Manatee approach; the mouth of Cockroach Bay channel - - particularly to the west; and the end of Port Manatee Road to the east.

(4) Cockroach Bay - Great shallow water (wade/pole) for Specs, Reds, and Snook in all but the coldest months of the year. The bay is full of potholes, island points, oyster bars, marine vegetation, and channels/cuts. Fish each and every one. Internal combustion engines are not allowed in the bay. In late August, check the C-Cut off Cockroach Bay for keeper Grouper.

(5) Piney Point - Grass beds to the north good for Trout early and late. Port Manatee, just around the corner to the south, offers a real mixed bag. Big Snook will be around the north shore spoil islands (May - Sep);Reds will also be there (Aug - Oct). Both fish will also hang out all summer in the

port's deeper holes. Spanish Mackerel become a possibility in the spring and fall. On channel rocky areas, don't be surprised to find Black Sea Bass, Mangrove Snapper, and occasionally legal Grouper.

(6) Bishop's Harbor - Specs, Reds, Snook, and Flounder usually cooperate around the harbor's oyster bars, mangrove shorelines, cuts, and creeks. Frog Creek, which can be accessed via Bishop's Harbor, is a particularly good area for winter Snook.

At this point in our discussion of area Bays, we need to shift our perspective just a bit. Up to this point, we've focused on proven spots - - as they relate to the shore and adjacent structure. Figure 3.8 highlights where we're going next. Yep, we're going fishing for sure. But this time, we'll focus on proven spots related to structure on the bottom rather than on the shore.

Figure 3.8 is, of necessity, busy. The amount of bottom structure available to the fisherman is really quite amazing - - and consistently productive. The dotted lines on the chart indicate dredged ship channels. The channel edges have drops that can be as much as 20 feet deeper than the surrounding bottom. And the edges are fishy. There are all kinds of undercuts, caves, holes, etc., in the limestone that provide perfect habitat for the whole local crowd. To put all this in perspective, it is 25 miles from Egmont Key (#1 in the figure) to where the main channel branches NW and NE in the upper bay. There are three additional channels that branch off the main channel that also have good fishy rock edges.

Collectively, you're now talking about 45 miles of main channel that offer potentially productive fishing on both sides of its entire length.

But there's more - - like the miles of lesser channels at the mouths of the area's rivers and into the nine major ports around the bay. It really is mind-boggling. Figure 3.8 also highlights two other aspects of Tampa Bay bottom structure. The eleven triangles indicate artificial reefs. Specifics on them are provided in Figure 3.9. The circled numbers identify several other natural bottom features that may be of interest to you. They're described below.

Egmont Key Lighthouse

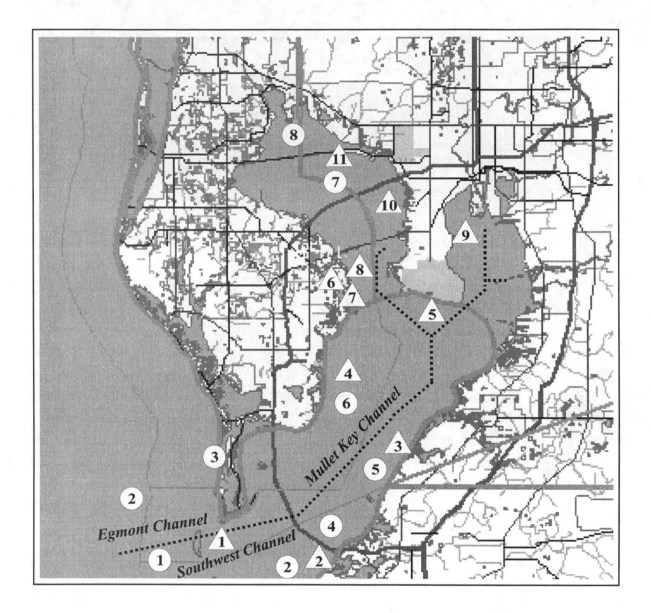

Figure 3.8 - Tampa Bay Bottom Structure

(**1**) Egmont Key State Park - This 440 acre island is the home of the only manned lighthouse in the U.S. Access to the park is by private boat only. Deep rocky ledges off the island's north point hold Grouper and Snapper. Giant Snook can often be found on the back side of the island.

(**2**) Egmont/Southwest Channels - These are super productive areas for lots of things, including smoker Kings in the spring and fall.

(**3**) North Channel/South Channel - Productive trolling for Kings, Spanish, and Grouper along the edges. Big Red Snapper are also a possibility.

④ East/West Cut - The cut runs between the south end of the Skyway causeway and Joe Island. It usually holds Snook, Reds, and Flounder, among others.

⑤ Good Stretch of Ship Channel - Rocky edges hold Grouper and Snapper; Spanish can usually be chummed up, and Cobia hang around the channel markers.

⑥ Big Tarpon - These guys are a late summer possibility in the 21 - 28 foot depression that starts a half mile off the St. Pete pier and extends south around Pinellas Point.

⑦ Old Bay Reef - A good area for Specs, Reds, Flounder, and large Tarpon.

⑧ Booth Point - There's a ledge just Offshore that produces good Spec fishing during much of the year.

Spot #	Name	LORAN Coordinates	Latitude Longitude	Depth (ft)	Structure
1	Egmont Key Reef	14193.5/44608.0	27/35.00 82/44.60	23	(Pending)
2	Sneads Point Reef	—	—	15	Tires, concrete rubble
3	Port Manatee Reef (.7 nm NE of Port Manatee ship channel)	14425.0/44557.4	27/39.68 82/34.87	21	8,000 tons of concrete bridge decking
4	St. Petersburg Reef	14242.6/44615.6	— —	34-36	Bridge rubble, concrete dolphins
5	Bahia Beach Reef (1.8 nm west of Mangrove Point)	14245.4/44560.2	27/44.85 82/31.00	24	Concrete pilings, slabs, pipe
6	Picnic Island Artificial Reef	14254.0/44619.4	27/51.390 82/33.200	26	Concrete/clay pipes
7	Picnic Island Pier Reef (100' off the end of the pier)	14257.9/44648.5	— ---	18	Prefab concrete pyramid units
8	Port of Tampa Reef (.6 nm west of Port Tampa)	14257.5/44632.3	27/51.65 82/33.84	24	Four barges, concrete pilings, bridge beams
9	Ballest Point Pier Reef	Four reef areas 50' from pier along both sides	27/53.36C 82/28.80C		Concrete pilings, slabs, pipe

Spot #	Name	LORAN Coordinates	Latitude Longitude	Depth (ft)	Structure
10	Howard Franklin Reef (1 nm west of Interbay Peninsula)	14266.2/44648.5	27/54.63 82/33.25	16	Bridge supports, rubble
11	Courtney Campbell Reef (.4 nm south of causeway)	14267.6/44701.9	27/57.75 82/36.86	16	Concrete pilings

Figure 3.9 - Tampa Bay Artificial Reefs

On a concluding note in this area, you might be interested in the census Hillsborough County officials have taken on the artificial reefs in their waters (#'s 1, 3, 5, 7-11 in Fig 3.8).

- Sheepshead - Year round on all reefs.

- Mangrove Snapper - Year round on all reefs.

- Black Grouper - Winter: Bahia Beach, Port Tampa, and Port Manatee.

- Gag Grouper - Fall and winter: Bahia Beach, Port Tampa and Port Manatee.

- Snook - Mid-summer: Bahia Beach and Port Manatee.

- Cobia - Summer: Port Tampa and Howard Franklin.

- Black Sea Bass - Spring: Port Tampa.

- Flounder - Year round: Port Tampa and Port Manatee.

- Black Drum - Spring and summer: Bahia Beach and Port Manatee.

- Permit - Spring: Port Tampa and Howard Franklin.

- Spanish Mackerel - Spring and fall; all reefs.

- Specs and Silver Trout - Winter: Ballast Point and Howard Franklin.

These are just the most frequent reef inhabitants. A total of 45 species have been identified on Hillsborough reefs at one time or another during a typical year.

Well, that's where the fish are. Now we need to get you to them. Figure 3.10 highlights public boat ramps that support Tampa Bay fishing.

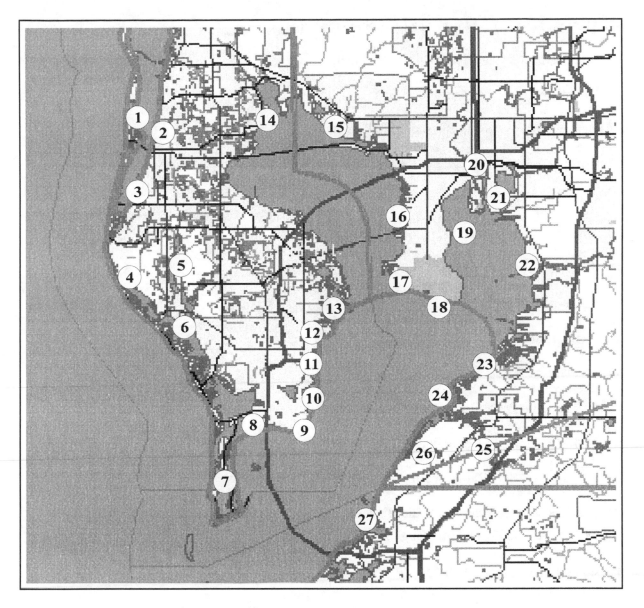

Figure 3.10 - Tampa Bay Area Public Boat Ramps

(1) Bay Esplande and the Intercoastal Waterway (ICW), Clearwater Beach.

(2) Hwy 60 and the ICW, Clearwater Beach.

(3) Bellaire Causeway and the ICW, Bellaire Bluffs.

(4) Park Blvd and the ICW, Indian Shores.

(5) Lake Seminole Park, Park Blvd, Seminole.

(6) War Veteran's Memorial Park, Bay Pines Blvd, St. Petersburg.

(7) Ft. DeSoto Park, Pinellas Bayway, Tierra Verde.

⑧ Maximo Park, off I-275 service road, St. Petersburg.

⑨ Bay Vista Park, Pinellas Pt Dr, St. Petersburg.

⑩ Grandview Park, 38th Ave and 6th St S, St. Petersburg.

⑪ Demens, 1st Ave S and Bayshore, St. Petersburg.

⑫ Coffee Pot Bayou, Coffee Pot Blvd. at 30th Ave NE, St. Petersburg.

⑬ Crisp Park, Poplar St and 35th Ave NE, St. Petersburg.

⑭ Philippe Park, Philippe Pkwy, Safety Harbor.

⑮ Rocky Creek, Rocky Creek Dr, Tampa.

⑯ Gandy Boat Ramp, Tampa.

⑰ Picnic Island Park, end of Commerce Rd, Port Tampa.

⑱ MacDill AFB Marina.

⑲ Ballast Point Park off Interbay Blvd, Tampa.

⑳ Marjorie Park, 115 Columbia Dr,Tampa.

㉑ Davis Island Boat Ramp, south end of Martinique Ave, Tampa.

㉒ Alafia River - Central and Alafia Blvds, Riverview: Riverview Civic Center east of Hwy 301 off MacMullen/Booth; and off Vaughn Ave in Gibsonton.

㉓ Apollo Beach - Two ramps: south side of Apollo Beach Blvd, and on the north side where the same road meets Surfside Dr.

㉔ E.G. Simmons Park - 19th Ave NW, two miles west of Hwy 41.

㉕ Little Manatee - east of Hwy 41 on Saffold Park Dr.

㉖ Cockroach Bay - Two ramps off Cockroach Bay Rd west of Hwy 41.

㉗ Bishop Harbor - End of Bishop Harbor Rd west of Hwy 41.

SURF

There are about 25 miles of potentially fishable surf between Clearwater Beach and the southern tip of Pass-A-Grille Beach - - including a mile or so on Ft. De Soto's west shore. Although this stretch is heavily developed, access to the water shouldn't be a problem. If you're staying on the beach, great, you've got fishing right out your backdoor. If you're not, still no problem. Given the ample number of parks and public accesses highlighted below, hitting the beach should be relatively easy.

Pinellas County Beach Parks (on-site parking)

1 Sand Key Park, 1060 Gulf Blvd.

2 Indian Rocks Beach Access, 1700 Gulf Blvd.

3 Tiki Gardens - Indian Shores Beach Access, 19601 Gulf Blvd.

4 Redington Shores Beach Access, 18200 Gulf Blvd.

5 Madeira Beach Access, 14400 Gulf Blvd.

6 Treasure Island Beach Access, 10400 Gulf Blvd.

7 St. Pete Beach Access, 4700 Gulf Blvd.

8 Fort De Soto Park.

✱ City Beach Accesses (north to south)

- Clearwater Beach - Many public accesses along Mandalay Ave with limited parking. Main access with metered parking at Pier 60.

- Indian Rocks Beach - Free parking along Gulf Blvd from Whitehurst to 28th Ave.

- Indian Shores - Access and parking at Tiki Park, 19601 Gulf Blvd. Metered parking is $1/hour.

- Redington Shores - Several accesses along Gulf Blvd between 174th and 183rd Aves. Free parking at the adjacent County park (#4 above).

- North Redington Beach - Six accesses between 164th and 174th Aves. Free parking on Gulf Blvd.

- Redington Beach - One public access at 160th Ave. Only parking is in the adjacent residential area.

- Madeira Beach - Several accesses between 128th (John's Pass) and 154th Avenues. Public parking only at John's Pass.

- St. Petersburg Municipal Beach - 11260 Gulf Blvd. Parking is $.50/hour.
- Upham Beach - Just south of Blind Pass, parking and access between 68th and 70th Avenues.

OK, now we're on the beach. Now let's talk about where to fish. From a surf fishing standpoint, bottom contour and any kind of structure are fundamentally important. Basically, they tell you where to look for the highest probability of success. Cuts, troughs, swash channels, groins, rock formations, and the areas around the jetties associated with area passes are all of great interest. Fish hang out in and around such things.

In addition to the surf fish identified in Figure 1.2 (Chapter 1), you can also expect to catch a variety of non-edible species, too. These include a variety of Jacks, Ladyfish, Sharks and Stingrays. And there's always a chance for surprise - - like the isolated Cobia or Tarpon that is caught now and then in the surf!

When to fish is an easy question to address for the area surf because the answer is clear-cut. Although something may bite throughout the day (and night), all fish seem to bite best at three specific times. The first is at sunup, regardless of what the tide is doing. The second is around sundown, also regardless of the tide. The third is during the two hour period that precedes the high tide. If you have to choose only one of these three periods to fish, sunup is absolutely the best.

To summarize, and at one time or another during a year, all of the following represent reasonable expectations in Tampa Bay area surf: Snook, Speckled and Silver Trout, Bluefish, Pompano, Permit, Redfish, Whiting, Flounder, and Spanish Mackerel. Tarpon, Sharks, and Cobia are also possible.

PIERS

Pier fishing in the Tampa Bay area can be and usually is world class. Tremendous diversity is available in the potential catch department, ranging from one pound Whiting to Tarpon and Sharks up in the hundreds of pounds. In between are some 15 other species of gamefish - - that are all great fighters and delicious to eat as well. And, given the number and location of available piers, the odds are very good that one or more kinds of fish you're after will be biting somewhere in the area. Figure 3.11 identifies the action.

① Pier 60 - 1 Causeway Blvd, Clearwater Beach. This 1,000 foot long pier is open 24 hours a day, seven days a week. Bait, tackle, a snack bar, and rod rentals are all available. Admission is most reasonable: Adults - $5.35, Seniors - $4.45, kids - $3.75, and lookers - $.50. No fishing license is required. At various times of the year, all of the following can be caught off Pier 60: Cobia, Mangrove Snapper, Whiting, Flounder, Silver and Speckled Trout, Sheepshead, Black Drum, Tripletail, Spanish and King Mackerel, Reds, Snook, and Tarpon. Check the free fishing pier at the Clearwater Municipal Marina while you're in the area (25 Causeway Blvd).

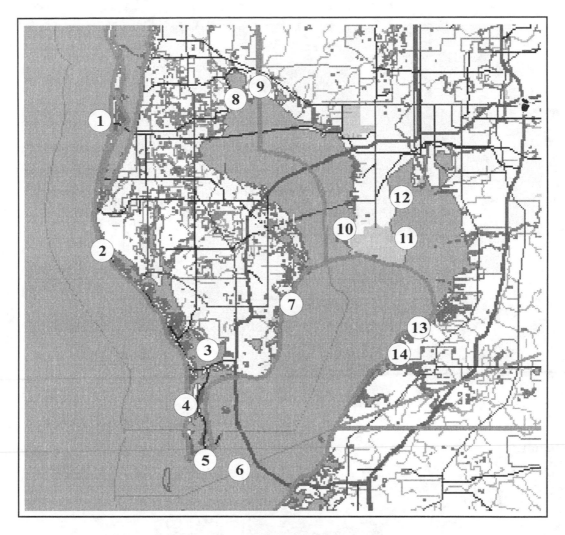

Figure 3.11 - Tampa Bay Area Piers

② Redington Long Pier - 17490 Gulf Blvd, Redington Shores. At 1,021 feet, this pier lives up to its name. It's open round-the-clock, seven days a week, offers a snack bar, bait and tackle, and rental rods and reels if you need them. Admission is $6.00 for adults and $5.00 for kids. Not surprisingly, the Long Pier's catch list is the same as Pier 60's.

Redington Long Pier

③ Gulfport Pier - Shore Blvd S. at the end of 58ᵗʰ Street S. Good access to the full variety of Boca Ciega Bay inhabitants. Try sunup and sundown for spring and summer top water action.

Gulfport Pier

④ Merry Pier - Pass-A-Grille. Superb access to all the guys who live in or transit North and Pass-A-Grille Channels. This can include: Mangrove Snapper, Black Grouper, Flounder, Sheepshead, Snook, Spanish, Pompano, Cobia, and Jack Cravalle. Other good spots in the immediate area: seawalls, gas dock, and close-by boat slips. There's no charge to fish either of the two piers but only metered parking is available. A super tackle shop with live bait is on site.

Merry Pier

⑤ Ft. De Soto Park - 3500 Pinellas Bayway S., Tierra Verde. An overview of the entire park was provided earlier in the Bay segment of this chapter. For our purposes here, we'll take a closer look at the two superb piers available to fishermen within the park. Their location is highlighted in the graphic. Both piers offer all the amenities, including baithouses. At different times of the year, you can expect to catch Spanish, Cobia, Snook, Sheepshead, Reds, Specs, etc., etc. Admission to the piers is free.

Ft. De Soto Fishing Piers

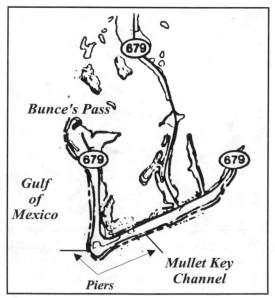

(6) Skyway Fishing Piers and other close-by opportunities. "Incredible" is clearly the operative word! Starting at the north end, let's work our way south on the Sunshine Skyway.

Skyway Bridge

- ICW Bridges - Just south of the toll booths on the causeway. Snook and wintertime Sheepshead.
- Bunce's Pass Bridges - Great summer night fishing for big Snook and a whole lot more.
- Causeway - Great wade fishing, particularly along the west side. A dredged boat channel parallels the causeway along this entire stretch and provides deep water for resident Reds, Specs, and Snook.
- North Pier - Exit 2B. Admission: $3 per car, $10 for an RV, and $2 per person over 13. About 3,360 feet of Bay, Inshore, and Offshore fishing. You can drive to your favorite spot. Catch possibilities are almost limitless: Snapper, Grouper, King and Spanish Mackerel, Bluefish, Tarpon,

North Fishing Pier

Pompano, Permit, Snook, Trout, Redfish, Cobia, Ladyfish, Jack Cravalle, Flounder, Sheepshead, Barracuda, and a whole variety of monster Sharks. There are bait shops at the ends of both North and South Piers and both piers have adjacent artificial reefs.
- South Pier - Exit 2A. Over 8,400 feet long. Same admission, convenience and incredible catch possibilities as the North Pier.
- South End Causeway Bridges. Just before you get to the shore. Although small, they're worth a try for Snook, Reds, Specs, Flounder, et al.

Bait is abundant with a throw net or gold hook/bait chaser rigs. Don't forget a bridge gaff if you're going to fish the piers.

(7) The Pier - St. Petersburg. This downtown landmark provides super year round bay fishing opportunities. Admission is free; there's a baithouse on the pier, and you can fish 24 hours a day if you like. Exit 10 off I-275 will take you there. Catch expectations include Bluefish, Redfish, Spanish, Snook, Sheepshead, Cobia, Black Drum and Trout. Try the NE corner at night for Snook. There is a rock pile adjacent to the pier. Its precise location is a closely guarded secret - - just ask around.

The Pier - St. Petersburg

Catching fish on the Pier

(8) Safety Harbor City Pier - This 450 foot long pier is part of a city park complex that also includes a marina and boat ramps. The park is located on Bayshore Dr, next door to the Safety Harbor Resort and Spa. The pier provides great access to the deeper water of the dredged boat channel into the marina. Reds, Specs, Snook, Sheepshead, and Sharks are all possibilities.

(9) Oldsmar Pier - Part of Olds Park which is located off Hwy 584 at the end of Bayview Blvd. This several hundred foot long concrete structure provides good access to all Safety Harbor inhabitants, including schooling Reds in the fall. No real fishing pressure due to the relatively isolated location.

(10) Picnic Island Pier - Just south of Port Tampa and west of MacDill AFB. Good access to the big guys that frequent the ship channel just Offshore and Port Tampa just to the north. The fact that there's

Safety Harbor City Pier

Oldsmar Pier

an artificial reef 100 feet off the end of the pier certainly doesn't hurt fishing either. The pier and boat ramp are open 24 hours a day.

11 Pelican Piers - MacDill Air Force Base. Located on the east side of the base adjacent to the Housing Office, these piers provide good access to deepwater. Snook, Reds, Specs, Sheepshead, Black Drum, Flounder, Spanish, and an occasional Cobia are all possibilities. Adjacent flats particularly productive in the late spring.

12 Ballast Point Pier - West shore of Hillsborough Bay in the Ballast Point Park. The artificial reef adjacent to the pier makes Ballast Point a fishy area indeed. The pier provides excellent fishing for Sheepshead, Snook, Specs, and Reds in the spring, summer, and fall. Specs are often available in the winter at night under the lights. The park also has a boat ramp, bait shop, and restaurant. There is no charge to fish the 1,000 foot long pier.

13 Apollo Beach Pier - At the end of Apollo Beach Blvd off Hwy 41. Rustic is probably a fair description. This free pier provides several hundred feet of wood structure out into Tampa Bay. There are several deep holes along the pier's north side. Free parking is available at the foot of the pier.

14 E.G. Simmons Park Piers - Just north of the Little Manatee River, two miles west on 19th Ave from Hwy 41. The park offers several small piers along the surrounding mangrove channels. There are also good shore fishing opportunities, flats access into Tampa Bay, and well maintained boat ramps. The park is open from 8 a.m. to 6 p.m.

A Superior Tampa Bay Pier Fisherman

INSHORE

Inshore small boat action between Clearwater and Palmetto is consistently good for both migrating pelagic species and year round bottom dwellers. As Figure 3.12 suggests, there is an excellent system of artificial reefs within easy reach of Inshore fishermen. At least 22 of the area's gamefish can be caught on these reefs, in area passes, or somewhere in between.

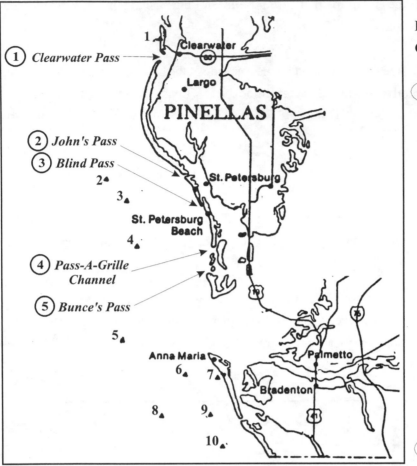

Figure 3.12 Inshore - Clearwater to Palmetto

① Clearwater Pass - The south jetty is productive for big Reds in the fall and early winter and Snook during the summer. King Mackerel are possible at the mouth of the pass in the spring and fall. (Sand Key Park provides great south jetty access for shore fishermen.) Shallows south of the pass are good for Tarpon (May - July) and Cobia frequent the jetties in season.

② John's Pass - Bridge over the pass is usually year-round Snook water. Specs and Reds join in during the winter. Tarpon hang out in the shallows just south of the mouth of the pass (shore fishing access via South Beach Park). The John's Pass islands are also great for giant Reds and Flounder in June, and large Specs frequent adjacent flats.

③ Blind Pass - Good for Winter Specs, Reds, and Snook (shore fishing access via Upham Park). Jetties are good for Snook in July, and Spanish wander through the pass in season.

④ Pass-A-Grille Channel - (North Channel). Very productive area for giant Snook around the tip of Pass-A-Grille Beach. Kings, Spanish, Cobia, and Sharks are also possibilities. Winter fishing for Snook, Reds, Specs, Sheepshead, Pompano, et al, is superb. Please see the "Merry Pier" write up in the previous Pier section for additional details on this area.

⑤ Bunce's Pass - Premier area Tarpon action (May - July). At one time of the year or another, all of the following can be found in the pass: Snook, Reds, Specs, Flounder, Spanish, Cobia, Pompano, and, occasionally, Permit.

Specifics on the Inshore artificial reef system are highlighted in the following legend. All of the spots on the chart are within seven miles of the beach.

Spot #	Name	LORAN Coordinates	Latitude Longitude	Depth (ft)	Structure
1	Pier 60 Fishing Reef	14245.0/44916.0	27/58.38C 82/49.50C	5-12	481 tons of concrete around the pier
2	Madeira Beach Reef	19201.0/44768.0	27/46.03C 82/54.90C	30-33	Concrete pyramids, culverts, rubble
3	Treasure Island Reef	14200.8/44738.7	27/44.50C 82/52.85C	29-33	Concrete pyramids, walls, culverts
4	St. Petersburg Beach Reef	14192.9/44694.1	27/40.60C 82/51.75C	34-36	Causeway and bridge rubble, 200' barge, 10 M60 Army tanks
5	Reef "A" 7 mile	14169.0/44655.0	27/32.216C 82/52.70C	40	Tires, concrete rubble
6	Reef "B" 3 mile	14175.8/44594.0	27/29.57C 82/47.00C	30	Tires, concrete rubble
7	One Mile Reef	14179.3/44564.2	27/29.390 82/44.050	21-27	Skyway bridge, many barges, tires, 1000 tons of concrete culverts
8	Reef "C" 7 mile	14162.4/44590.5	27/26.703C 82/49.165C	40	Tires, concrete rubble
9	Reef "D" 3 mile	14172.0/44555.0	27/26.753C 82/44.785C	25	525 tons concrete culverts, rubble
10	Funerarius Reef	14166.6/44521.4	---- ----	35	Concrete rubble

Legend - Figure 3.12

Enough numbers. These spots are proven producers. Try one. Better yet, weather permitting, try several. And, while you're trying things, here are some final Inshore thoughts you might want to check out.

- Inshore Trolling Patterns - Knowledgeable area small boat fishermen have developed consistently productive routes Inshore for visiting pelagic species. When Kings visit the area in April and November, one good pattern racetracks between the Pass-A-Grille North Channel marker #2 and John's Pass to the north in 10 - 25 feet of water. Another consistently productive area is off Indian

Rocks Beach. For several miles off the beach, there are shoals that attract bait fish - - that migrating Spanish, Kings, and Cobia can't resist.

- Snook - To re-emphasize a point, area passes can be where the action is. Between May and September, spawning Snook stack up in Clearwater, John's, Blind, Pass-A-Grille, and Bunce's Passes.

- Fall Smoker Kings - One good area is called Sand Key and it's about a mile off Clearwater. This 18 - 23 foot deep, mile square plus area of limestone hard bottom produces big Kings from mid-October to around the first of the year. Slow trolled live threadfin (greenbacks) is one preferred approach.

- Other Good Smoker Spots/Areas- Pasco Artificial Reef #1, Egmont Channel edges, Dunedin Reef, Betty Rose, and the Mandalay hard bottom.

- Clearwater Pass - The area around the bridge has consistently produced monster Reds, Snook, Cobia, Sharks, and Tarpon. Kings, Pompano, Permit, Specs, Grouper, and Jewfish are also possibilities. One of the largest and most cooperative residents of the area, however, is the Black Drum. There are lots of them and 50 pounders aren't extraordinary.

- Skyway Tarpon - They're dependably present between April and September. You can tie up to the wood and concrete bumpers around the bridge's main center supports. After a fish is hooked, the fun begins. You've got to chase him for any chance of preventing a cut-off on the bridge pilings.

OK, its time to begin wrapping up our discussion of when and where to fish the Tampa Bay area. We'll close out this segment with a quick trip Offshore. There are some great opportunities out there, too.

OFFSHORE

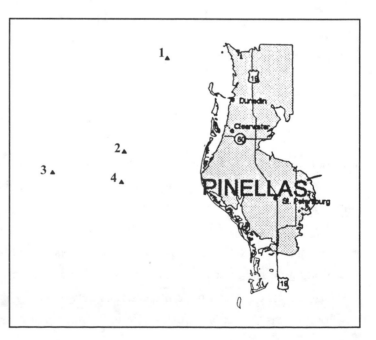

Actually, our trip Offshore won't be that quick, despite what I just said. That's because you've got to go a ways to get to the deeper water associated with Offshore fishing opportunities. Along this stretch of the West Coast, the bottom drops off slowly as you head out. At nine miles off the beach, the depth averages only 36 feet. Double the distance out, and you're still only talking about 60 feet

**Figure 3.13 - Tampa Bay
Area Offshore Spots**

of water. Real big gamefishing is much farther out still. You start to find the big guys about 80 miles off St. Petersburg Beach in an area known as the "Elbow." Wahoo, Yellowfin Tuna, Dolphin, Sails and White Marlin are possibilities. Go 20 miles farther west and you should be close to the 100 fathom curve. If you're lucky, the Loop Current will have loaded the area with bait and you'll catch your Blue Marlin. Closer to home, there are four artificial reefs worthy of attention. Figure 3.13 provides the details.

Spot #	Name	LORAN Coordinates	Latitude Longitude	Depth (ft)	Structure
1	Tarpon Springs Reef	14259.3/44935.6	28/08.25C 82/5581.C	26-28	Cement pyramids
2	Rube Allyn Reef	14211.2/44884.6	27/55.194 83/01.586	50	Concrete culverts
		14212.4/44885.9	27/55.540 83/01.450	50	Concrete culverts
		14212.4/44885.8	27/55.550C 83/01.440C	50	Concrete culverts
		14212.4/44885.9	27/55.560 83/01.450	50	Concrete culverts
		14212.4/44886.0	27/55.560 83/01.450	50	Barge, 2 steel vessels, Japanese fish attractors
		14212.3/44886.6	27/55.60C 83/01340C		
3	Pinellas II Reef	14181.6/44943.3	27/52.56C 83/11.18C	80	Tires, 250' steel barge. Tug "DT Sheridan," 180' Coast Guard cutter "Blackthorn"
			27/52.57 83/11.28		
4	Indian Shores Reef	14200.0/44859.7	27/51.40C 83/01.75C	44-46	Two LSM's, salt hopper barge

Legend - Figure 3.13

Before leaving Offshore, here are several more bits of random information. We'll start with some additional spots.

Name	LORAN	Latitude	Longitude	Depth	Structure
Bay Rando	14057.1/44375.5	26/45.85	82/50.87	90	Barge
Mexican Pride	14089.6/44898.6	27/31.38	83/24.38	125	Steamer
Shrimp Boat	14149.1/44694.5	27/30.32	82/59.20	60	Shrimpboat
Wreckage	14098.0/44898.0	--	--	125	--
The Airplane	14068.9/44874.2	--	--	138	--
Sailboat	14097.1/45091.8	--	--	138	--
Shrimp Boat	14084.1/44957.8	--	--	126	--

Name	LORAN	Latitude	Longitude	Depth	Structure
Wreck	13930.8/45250.2	--	--	240	--
Gunsmoke	14184.3/44762.4	--	--	--	--
Steamer	14162.3/44755.8	--	--	--	--
Betty Rose	14184.3/44769.2	--	--	--	--
Wreck	14203.8/44944.9	--	--	--	--

Figure 3.14 - Additional Tampa Bay Offshore Structure

- Who Lives Where and When - There seems to be a consensus in the Tampa Bay area that bluewater fishing may start as close as 30 miles west of the beach. But, for dependable access to Offshore pelagic species, 50 - 80 miles out is probably required. Water depths at these distances (150-180 feet) probably hold Blue Marlin, White Marlin, Yellowfin and Blackfin Tuna, Sailfish, Wahoo, and Dolphin nearly year round. About the only rule of thumb, however, is more Tuna and Sails fall through spring and "Hoo's" in the summer.

- Florida Middlegrounds - Please see write-up in the previous Cedar Key - Dunedin Offshore section. The Middlegrounds are roughly 100 miles off Tampa Bay.

- Loop Current - A river of relatively cool water that tracks Offshore north up the Mexican Gulf Coast, east along the US Gulf Coast, and then south down the west coast of Florida. At times, it comes within 40 miles of the central Florida coast. You need a good thermometer because you're looking for relatively small temperature differentials. When you find the "Loop" in 60 feet or more water, look for Marlin, Sails, Tuna, Wahoo and Dolphin.

And that's all there is to say about Offshore and all the rest of the super fishing opportunities between Clearwater and Palmetto. It's time to continue south along Florida's West Coast. Our next stop will be the area between Bradenton and Englewood.

-PERSONAL NOTES-

CHAPTER 4

BRADENTON TO ENGLEWOOD

This stretch of Florida's West Coast is amazingly fishy despite its lack of a monster bay like Tampa's. It does, however, have some very special features of its own - - like 30 miles of barrier keys, six consistently productive passes into the Gulf of Mexico, two immensely fertile bays, and an extensive array of both Inshore and Offshore bottom structure. Major segments of this stretch are also lightly populated. That can significantly reduce fishing pressure and sometimes provides unique moments of solitude with nature.

As we noted above, this is a very fishy stretch of coast. Figure 4.1 makes the point. As we move farther south, more and more of the resident species are available on a year round basis, without the benefit of warm water discharge canals from power plants.

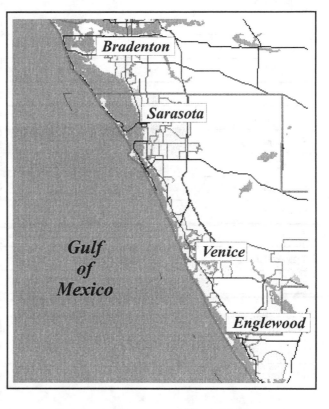

Figure 4.0 - Bradenton to Englewood

Possibilities	Best Time To Try
Amberjack	Available year round - late Spring through Early Fall
Barracuda	Available year round - Summer/Early Fall
Black Drum	Available year round - Fall/Winter/Early Spring
Black Sea Bass	Available year round
Blackfin Tuna	Summer/Early Fall
Bluefish	Available year round
Blue Marlin	Late Summer/Early Fall
Bonito	Available year round
Cobia	Migratory - available year round - Spring

Possibilities	Best Time To Try
Dolphin	Summer/Early Fall
Flounder	Available year round - Fall/Winter
Grouper	Available year round
Jack Cravalle	Available year round
King Mackerel	Migratory - Spring and Fall
Permit	Available year round - Spring/Summer
Pompano	Available year round - Summer/Fall
Redfish	Available year round
Sailfish	Summer/Fall
Sheepshead	Available year round
Snapper	Available year round
Snook*	Available year round
Spanish Mackerel	Migratory - Available year round
Swordfish	Late Summer/Early Fall
Tarpon	Migratory - Available year round - Summer
Triggerfish	Available year round
Tripletail	Available year round - Summer/Fall
Trout*	Available year round
Wahoo	Spring through early Fall
White Marlin	Late Spring through early Fall
Whiting	Available year round
Yellowfin Tuna	Late Summer/Fall
* Subject to closed season. Catch and release OK. Please see Appendix for dates.	

Figure 4.1 - Gamefish Availability

As in previous chapters, a couple of words of explanation about Figure 4.1 might be helpful. Specifically, if there isn't a qualifier after a "Best Time to Try" recommendation, that means the whole period is good. Black Sea Bass is a good example of this. On the other hand, if there is a qualifier, it simply indicates the very best time within a particular period. Mr. Amberjack can help us here. You can catch him every month of the year. But he seems to be the most hungry and aggressive from late Spring to early Fall.

OK, with that top level summary in mind, let's take a look at fishing action on a month-to-month basis. The following narrative is only supposed to give you a feel for what typically goes on between Bradenton and Englewood. It is certainly not all inclusive.

January

- Reefs in 40 - 50 feet of water off Englewood producing Blackfin Tuna, Red and Gag Grouper, Black Sea Bass, Snapper, and bull Reds. AJ's around warm water springs.
- Big Grouper 27 miles off Venice and close in at Longboat Pass.
- Specs, Reds, and Snook in area creeks, rivers, and bayous.
- Snook at night in Venice canals.
- Reds and Trout active on oyster bars in Little Sarasota Bay from Stickney Pt south.
- Inshore reefs producing Sheepshead and Triggerfish.
- M-6 holding Snapper and Flounder.
- Bluefish along the docks and under the bridge in New Pass.

February

- M-Reefs off Sarasota starting to hold Grouper and Snapper.
- Grouper cooperating on live coral bottom five to eight miles west of Anna Maria Island.
- Reds in area residential canals and coastal rivers and creeks. Snook, too.
- Very big Sheepshead on the docks and bridges around Bird Key.
- Tripletail around stone crab trap buoy lines.
- Whiting and Silver Trout on the north side of New Pass by Sand Point. Bluefish in the Pass around the bridge.
- The I-3 Roehr artificial reef loaded up with Spanish and Bluefish.
- Big Specs possible in Zwicks Channel.
- Snook along area beaches and Pompano from the beaches to the grass flats.

March

- Spanish are all over Sarasota's Ringling Bridge. Kings in 25 - 40 feet of water moving north.
- Grouper, Sea Bass, AJ's, Mangrove Snapper, Flounder, and Sheepshead on Sarasota's three mile reefs.
- Snook starting to show on the flats in Sarasota and Lemon Bays.
- Kings and Spanish active off Englewood's Anglers Pier.
- Spanish Mackerel starting to show off Sarasota and Venice municipal piers.
- The first Kings arriving on the M-reefs.
- Gator Trout on the oyster bars in Lemon Bay.
- Strong run of Kings from the "Cuda Hole" to the M-6.

April

- Spanish, Bluefish, Specs, and Pompano on the west side flats in Sarasota Bay.
- Big Cobia and big Tarpon in Sarasota and Lemon Bays.
- Offshore from Sarasota, D-6 and D-9 (105 ft) reefs producing some large AJ's and an abundance of Snapper and Grouper.

- Snook and Reds hitting the flats.
- "Cuda Hole" off Sarasota producing intermittent Kings.
- Tarpon and Jack Cravalle possible around the New Pass bridge.

May

- Permit starting to show on the M-Reefs off Sarasota.
- AJ's, Grouper, and Wahoo on the wreck "Mexican Pride."
- Big Cobia at creek mouths eating Blue Crabs.
- Snook in the surf at Bean Pt and Sarasota beaches.
- Tarpon running the beaches and in area passes.
- Kings still running on the M-7, 12 miles west of the New Pass bell.
- Smallish Specs active in Sarasota Bay grass flats.
- Offshore on the D-9, 30 miles west of New Pass - - Dolphin, Blackfin, and possibly Wahoo.
- Bonito and Barracuda working hard on the M-3.
- Spanish, Blues, Jack Cravalle, Reds, and Flounder available in area bays.
- Inshore (I) reefs in 20 - 30 feet of water yielding Grouper, Snapper, and Flounder.

June

- Giant Tarpon moving north just off Sarasota area beaches along Casey and Siesta Keys.
- Catch and release Snook easy on the points and mouth of the Manatee River.
- Nice Grouper in the natural breaks in 40 - 50 feet of water around the "Cuda Hole."
- Offshore in 120 feet and closer in at 45 feet on the 3 and 7 mile reefs, Red and Gag Grouper, Mangrove Snapper, Blackfin Tuna, Dolphin and schools of Bonito are all active. Barracuda cooperating, too.
- Specs, Reds, and Snook possible around area docks.
- Spanish Mackerel thick Inshore.
- Permit are active on most M-reefs, and Snapper, Grouper, and Flounder good on M-6, 7, and 8.

July

- Dolphin in 50 feet of water off Sarasota on floating grass.
- Lemon Bay yielding gator Specs.
- Snook stacked up in area passes.
- Tarpon in the swash channels (8-20 ft) within 100 yds of Manatee beaches.
- Cobia frequently found on area channel markers.
- Superior Spec fishing on grass flats early and late.
- Permit, lots of Barracuda, and an occasional Cobia cooperating on the 1, 3, and 7 mile artificial reefs.
- Reds are in the mangroves in Terra Ceia and Miguel Bays, and starting to school in Sarasota Bay.
- Pompano and Bluefish sharing area grass flats with big Specs.
- Spanish and Barracuda on the I-3 artificial reef.

August
- Tarpon working early mornings around Bean Pt and Siesta Key.
- All area flats infested with Redfish.
- Off Sarasota, Blackfin Tuna, Sails, Wahoo, Dolphin, Grouper and Snapper are available in 120 feet of water around fresh water springs.
- Redfish and Cobia being taken by waders on Manatee County's Emerson Pt.
- Amberjack 25 miles due west of Sarasota.
- Reds aggressive in the mouth of the Manatee River.
- Large Dolphin in 120 - 150 feet of water and Kings in 80 feet.
- Permit still aggressive on the close-in reefs and continue to have a few Cobia for company.
- Spanish and Barracuda on Inshore artificial reefs.
- Pompano stealing the show in Big Pass and adjacent flats.
- Big Specs and Bluefish in Zwick Channel.

September
- Specs, Pompano, Bluefish, and Spanish starting to show well in Sarasota Bay.
- Lots of big Snook on artificial reefs off Englewood Beach.
- Barracuda eating everything in sight on Offshore wrecks.
- Tarpon off Venice beaches.
- Big Reds by the school in area passes.
- Offshore trolling provides excellent and larger Dolphin, Wahoo, and Sailfish in 80-120 feet of water.

October
- Pompano making good runs in Sarasota Bay.
- Sheepshead and Flounder cooperating on area docks and seawalls.
- King Mackerel 5 to 12 miles off Sarasota mixed in with Spanish.
- Offshore in 90 -120 feet of water, Sailfish and Dolphin are still around.
- Cobia and Tripletail are marker - hopping on their way south.
- Longboat Pass producing Grouper to 30 pounds.
- Area piers active with Mangrove Snapper, Spanish, Specs, Snook, Reds, Black Drum, and Sheepshead.

November
- Grouper, Kings, Spanish, and Cobia in 36 - 40 feet of water on hard bottoms off Sarasota. Many Kings closer in 30 feet of water.
- Gag Grouper in 20 - 30 feet of water off the Venice jetty.
- Snook in usual deep water holding areas and on the docks behind Otter Key.
- Tripletail starting to show up on Stone Crab trap buoys.
- Big Permit hungry in Longboat Pass.

- Seven Mile Reef west of Manatee County producing smoker Kings.
- Bluefish, some Spanish and a few bull Reds on the I-2 artificial reef.
- Specs on the flats in south Sarasota Bay.

December
- Bluefish and Spanish in area passes, particularly Sarasota's Big and New Passes.
- Tripletail around and along Stone Crab trap line buoys.
- Pompano in Sarasota passes and grass flats in the bay.
- Grouper in 25 feet or less water off Venice and in the holes off the jetties.
- Redfish still active in Lemon Bay.
- Snook in residential canals off Sarasota Bay.
- Offshore, in 25 - 40 feet of water on rocky ledges, all of the following are possibilities: Grouper, Cobia, Kings, Spanish, AJ's and Barracuda.
- Triggerfish thick on Inshore reefs. The I-3 producing Bluefish and Cobia.

As in previous chapters, about five years of data were synthesized to compile this monthly narrative. Obviously, it is not a current fishing report. But it does provide some useful insights into year round fishing action between Bradenton and Englewood. Now we'll focus on more specific spots and areas that have a demonstrated record of producing fish. We'll begin with a look at the area's bays and adjacent and contiguous water like the Manatee River and Intercoastal Waterway. That will be followed by similar coverage of Surf, Pier, Inshore (including passes), and Offshore fishing opportunities.

BAYS

Before we really jump in this water, let's talk shore fishing opportunities. Having a boat is great, but it certainly isn't necessary to fish some of the best spots between Bradenton and Englewood. Here are some super bridge and other shore fishing areas to keep in mind on the northern end of this stretch.

Bradenton Mainland
- Manatee Ave Bridges and Causeways - Three bridges: Palma Sola Bay, Perico Bayou and Anna Maria Sound, and their adjacent flats and channels, make up this system. Even though boaters can and do take advantage of the fishing here, this area is better suited for land-based anglers and waders. Specs, Sheepshead, Snook, Redfish and Flounder will be hitting. The Anna Maria Sound and Palma Sola Bay waters offer wading along channels and across great expanses of grass flats. Perico Bayou is a rocky, oyster barred flowage where a wading angler can cast beneath the mangroves. There is far better fishing here than you might imagine while driving by on Manatee Ave.
- Braden River Bridge - Head east on Manatee Ave from downtown. It isn't far. There are boat ramps at the bridge and a wide variety of species available year round.

Sarasota Mainland

- Siesta Dr Bridge - Over the ICW from the mainland to Siesta Key. Park along the road.
- Island Park - Downtown bayfront, Marina Jack. Fish from the seawall.
- Phillippi Creek - Bridge is near The Landings on Hwy 41.
- Stickney Point - At the end of Stickney Point Rd. You can fish off either the bridge or adjacent seawall. There's a close-by tackle shop.

The Keys

- Anna Maria Bayfront Park - On Bay Blvd North, the park provides good access for wade fishing the flats along Anna Maria Sound.
- Longboat Pass Bridge - Literally, almost every species in the Gulf except the billfish wander through here at one time or another.
- Beer Can Island - Located in the center of Longboat Pass. You can walk out to it at low tide. Limited parking on Gulfside Drive.
- New Pass Bridge - This record-producing span connects Longboat and Lido Keys. Year-round action!
- Bay Island - On the Gulf side of the Siesta Bridge. Its seawalls are always productive spots.
- Turtle Beach Lagoon - On the south end of Siesta Key, you can fish from the shore, off the seawall or the pier.
- Old Midnight Pass - Walk south from Turtle Beach about a half a mile and you can fish either the Gulf, pass or bay.
- City Island - On Lido Key. Fish off the north seawall or small docks.

Those are just a few of the productive shore fishing spots in Bradenton and Sarasota. We'll visit the piers in the area later in this chapter. Right now, lets check out some of the almost limitless bay fishing opportunities.

Bridge Street, Anna Maria Island - Bradenton Beach Pier in the background

(Located on the map in Figure 4.2 on the following page.)

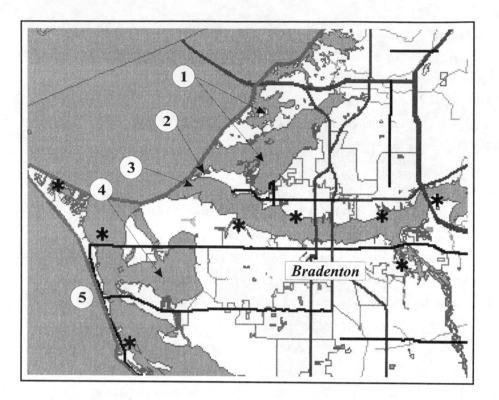

Figure 4.2 - Bradenton Area

Convenient Boat Ramps (✱)

✱ NE side of the I-75 bridge.
✱ Hwy 64 at the Braden River bridge.
✱ Highland Shores on Shore Dr, Ellenton.
✱ North side of the Anna Maria bridge.
✱ 63ʳᵈ St Memorial Park, Holmes Beach.
✱ Coquina Bayside Park, Anna Maria Island.
✱ Riverside Park, Riverside Dr, Palmetto.
✱ Warners Bayou, County Park, NW Riverview Blvd, Bradenton.

① Terra Ceia and Miguel Bays - Productive water for Snook, Reds, and Specs almost year round. In the summer, check the points at the mouths of the bays for Snook; hard bottom / oyster bars / mangroves for Reds; and in the holes on deeper grass flats for Specs. Winter Snook in Terra Ceia canals and Frog Creek.

② Emerson Point - The western tip of Snead Island at the mouth of the Manatee River is a favorite of both wading and boating anglers. A host of marine species feed here, but Snook is the target for most fishermen. Redfish, Sheepshead and Speckled Trout are available. During spring and summer, a good concentration of Sharks can be found in the deeper river channel.

③ Manatee River

• Twenty two free flowing miles long, and full of fish. Snook, Tarpon, Cobia, Jack Cravalle, Sharks, Reds, Specs, Spanish, Flounder, Sheepshead, Black Drum, etc., etc.

- Spring and fall - Check the river mouth for Snook.
- Summer - Tarpon, Jack Cravalle, Snook, Cobia, Sharks, Reds, and Specs on the flats adjacent to the mouth. Cobia on the markers.
- Shore fishing - Try De Soto National Memorial Park (De Soto Memorial Hwy off Manatee Ave W) and Emerson Point area (western tip of Snead's Island).
- Mid-River Hot Spots - Snead Island Boat Works (north shore adjacent to McKay Pt), Warner's Bayou (south shore just east of McNeil Pt), the new Green Bridge between Palmetto and Bradenton, pilings of the old ferry dock, the Clyde Fore Holes, and the mid-river railroad trestle.
- Upper Braden and Manatee Rivers - Good winter Snook fishing.

- Port Manatee - A spectacular area. They're all here during the year (Snook, Reds, Specs, Jewfish, Grouper, Sheepshead, Mangrove Snapper, Cobia, Flounder, Sharks, and Spanish Mackerel).

Port Manatee

- Swash Channels and Docks - This is a fairly broad area which includes both sides of the river from the Green Bridge to its mouth. Snook and Redfish are the primary targets around the piers and docks, while Reds and Specs can be caught in the swash channels 12 months out of the year. This is a boating area, for the most part, but access is available at the foot of streets and avenues on both sides of the river.

(4) Palma Sola Bay - Good structure and habitat make this mile wide area a consistent producer of Reds, Specs, Flounder, Grouper, Snapper, Jack Cravalle, and Snook.

(5) Cortez Bridge to Leffis Key - Deeper holes and shoal along the western side of the ICW are good areas for Reds, Specs, and large Flounder in fall and winter months. The Coquina ramp is convenient.

**Looking North
Up The Bay**

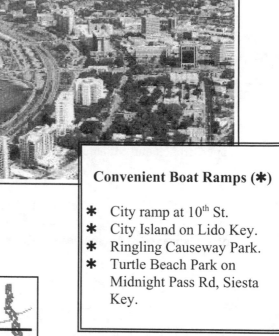

Convenient Boat Ramps (✱)

✱ City ramp at 10th St.
✱ City Island on Lido Key.
✱ Ringling Causeway Park.
✱ Turtle Beach Park on Midnight Pass Rd, Siesta Key.

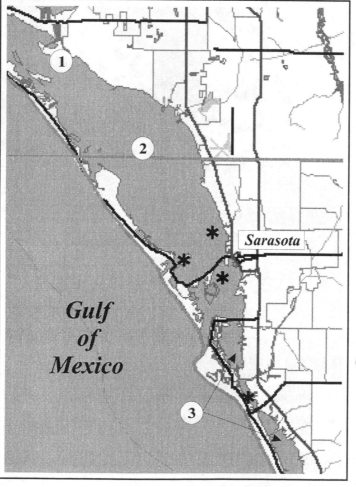

Figure 4.3 - Sarasota Area

① Tidy Island - Sister Eys Flats - To a large portion of Manatee County's recreational anglers, this is the bread and butter area of fishing. For the most part, only three species are sought here - Snook, Reds, and Specs. The area is roughly three square miles and consists of shallow grass flats, some pot holes, and the vestiges of the old Sarasota Bay Channel.

② Sarasota Bay

• Specs - good areas to try:
  – On the north end, the series of mangrove islets on the west side that surround Longboat Key's Buttonwood Harbor.

- On the east side, the deep grass flats off the Ringling Museum and farther north at the mouth of Bowlees Creek.
- On the west side, the grass flats off the Mote Marine Laboratory and the Zwick Channel area adjacent to and north of New Pass.
- Reds - Try these, too:
  - The flats on the north end of the bay and around oyster bars, too.
  - Canal seawalls on Bird, Lido, and Siesta Keys (winter).
  - Transition zones between channels and grass flats.
- Cobia - In the fall/winter, check the "middlegrounds" on the south end of the bay, just east of New Pass.
- Pompano - During the winter, check the flats just inside the passes.
- Tarpon - Available between early spring and fall. Check the Jim Evans Reef just south of the west end of the Ringling Bridge and around the bridge itself.
- General Comment - The spoil islands, dredged channels, and residential canals on the northwestern section of the bay are all worthy of exploration year-round. At any given time, you may find Reds, Specs, Snook, and Flounder. In the fall, check for schools of Bluefish, Spanish, Trout, and Jack Cravalle on the bay sides of area passes.
- Sarasota's Urban Creeks - Phillippi and Bowlee's Creeks and Hudson Bayou are good for winter Snook.
- Intracoastal Waterway Edges - The rocks separating Sarasota Bay and the federal inside channel meander southward from markers 45 and 46 at Longboat Pass to marker 15. They hold Sheepshead and Black Drum in the winter, and Mangrove Snapper, Redfish, Flounder and some surprisingly big Gag Grouper in the summer.

(3) Roberts Bay/Little Sarasota Bay - The grassy points on the west side of Roberts Bay produce springtime gator Trout. The dredged boat basins in The Landings area should be checked in the fall and winter for larger Reds, Specs, and Snook. In Little Sarasota Bay to the south, work the channels inside Midnight Pass for Snook and Specs. Fall Flounder (big) along the edges of the ICW are always a possibility.

Lemon Bay

(Number 3 on the map on the following page.)

Figure 4.4 - Venice and Englewood Areas

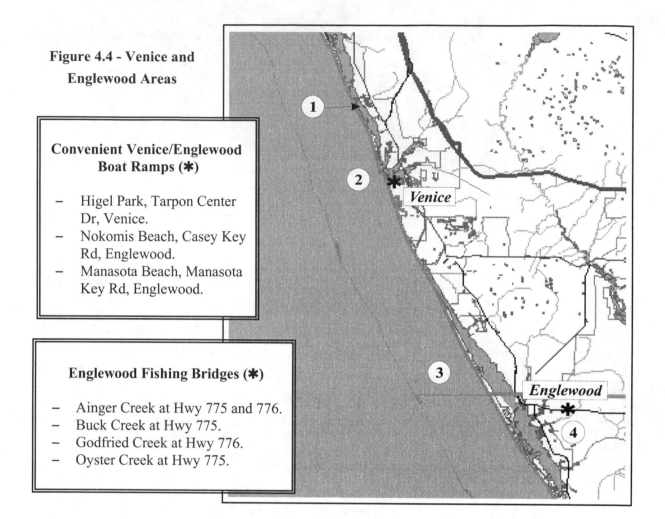

Convenient Venice/Englewood Boat Ramps (✳)

– Higel Park, Tarpon Center Dr, Venice.
– Nokomis Beach, Casey Key Rd, Englewood.
– Manasota Beach, Manasota Key Rd, Englewood.

Englewood Fishing Bridges (✳)

– Ainger Creek at Hwy 775 and 776.
– Buck Creek at Hwy 775.
– Godfried Creek at Hwy 776.
– Oyster Creek at Hwy 775.

(1) Oscar Scherer State Park - Two miles south of Osprey on Hwy 41. Off Little Sarasota Bay, it's a good place to fish South Creek from the shore or rent a canoe to cover more water. Very Snooky area.

(2) Albee Road Bridge - Good spot near the Venice Inlet. Particularly productive for big Reds in the fall. Venice pier and jetties on the inlet are equally productive. All will produce the full group of players, including Tarpon, Snook, Reds, Specs, Flounder, Blues, Spanish, Jack Cravalle, Cobia, and Sheepshead to name just a few.

(3) Lemon Bay - This Englewood area bay provides extraordinary fishing for Flounder, Pompano, Snook, Grouper, Redfish, Mangrove Snapper, Specs, Sheepshead, Bluefish, Spanish, et al. The bay is a unique, submerged ecosystem of mangroves, seagrass, and oyster biological communities. Its uniqueness was recognized with its designation as an Aquatic Preserve and an "Outstanding Florida Water." All told, the preserve encompasses some 7,667 areas of Lemon Bay. Public boat ramps (and good places to fish) are located at the Manasota Key Bridge, Indian Mound Park and the Tom Adams Bridge.

④ South Gulf Cove Canals - This Englewood area canal network was constructed during the 1960's. The network is still mostly undeveloped and both shore and boat fishing opportunities are outstanding. Small boats can be launched at a number of satisfactory dirt ramps at several locations. Snook, Reds, Jacks, and Tarpon all enter the canals from the Myakka River.

SURF

The entire stretch of beach from the tip of Anna Maria Island in the north all the way south to Englewood is potentially excellent for surf fishing. While there are several obvious reasons for this, one that may not be obvious is probably the most important. Specifically, there are narrow strips of flat rock formations that essentially parallel the beach - - within casting distance - - all the way from the mouth of Tampa Bay south to Boca Grande. This rock structure is particularly pronounced along Siesta Key and Anna Maria Island. In many places, it is clearly visible.

Snook and Mangrove Snapper are prime targets in the surf in the spring and summer. They are joined at various times by Flounder, Spanish, and Bluefish. Bigger prey such as Tarpon, Cobia, and Barracuda are also distinct possibilities from the beach.

In the winter, a slightly different cast of characters takes over. Sheepshead, Pompano, Reds, and Specs become prime targets. They are frequently joined, however, by Blues, Spanish, Bonito, Black Drum, and the always cooperative Whiting.

Working north to south, good rock structure (and surf fishing) may be found in the following areas:

- Bradenton Beach to the southern tip of Anna Maria Island.
- The south end of Longboat Key.
- "Point of Rocks" on Siesta Key.
- All along Casey Key.
- Venice's Casperson Beach.
- All along Manasota Key.

Two other spots are worthy of specific mention. The first is Whitney Beach. It's located about a mile south of Longboat Pass and is tough for a shore fisherman to get to. You'll have to wade because the beachfront is private property. But it's worth the effort. Whitney Beach is a mess of rocks, crumbling seawalls, and what have you, that really hold the fish. In warmer weather, look for Snook, Reds, and

Mangrove Snapper. In the winter, Whitney is always a good bet for Sheepshead, Specs, Black Drum, and Pompano. Farther south, a second spot to check is Casperson Beach. It is alleged that some really, really big Snook hang out on this beach in the spring and summer.

So, OK, there are fish in the surf. Now, how do I get at them? Glad you asked. Figure 4.5 should be of some help.

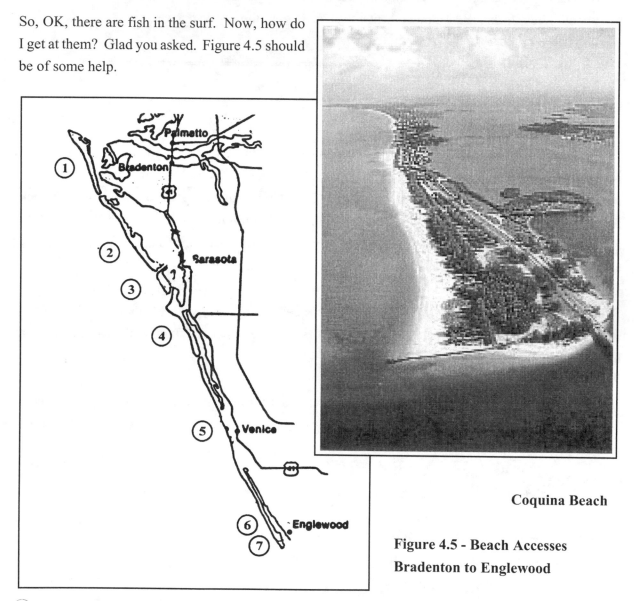

Coquina Beach

**Figure 4.5 - Beach Accesses
Bradenton to Englewood**

① Anna Maria Island -

- Bean Point - Northern tip of the island. Passage and Egmont Keys and the mouth of Tampa Bay are right there. Parking not too bad.
- Manatee County Public Beach - South a bit on Gulf Dr. Plenty of parking.
- Coquina Beach - A little farther south in Bradenton Beach. There are three beach parks within a mile or so of each other. The first is a city park, the second is called Coquina Beach, and the third (city) is adjacent to the north jetty of Longboat Pass.

(2) Longboat Key - Beach accesses on this key are just that - - accesses! You'll have to look hard, but there are some, and they include the following:

- North Shore Rd.
- Coral Ave.
- Palmetto and Seabreeze.
- Broadway.
- Beachwalk (6900 block of Gulf of Mexico Dr).
- Gulfside Rd.
- Atlas St (4800 block of Gulf of Mexico Dr).
- Hilton.
- Longview Dr.
- Mayfield St.
- Westfield St.
- Triton St.
- Neptune St.

All are off Gulf of Mexico Dr (Hwy 789, which is called Gulf Dr on Anna Maria Island).

(3) Lido Key - Continuing south on Hwy 789 over New Pass, there are two beach parks on this key. The first, North Lido Beach, is reached by going west from the traffic circle and then just bearing right. Parking is limited at this formerly "topless" beach. A half mile south is South Lido Park. Parking is usually not a problem. The park provides surf fishing opportunities and superb access to the big guys that live in Big Sarasota Pass.

(4) Siesta Key - From the mainland, take Hwy 789 out to the key. There are three parks there that are worthy of your consideration:

- Siesta Beach - On the northern end of the key, it has award winning white sand, ample parking, and all the amenities.
- Turtle Beach - Farther south, it, too, has good surf access and all the amenities.

Lido Key

- Palmer Point Park North - Literally at the end of the road, it provides great access to the waters of Midnight Pass as well as the Gulf surf.

(5) Venice Area - Still working north to south, there are five possibilities in the area:

- Nokomis Beach - Take Hwy 789 to Casey Key Rd. Good facilities, including a boat ramp.
- North Jetty Park - At the south end of North Jetty Rd, the park provides great access to both the surf and the very fishy waters of Venice Inlet. There's a bait shop on site.
- Venice Municipal Beach - Located at the end of W Venice Ave. There's a coral reef less than a quarter mile off the beach.
- Brohard Park Beach - Just south of Venice Harbor Airport on Harbor Dr, the park is well equipped, including a fishing pier and bait shop.
- Casperson Beach - Next door to Brohard, this is allegedly one of the longest beaches in the state. It's partially undeveloped and, with a little walking, can provide surf fishing without distractions. As noted earlier, be prepared for giant Snook in the spring and summer.

(6) Manasota Beach - Off Hwy 776 on Manasota Key, this park provides all the amenities, including a boat ramp and dock on the ICW. There's another park close by at Blind Pass. Both of these parks provide great surf fishing access to near shore rock structures.

(7) Englewood Area - Farther south on Manasota Key (Hwy 776), there are two more beach accesses before the road ends short of Stump Pass. The first is adjacent to what some maps call Alexander Island. The second, Englewood Beach, is located where Hwy 776 turns left to cross Lemon Bay and returns to the mainland.

By way of summary in the surf department, the answer on what time to fish is pretty straightforward. Although something may bite throughout the day (and night), all fish seem to bite best during three specific periods. The first is sunup, regardless of what the tide is doing. The second is around sundown, again regardless of tide. The third is during the two hour period that precedes high tide. The question of potential catch is also easy to answer. Depending on time of year, all of the following are reasonable expectations: Snook, Specs, Silver Trout, Sheepshead, Bluefish, Black Drum, Reds, Pompano, Flounder, and Spanish Mackerel. And there's always a chance for Tarpon, Sharks, Cobia - - and Stingrays, Ladyfish, and Jacks of all kinds.

PIERS

There are diverse opportunities for potential pier fishing between Bradenton and Englewood. On the north end of this section, two piers on Anna Maria Island provide access to all the Inshore species that inhabit the mouth of Tampa Bay. Moving south from there, six other piers offer great access to area estuaries, including Sarasota and Lemon Bays. Two additional piers provide superb fishing in the

Manatee River, while the Venice Pier offers year round possibilities in the Gulf of Mexico. Figure 4.6 highlights the location of all of these.

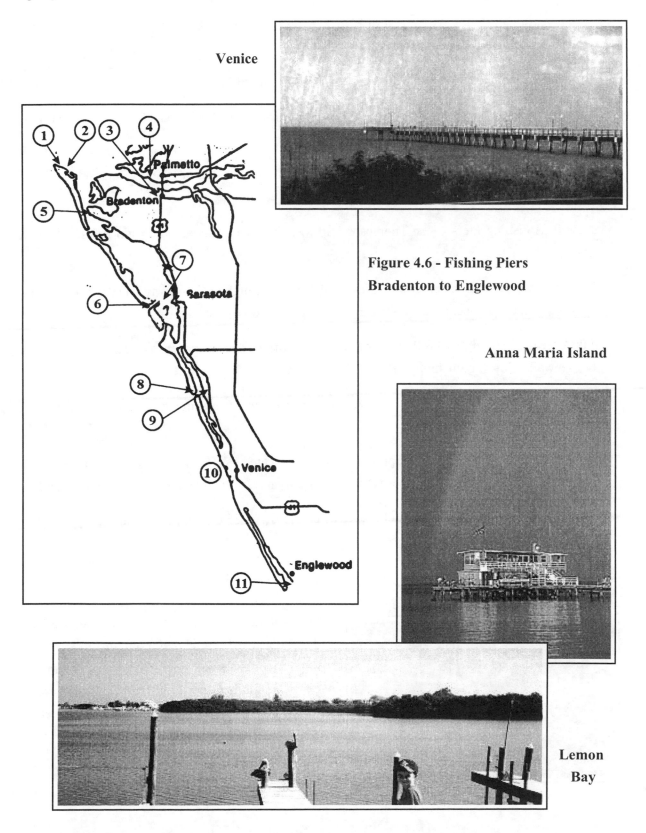

Venice

**Figure 4.6 - Fishing Piers
Bradenton to Englewood**

Anna Maria Island

**Lemon
Bay**

(1) Rod and Reel Pier - 875 North Shore Dr, Anna Maria Island. Bait, tackle, and rental rods and reels are available. Mouth of Tampa Bay.

(2) Anna Maria City Pier - At the end of Pine Ave across from the Anchorage restaurant. Bait and tackle are available. Mouth of Tampa Bay.

(3) Bradenton Fishing Pier - On the Manatee River at the end of 12th St.

(4) Green Bridge Fishing Pier - Riverside Dr at 8th Ave in Palmetto. On the Manatee River across from the Bradenton Pier.

(5) Bradenton Beach City Pier - At the end of Bridge St on Anna Maria Island. Bait and tackle are available. Fish the Sound and ICW.

(6) New Pass Fishing Piers - Ken Thompson Parkway between Longboat and Lido Keys. Off road parking.

(7) Tony Saprito Pier - Located at the east end of the John Ringling Causeway. There's a bait shop close by and the adjacent seawalls are also productive spots to fish.

(8) Turtle Beach - Midnight Pass Rd on Siesta Key. Fish off the docks adjacent to the boat ramp or from the seawall. You'll be fishing in Blind Pass Lagoon.

(9) Osprey Fishing Pier - West end of Main St. Good access to a fishy stretch of Sarasota Bay and the ICW.

(10) Venice City Pier - Great Gulf opportunities. It's located on South Harbor Drive at Sharky's restaurant. There's an on-site tackle shop that usually has live bait and always has rental tackle.

(11) Angler Pier - An Englewood attraction. Located off Hwy 776 on Lemon Bay at the Tom Adams bridge. There's an adjacent boat ramp.

INSHORE

With six immensely productive passes into the Gulf and an extensive artificial reef program, this stretch of Inshore water is a small boat fisherman's dream. At one time or another during the year, 22 of the area's gamefish can be caught within five miles of the beach. Figure 4.7 highlights the area's attractions.

Venice Inlet

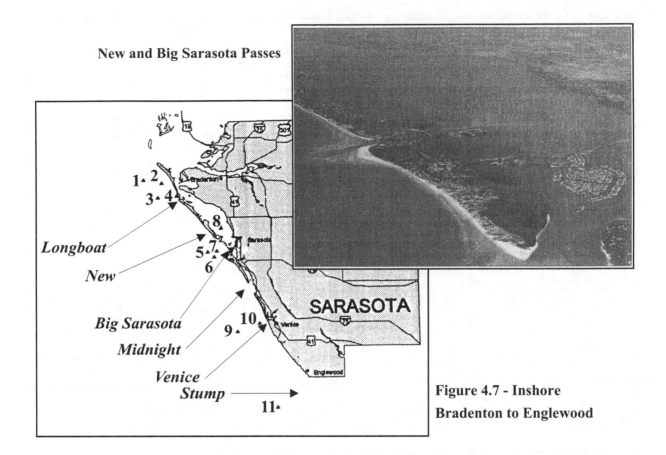

New and Big Sarasota Passes

Longboat

New

Big Sarasota

Midnight

Venice

Stump

**Figure 4.7 - Inshore
Bradenton to Englewood**

Spot #	Name	LORAN Coordinates	Latitude Longitude	Depth (ft)	Structure
1	Reef 'B' 3 mile	14175.8/44594.0	27/29.57C 82/47.00C	30	Tires, concrete rubble
2	One Mile Reef	14179.3/44564.2	27/29.390 82/44.050 27/29.059C 82/44.119C	27	1000 tons concrete culverts
3	Reef 'D' 3 mile	14172.0/44555.0	27/26.753C 82/44.785C	25	525 tons concrete culverts
4	Near Shore Reef	14178.0/44533.2	27/26.94C 82/41.85C	16	Skyway bridge material
5	Alan E. Fisher	14166.1/44437.4	27/17.72C 82/37.17C	30	New Pass bridge material, concrete rubble
6	Lynn Silvertooth	14166.1/44423.6	27/16.84C 82/36.14C	30	Concrete piles, boxes, rubble
7	Donald Roehr	14169.5/44425.8	27/17.84C 82/35.68C	22	Orange Ave bridge pilings

CATCH FISH NOW! *on Florida's West Coast*

Spot #	Name	LORAN Coordinates	Latitude Longitude	Depth (ft)	Structure
8	Deamus Hart	14181.4/44441.1	27/22.015C 82/34.574C	10	Concrete blocks, FPL insulators
	O.D. Miller	14176.5/44430.0	27/20.075C 82/34.671C	9-21	Concrete blocks, FPL insulators
	L.D. Byrd	14175.4/44429.5	27/19.816C 82/34.783C	7	Concrete, FPL insulators
	Jim Evans	14177.6/44418.0	27/19.626C 82/33.543C	10	Concrete blocks, FPL insulators
	Pop Jantzen	14176.7/44421.0	27/19.584C 82/33.934C	7	861 cu. yds. concrete blocks
	Bully Powers	14173.7/44418.8	27/18.686C 82/34.318C	12	Concrete blocks
	Rose Coker	14176.9/44404.0	27/18.61C 82/32.61C	7	Concrete, FPL insulators
9	MIS Reef	14143.6/44325.8	27/04.63C 82/32.69C	38	Concrete culverts, mixing drums, steel racks
10	14 Reef	14154.2/44302.6	27/05.091C 82/29.06C	25	Venice bridge and fishing pier
11	M14 Reef	14126.3/44209.7	26/51.86C 82/26.54C	43	Concrete rubble

Legend - Figure 4.7

Enough numbers. These spots are proven producers. Try one. Better yet, try them all. And while you're trying things, here are a few additional bits and pieces that may be of interest.

- Hardbottom - Among other places, Grouper trollers do well on the hardbottom in Longboat and New Passes.
- Rocks - Narrow bands of relatively flat rock structure parallel the coast all the way from Charlotte Harbor to Tampa Bay. This structure, which occurs roughly a half mile to a mile off the beach, is a great fish attractor. Tarpon love it in the summer. At other times of the year, it attracts Kings, Spanish, Permit, Sheepshead, Cobia, Bonito, Blackfin Tuna, Snapper, Grouper, Barracuda, and Tripletail, to name just a few.
- Cobia - Off Sarasota County, there are a number of nearshore reefs within .8 - 1.6 miles of the beach. Cobia are annual visitors, particularly in the months of April and November.
- Tarpon - The month of June is magic for area Tarpon fishermen. Why? Simple. Lots and lots of very big fish are running the beaches, anywhere from a couple of hundred feet out to a couple of miles Offshore. Look for them all the way from Anna Maria Island south to Englewood and beyond.

- Snook - From the full moon in May to the full moon in September, spawning Snook stack up in area passes. Although this period is catch and release fishing only, it provides a great opportunity for the fisherman. Literally thousands of line-siders get together in the following hot spots:
  - Passage Key Inlet off the northern tip of Anna Maria Island.
  - Around the two fishing piers on the island's Bean Pt.
  - Inside Longboat, New, and Big Sarasota Passes.
  - The Venice Inlet.

  Snook up to 20 - 25 pounds are almost the rule rather than the exception during this period.

So much for Inshore opportunities. There are lots of them - - for both bottom feeders and the pelagic species. That's equally true for Offshore, too. We'll check that out next.

OFFSHORE

Without belaboring the obvious, there is an extensive array of Offshore artificial structure off Sarasota and Venice. The 14 mid-range reefs off Sarasota range from 6.3 to 13.8 miles off the beach. At various times of the year, these reefs consistently provide outstanding King Mackerel action. In addition to lots of bottom dwellers, Barracuda usually add to the excitement. Farther out, from 24 - 28 miles off the beach, the fun really

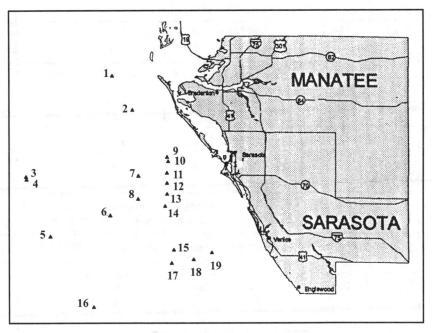

Figure 4.8 - Offshore Bradenton to Englewood

begins. The four deep water reefs consistently produce AJ's, Grouper, Cobia, Blackfin Tuna, Kings, and big Snapper. An occasional Sailfish is also a possibility. Figure 4.8 tells the Offshore story.

Spot #	Name	LORAN Coordinates	Latitude Longitude	Depth (ft)	Structure
1	Reef 'A' 7 Mile	14169.0/44655.0	27/32.216C 82/52.70C	40	Tires, concrete rubble
2	Reef 'C' 7 Mile	14162.4/44590.5	27/26.703C 82/49.165C	40	Tires, concrete culverts, rubble
3	D3 Reef	14091.7/44668.4 14091.9/44668.1	27/15.59C 82/07.36C 27/15.59 83/07.36	105 105	Steel CSX boxcars Steel CSX boxcars

Spot #	Name	LORAN Coordinates	Latitude Longitude	Depth (ft)	Structure
4	D4 Reef	14090.9/44664.6	27/15.12C 83/07.27C	103	10 steel CSX boxcars
5	D6 Reef	14076.8/44579.7	27/05.84C 83/03.36C	110	Fiberglass boats and molds
6	MD1 Reef	14108.9/44518.8	27/09.35C 82/53.20C	80	Barge, concrete hopper
7	M7 Reef	14137.8/44517.1	27/15.92C 82/48.20C	50	Boxcars, concrete culverts
8	M8 Reef	14128.1/44495.5 14128.2/44495.6	27/12.13 82/48.28 27/12.13 82/48.28	55 65	Steel landing craft 10 steel boxcars
9	M1 Reef	14155.7/44495.1 14155.8/44495.2	27/19.043 82/43.295 27/19.073C 82/43.284C	42 42	Concrete culverts, catch basins 120' steel barge, fiberglass boats
10	M2 Reef	14155.1/44490.4	27/18.38C 82/43.13C	42	Concrete culverts, boxes, drums
11	M3 Reef	1414938/44480.5	27/16.44C 82/43.33C	43	Concrete culverts, boxes, drums
12	M4 Reef	14145.7/44470.7	27/14.79C 82/43.33C	42	Concrete rubble
13	M5 Reef	14141.4/44460.5	27/12.98C 82/43.37C	43	Concrete culverts
14	M6 Reef	14135.4/44451.7	27/10.98C 82/43.71C	55	Fiberglass boats, concrete culverts
15	M9 Reef	14121.0/44399.9 14121.0/44400.0	27/04.046 82/42.198 27/03.83 82/42.27	61 61	Concrete rubble, rock 5 M-60 Army tanks
16	D9 Reef	14066.1/44459.5	26/54.33 82/56.02C	100	Steel crane barge, fiberglass boats
17	M10 Reef	14114.7/44390.9 14114.8/44391.5	27.01.65 82/42.68 27/01.65C 82/42.68C	65 65	100' steel barge Sailboat, fiberglass boats and molds
18	M17 Reef	14124.5/44364.6	27/02.27C 82/38.96C	63	200 reef balls
19	M16 Reef	14134.1/44345.1	27/03.44C 82/35.88C	49	Concrete culverts, catch basins

Legend - Figure 4.8

And that's Offshore for this stretch of the West Coast. . . almost. We can't leave, however, without at least mentioning one other legendary bottom spot. Its called the "Cuda Hole" and all kinds of big fish have been taken there. The "Cuda" is about 10 miles off the New Pass bell at latitude 27/15.12 and longitude 82/44.73. The hole is roughly 50 feet deep, has a natural jagged bottom with breaks and limestone ledges, and is probably a couple of miles wide. Check it out. Now, let's head farther south for our final segment of the West Coast - - between Port Charlotte and Naples.

CHAPTER 5

PORT CHARLOTTE TO NAPLES

It's about 75 miles from Port Charlotte to Naples. That's not a great distance in this day and age. But, from a fisherman's perspective, those 75 miles encompass an absolutely huge area of superior - - actually world class - - saltwater sportfishing opportunities. Knowledgeable fishermen, intent on an experience of a lifetime, come to the area to sample the best that places like Boca Grande, Charlotte Harbor, and Sanibel Island, have to offer. Let's take a closer look.

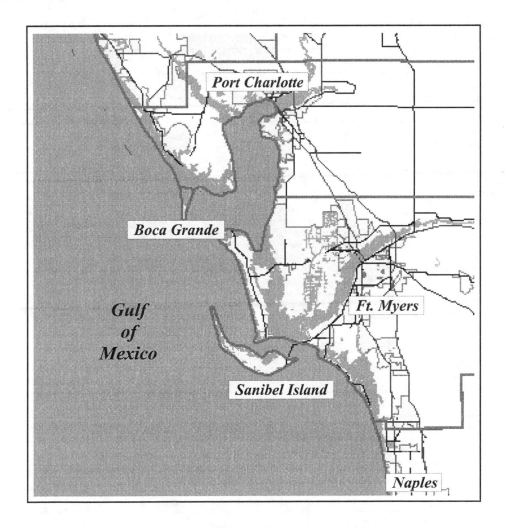

Figure 5.0 - Port Charlotte to Naples

This fourth and final stretch of Florida's West Coast has it all. There are three significant rivers (Myakka, Peace, and Caloosahatchee) which empty into two famous bays (Charlotte Harbor and San Carlos Bay). These features are complemented with eight barrier islands, 12 passes into the Gulf of Mexico, several sounds, miles and miles of fishy surf, and a superb system of fishing piers, bridges, parks, and boat ramps. And, not surprisingly, lots of fish are year round residents of the area. Figure 5.1 summarizes the situation.

Possibilities	Best Time To Try
Amberjack	Available year round - Fall/Winter/early Spring
Barracuda	Available year round - Summer/Fall
Black Drum	Available year round - Fall/Winter
Black Sea Bass	Available year round
Blackfin Tuna	Late Spring through early Fall
Bluefish	Available year round
Blue Marlin	Late Summer/Fall
Bonito	Available year round
Cobia	Migratory - Available year round-Spring/Summer/Fall
Dolphin	Late Spring through early Fall
Flounder	Available year round
Grouper	Available year round
Jack Cravalle	Available year round
King Mackerel	Migratory - Spring and Fall
Permit	Available year round - Summer
Pompano	Available year round - Summer/Winter
Redfish	Available year round - Spring through Fall
Sailfish	Summer/Early Fall
Sheepshead	Available year round
Snapper	Available year round
Snook*	Available year round - Spring through Fall
Spanish Mackerel	Migratory - Available year round - Winter
Swordfish	Late Summer/early Fall
Tarpon	Migratory - Available year round - Spring
Triggerfish	Available year round
Tripletail	Available year round
Trout*	Available year round

Possibilities	Best Time To Try
Wahoo	Summer/early Fall
White Marlin	Late Spring through early Fall
Whiting	Available year round
Yellowfin Tuna	Summer
* Subject to closed season. Catch and release OK. Please see Appendix for dates.	

Figure 5.1 - Gamefish Availability

There are a few words of explanation that go with the figure. If you didn't read them in previous chapters, here they are. If there isn't a qualifier after a "Best Time to Try" recommendation, that means the whole period is good. Bluefish are a good example of this. On the other hand, if there is a qualifier, it simply indicates the very best time within a particular period. Mr. Amberjack can help us here. You can catch him every month of the year. But he seems to be the most hungry and aggressive in the fall, winter, and early spring.

OK, with that top level summary in mind, let's take a look at fishing action on a month-to-month basis. The following narrative is only supposed to give you a feel for what typically goes on between Port Charlotte and Naples. It is certainly not all inclusive.

January
- Well Offshore (40 miles) in 75 - 90 feet, Grouper and Snapper make the trip worthwhile.
- Kings still available on the Edison Reef off Sanibel and the rocks in 40 feet of water off Englewood.
- Reds, Specs, and Flounder on Charlotte Harbor Reef below Alligator Creek, and Whiting and Silver Trout on many harbor markers.
- Tough to catch Tarpon in Port Charlotte, Punta Gorda Isles, and Cape Coral canals.
- Snapper, Sheepshead, Reds, Specs, and Flounder in areas with relatively deep channels protected from the wind by mangroves - - with some sort of structure.
- Snook, Jack Cravalle (and Tarpon) hanging around the railroad trestle and Interstate bridge over the Caloosahatchee river.
- Cobia off Naples beaches in schools of Silver Trout. Bluefish there, too.

February
- Sheepshead thick on near shore artificial and natural limestone reefs.
- Grouper and Amberjack hungry on Offshore wrecks and ledges.
- Tripletail around Stone Crab trap buoys.
- Specs spreading out on grass flats.

- Inshore big Sheepshead a distinct possibility at the El Jobean and Placida fishing trestles, Matlacha Pass Bridge, and Boca Grande phosphate dock.
- Snook cooperating in area residential canals.
- King Mackerel back in force off Ft. Myers Beach in 40 - 70 feet of water.
- Triggerfish active on Inshore and Offshore structure.

March
- Tarpon well up coastal rivers including Peace, Myakka, and Caloosahatchee.
- Snook around bridges over the same rivers.
- A few really big Specs in Matlacha Pass.
- Sheepshead still biting well around area piers and bridges.
- Black Drum, Whiting, and Silver Trout in coastal rivers.
- Spanish starting to show well around the San Carlos Bay causeway.
- Kings, AJ's, and Cobia at the ARCOA reef 12 miles west of Redfish Pass.
- Snook in Port Charlotte, Punta Gorda Isles, and Cape Coral canals.
- Reds very active around Estero Bay oyster bars, with Snook and Jack Cravalle also in the area.

April
- Kings and Tarpon in 40 feet of water south of Sanibel Island on Edison Reef.
- Big Snook at the Cape Coral Bridge and at Cattledock Pt and Shell Creek at the mouth of Caloosahatchee River.
- Cobia in Charlotte Harbor at the artificial reef south of Alligator Creek, along the Sanibel Causeway, and at the Cape Coral Bridge.
- Cobia, AJ's, Barracuda, and Snapper on Offshore wrecks and ledges.
- Very big Black Drum from the Hwy 41 bridges over Peace and Caloosahatchee Rivers.
- Sheepshead and Snapper between the goal posts south of Alligator Creek.
- Flounder and Pompano widely scattered across the area.
- Specs and Reds on almost all flats.
- Giant Jack Cravalle, AJ's, Cobia, and Barracuda all over Offshore reefs.
- Snook have infested Estero Bay mangrove islands and oyster bars.

May
- Kings thinning out with northward migration.
- Tarpon south of Sanibel in 25 - 40 feet of water and upper Charlotte Harbor. Trophy Snook starting to spawn with big fish along the bar on the eastern shore of Charlotte Harbor and Blind and Captiva Passes.
- Spanish in the bays and along the beaches.
- Tarpon and Snook on US 41 bridges over the Peace River and off the Sanibel causeway.
- Cobia at the Cape Coral Bridge and on Naples area flats.

- Grouper and Snapper moving farther Offshore.
- Naples area grass flats loaded with big Specs and Pompano.

June
- AJ's on Offshore wrecks.
- Snook in all the passes and along the beaches on any kind of structure.
- Tarpon out of control in Boca Grande Pass and at the mouth of the Myakka River in Charlotte Harbor - - and everywhere else.
- Grouper in 100 feet of water off Venice.
- Schoolie Dolphin Offshore.
- Reds on shallow flats.
- Offshore wrecks holding Barracuda, big Kings, Spanish, Snapper, and Permit.
- Naples' Gordon's Pass area producing Snook, Tarpon, Jacks, Snapper, Sharks, Specs, and an occasional Cobia.

July
- Tarpon stacked up in Boca Grande Pass.
- Reds starting to school on many flats.
- Snook still spawning in Gulf Passes and along beaches.
- Offshore Grouper from 50 feet of water to over 100.
- Dolphin on weedlines and floating objects Offshore.
- Specs in Bull and Turtle Bays off Charlotte Harbor and along area beaches.
- Bonito and Barracuda widely scattered Offshore.

August
- Grouper and Snapper Offshore in 40 - 50 feet.
- Snappers thick in Boca Grande Pass in 30 - 40 feet of water and Tarpon in 70 feet of water.
- Specs active in Gasparilla and Pine Island Sounds and in San Carlos Bay around spoil islands.
- Pompano, Snook, Flounder, Specs, and Spanish along drop offs.
- Jack Cravalle and big Black Drum around most coastal bridges.
- Dolphin Offshore in 50+ feet of water.
- Schooling Redfish on most flats.

September
- Mr. Snook is everywhere - - from Offshore in 20 - 30 feet of water on structure to well inland.
- Redfish schooling on flats along the Intercoastal Waterway.
- Cobia and Tripletail around Inshore markers, power poles, and pilings.
- Spanish widely scattered in Charlotte Harbor and San Carlos Bay.
- Pompano, Specs, and Flounder biting well in larger bays.

- Grouper and Snapper at the 25 foot contour on ledges and reefs.
- Specs, big Snook, Spanish, Reds, and Snapper in the Captiva Pass area.

October

- Snook good around Boca Grande phosphate dock, Sanibel pier, Cattledock Point, and the mouth of the Caloosahatchee River.
- Jack Cravalle, Spanish Mackerel, and Ladyfish in Charlotte Harbor.
- Cobia also in Charlotte Harbor around markers.
- Edison Reef West of Sanibel holding increasing numbers of Kings and lots of Barracuda, Jack Cravalle, and Mangrove Snapper.
- Reds on most flats and heading into the back country.
- Tarpon available in Charlotte Harbor.
- Pompano along the barrier islands and in area passes.
- Estero Bay full of bait - - and Snook, Reds, Specs, and huge Jack Cravalle.

November

- Kings as far south as Boca Grande (CSX Boxcar Reef). The Edison Reef a little farther north is also good. Snapper and Triggers are there, too.
- Good for Grouper around the 70 foot contour on rocky ledges.
- Reds on most oyster bars in Estero Bay.
- Snook moving into coastal rivers and canals. Matlacha Pass Bridge a hot spot for big fish.
- Trout, Flounder, and Pompano around the Sanibel Causeway spoil island.
- Sheepshead on all area piers.
- Tripletail on many crab trap floats.
- Offshore wrecks and reefs hold great numbers of Kings, Spanish, AJ's and Barracuda.
- Specs are hungry in the Little Carlos Pass hole and surrounding Estero Bay water.

December

- Specs on the flats in San Carlos Bay and bridges on the Sanibel Causeway.
- Whiting, Sand and Speckled Trout off the bridges over the Myakka, Peace, and Caloosahatchee Rivers.
- Sheepshead on the Coral Creek and Cape Coral Piers.
- Snook around coastal river bridges and deeper canal bridges in Port Charlotte, Punta Gorda Isles and Cape Coral.
- Tarpon around Orange River Power Plant.
- Cobia (big), Snapper, Flounder, Specs, and Pompano on and around the Charlotte Harbor Reef rubble below Alligator Creek.
- King Mackerel scattered on artificial reefs off Lee, Charlotte, and Sarasota counties.
- Grouper and Snapper on the Edison Reef off Sanibel.

- Tripletail just off the coast from Boca Grande south in 10 - 40 feet of water around Stone Crab trap buoys.

As in previous chapters, about five years of data were synthesized to compile this monthly narrative. Although it's not a complete, current fishing report, it does provide some useful insights into year round fishing action from Port Charlotte to Naples.   Now, let's take a closer look at more specific spots that have a demonstrated record of producing good fish. We'll start with the area's bays and contiguous waters.

BAYS

Before we visit the bigger estuaries, there are a couple of spots on Lemon Bay and the ICW that need to be mentioned. They're identified next and are really just good starting points for working the whole stretch between Grove City and Placida Harbor. For what it's worth, everything except Billfish can be caught along this stretch.

Stump Pass Area

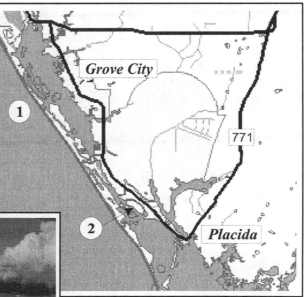

Figure 5.2 - Lemon Bay/Cape Haze

Placida Harbor

(1) Stump Pass - Flats adjacent to the inside of the pass are prime territory for spring Snook. During the summer, the pass holds a spawning school of Snook that experts estimate exceeds 1,000 fish.

(2) Cape Haze Flats - Rich flats of mixed seagrasses, sand, and oysters. Consistently productive area for Reds, Snook, Tarpon, Specs, and Pompano.

Figure 5.3 - Port Charlotte Area

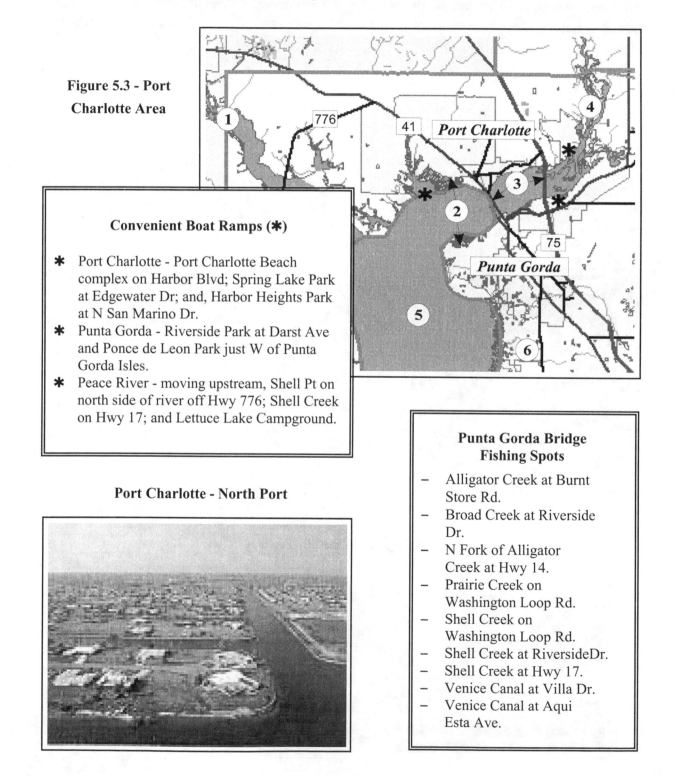

Convenient Boat Ramps (✱)

✱ Port Charlotte - Port Charlotte Beach complex on Harbor Blvd; Spring Lake Park at Edgewater Dr; and, Harbor Heights Park at N San Marino Dr.

✱ Punta Gorda - Riverside Park at Darst Ave and Ponce de Leon Park just W of Punta Gorda Isles.

✱ Peace River - moving upstream, Shell Pt on north side of river off Hwy 776; Shell Creek on Hwy 17; and Lettuce Lake Campground.

Punta Gorda Bridge Fishing Spots

- Alligator Creek at Burnt Store Rd.
- Broad Creek at Riverside Dr.
- N Fork of Alligator Creek at Hwy 14.
- Prairie Creek on Washington Loop Rd.
- Shell Creek on Washington Loop Rd.
- Shell Creek at RiversideDr.
- Shell Creek at Hwy 17.
- Venice Canal at Villa Dr.
- Venice Canal at Aqui Esta Ave.

Port Charlotte - North Port

Punta Gorda

Charlotte Harbor

(1) Myakka River - Great fishing going upriver from Charlotte Harbor. Tarpon, Snook, Trout, and Reds go upstream substantial distances (i.e., Snook - 20 miles, Reds - 10 miles). El Jobean trestle is a good spot for big Reds and Mangrove Snapper in August and September. Snook are there too. Snapper are also available at the Myakka River Cutoff.

(2) Port Charlotte and Punta Gorda Canals - North and south sides of the mouth of the Peace River. There are allegedly more than 100 miles of canals in Punta Gorda Isles alone. Among others, Tarpon cooperate in the canals from April through November. Snook fishing is very good in May. Huge schools of Jack Cravalle destroy tackle in the canals in early fall. Snook live in the canals in the winter.

(3) Hwy 41 and 75 Bridges - There's always something available. In the summer months, the big guys, including Tarpon, Cobia, and Black Drum, are there.

(4) Headwaters of the Peace River - Tarpon come up the river to beyond the Ft. Ogden bridge. Some of the fish, up to 80 pounds, may stay in the river year round.   Your highest probability for success, however, is in late summer, early fall. Convenient boat ramps include the Ft. Ogden public ramp off Hwy 769 and the Nocatee public ramp off Hwy 760 on the east side of the river. Big Snook winter-over in the upper Peace River.

Burnt Store Area

(5) Charlotte Harbor - Something for everyone:

- Good flats for Redfish around Hog Key and at the mouth of Alligator Creek. Equally good flats run along the entire eleven mile eastern shore of the harbor. Try around Two Pines and Burnt Store.

- Equally superior flats for Snook include Whidden's Creek, Bull Bay, Cayo Pelau, and Turtle Bay on the west side. On the east side, the flats in the Burnt Store area are consistently good. Always check deep white sand potholes, swash channels, and around oyster bars.

- Cape Haze (the other one) - On the SW corner of the harbor, a very fishy flat of sand, oysters, and seagrass extends out from shore several hundred yards. At one time or another, it's a good area for Reds, Tarpon, Specs, Snook, Pompano, Jack Cravalle, and some large Sharks.

- Random Appearances/Locations - Schools of Permit wander the harbor during mid-winter. Tarpon fishing is great spring - fall. Other transients include Cobia, Sharks, and Tripletail. Try the Harbor's "West Wall" for big Reds in August and September.

(6) Burnt Store Area - The canals along Burnt Store Road (Hwy 765) are very productive for winter Snook, among other things. Good shore fishing spots, or you can launch a small boat along the road. Also, check the Burnt Store Marina for big winter Snook while you're in the area.

Figure 5.4 - Boca Grande Area

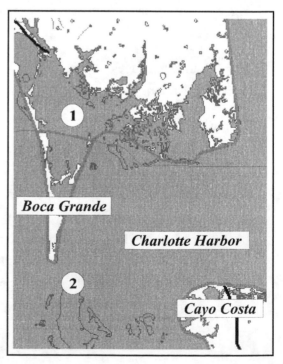

(1) Gasparilla Island Area -

- Boca Grande Canal, hardbottom near the golf course, and passes into Bull and Turtle Bays produce nice winter Grouper.
- Gasparilla Sound - Redfish frequent the bar between Catfish Creek south to Sandfly Key and then east in a natural cut to the mouth of Whidden's Creek. Just east of there, the bar at the mouth of the Bull Bay mentioned above is also a popular area for Reds. In the winter, Sheepshead, among others, like the old

railroad trestle that parallels the east shore of the island. Specs can be found in almost all the areas holding Reds.

Boca Grande Pass

- Downtown Boca Grande Boat Channels - Lots of deep water and docks. Great area for cold weather Snook, Sheepshead, and Mangrove Snapper. You'll find Flounder along channel edges, too.

- Boca Grande Yacht Basin - Check the grass flats adjacent to the channel for Specs most of the year.

- Phosphate Docks - Legendary. Southern tip of Gasparilla Island. Giant Snook, giant Reds - - and who knows what else!

Gasparilla Island

(2) Boca Grande Pass - Also legendary. The following words were provided by the Boca Grande Fishing Guides Association (BGFGA). What they have to say should really be mandatory reading for anyone intent on fishing the Pass without a professional guide on board.

- Boat operation at the Pass:

Boat traffic in Boca Grande Pass has increased at an alarming rate. Enthusiasts who are not aware of the established methods and procedures for boat operation in the pass are creating an unsafe and frustrating situation for the guides who are trying to give their clients the best possible trip. We suggest you hire a BGFGA member for an enjoyable day of fishing. If you must use your own boat, we would greatly appreciate your use of the following information.

Drifting the pass requires "team" effort!!! Keep your engine(s) running at all times. Try and keep your boat in a drift such that it is in line with the drift, not sideways. Unless your boat is keeled, you will most likely have the best luck in drifting stern to the wind. In this manner, your boat will be more easily controlled. Easing the engine(s) in and out of gear so as to keep the boat straight with lines running almost straight down is necessary and requires the full attention of someone aboard. That person should be the one running the boat and calling out designation of line depths . . . green or red marker. (This will be explained shortly.)

If you see a fish "ON" in close proximity to your boat, REEL UP & MOVE as quickly as possible.

When you have completed a drift, move back to the head (start) of the drift by going outside the pack at a rate of speed that does not create a lot of wake or noise. Moving back through the pack is WRONG.

Generally, you will find the greatest congregation of fish on the drop off ledges at the end of the hole on incoming water movement (outgoing tide = east end of hole . . incoming tide = west end of hole).

DO NOT ANCHOR IN THE PASS!!! It's dangerous and it's a "pain" to those drifting. Anchored boats have been "sucked" under on hard outgoing tides. Boca Grande Pass is predominately coral bottom and anchors are frequently lost.

If you snag bottom, break off as quickly as possible as the tide will move you away from the snag point at a much faster rate of speed than you can imagine. Tides of 4 to 6 knots are standard, particularly the outgoing tides. Do not attempt to pull or break off bare handed. Use gloves or a towel for protection.

At night the pass can be a very dark place. Make sure all of your lights are in good working order and "ON" at all times. Flood lights used for rigging should be turned off except when absolutely needed.

- Emergency Help - Call for help on Channel 16 and/or hail nearby guide boats for assistance.

- Tarpon Release:

Please do not waste a Tarpon unless you wish it for a mount. Even if you wish to mount your catch, a length and girth measurement can result in a plastic mount (most Tarpon mounts are plastic anyway, unless you specify a "skin" mount which is more expensive and does not last as long). If you are going to release the fish, DO NOT attempt to gaff it and/or bring it in the boat. Take your pictures and break the fish off as quickly as possible.

Once at the boat, the wire leader can be snapped (use gloves or towel) and the fish released without the need for a gaff. Do not try and retrieve your hook. Make sure the leader wire is not wrapped around the fish's gills.

Remember, if you should decide to keep your fish, IT MUST BE TAGGED at the time of capture.

- Fishing Boca Grande Pass:

The average Tarpon at Boca Grande weighs about 75 to 85 pounds, with numerous fish well over 100 pounds. Catches of fish over 200 pounds have occurred at Boca Grande. A fish over 100 pounds is generally a female, and the rate of growth is very slow, taking 8 to 10 years to reach sexual maturity. Tarpon can live to 55 or 60 years.

For the pass, rods preferably in the 6 to 8 foot range with either rollerized or ceramic guides should be used.

Fishing reels such as the 3/0 and 4/0 Penn models are popular and effective. Reels should have a good drag system and be wound with 50 or 80 pound Dacron line, which will give the angler more chance of controlling the fish with minimal stretch for a better chance of a good hook-up. Lines should be marked at the 42 and 60 foot distances from the swivel with red and green yarn spliced in the Dacron line (green at 42 feet and red at 60 feet).

Swivels should be the 5/0 size, and leaders should be 10 to 12 feet long with a rating of about 70 pounds. It is important to use the Mustad forged needle eye hook in 4/0 or 5/0 size, such as the #7690.

When sinkers are necessary, use copper wire attached and twisted tightly to the bottom eye of the swivel. The sinker should be slid on to the copper wire and the tail of the wire loosely wrapped around the leader wire. The loose wrap will allow the sinker to be thrown when the fish is hooked.

In the pass, there are four standard live baits used: squirrel fish, mutton minnows, crabs, and shrimp. Squirrel fish and mutton minnows should be hooked between the head and dorsal fin, crabs should be hooked through either "point" of the shell, and shrimp should be hooked just in front of the "dark spot" in the head.

Tarpon generally congregate in mass at the deepest areas of the pass. The "hole" (Boca Grande Hole) is approximately 100 yards wide and 250 yards long. It runs lengthwise with the pass just south of the lighthouse which is located at the south end of the island. There is a smaller hole referred to as the "Coast Guard Hole" which is closer yet to the beach. The Boca Grande Hole is 65 to 70 feet deep and the Coast Guard Hole is about 70 feet. The remainder of the pass bottom surrounding the holes is about 40 feet. Fishing the pass requires a good fish recorder.

When fishing outside the hole, the "green" marker on the reel will keep you generally safe from snagging the bottom. When in the hole, "red" on the reel or at the tip of the rod is suggested, depending upon the actual depth reading. You must pay attention to the recorder and adjust your reel settings accordingly.

(Thanks again to the Boca Grande Fishing Guides Association for those invaluable insights.)

**Figure 5.5 -
Ft. Myers
Cape Coral
Area**

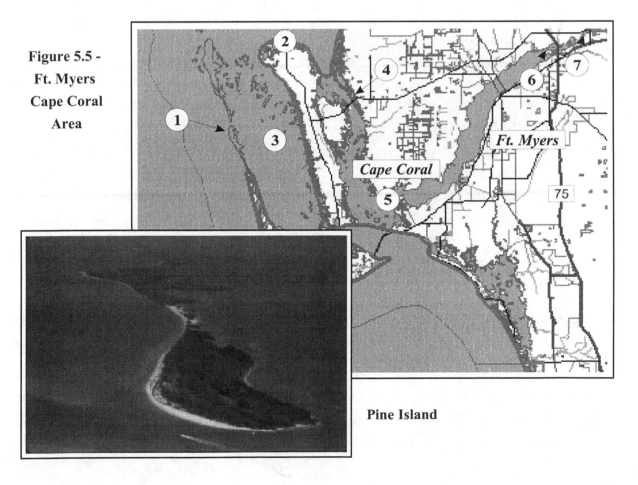

Pine Island

Matlacha Pass Area

Caloosahatchee River - Cape Coral

(**1**) Redfish, Captiva and Blind Passes - Fall Snook and huge schools of Reds are only two of many world class opportunities in these passes.

(**2**) Bokellia Area - The whole crowd is here year round. But Sharks are something special in August and September. Count on Blacktips, Hammerheads, and Lemons for starters.

(**3**) Pine Island Sound -

- Flats - Fish due south from Regla Island about 3/4 of a mile to McKeever Keys. Area is often called "The Hump." Other consistently good areas, particularly for Reds, include around Cabbage Key and Useppa Island to the west and Port Island and Black, Wood, and Little Wood keys to the east. Also check Demre Key for Snook, Specs, and Reds.
- Foster's Point on the east side of North Captiva Island. Dependable Reds loiter in the area, particularly on higher tides.
- Tarpon - Fishing for these guys is alive and well in the Sound from April through September. Several specific areas/spots are worth checking out: SE side of Useppa Island; Cabbage Key just to the west; the old bombing range just south of that; the flats just inside Captiva Pass; Foster's Point (mentioned above for Reds); the channel just north of Buck Key; and the east side of Chino Island.

(**4**) Matlacha Pass - Always a very fishy area. Summer and fall fishing for Reds, Snook (around sandy bottoms), Specs, and large schools of Jack Cravalle, is superior. Sheepshead, Tarpon, Shark, and Mangrove Snapper are also possibilities. Pompano is a local (and dependable) favorite.

(**5**) Mouth of the Caloosahatchee River - Cattledock Pt and Shell Creek are good areas for Snook. Fish an incoming tide and use "shiners" for bait. Adjacent Cape Coral canals offer a variety of species year round. Big Mangrove Snappers, particularly in August, are a local favorite.

⑥ Caloosahatchee River at the I-75 bridge - The Orange River dumps into the main river channel just east of the bridge. Orange River water is always warm since it's used for cooling by the resident power plant. The warmed water funnels through a relatively narrow channel for about a mile before passing under a railroad trestle at Beautiful Island, expanding and heading on downstream. The relatively warm, relatively narrow part of the river at the bridge holds lots of bait and lots of Tarpon, Snook, and Jack Cravalle year round.

⑦ Caloosahatchee River Headwaters - The river connects Lake Okeechobee and Charlotte Harbor via a series of locks on the channel. Shore fishing is possible at Moore Haven, Labelle, and Alva. Both saltwater and freshwater species are possible.

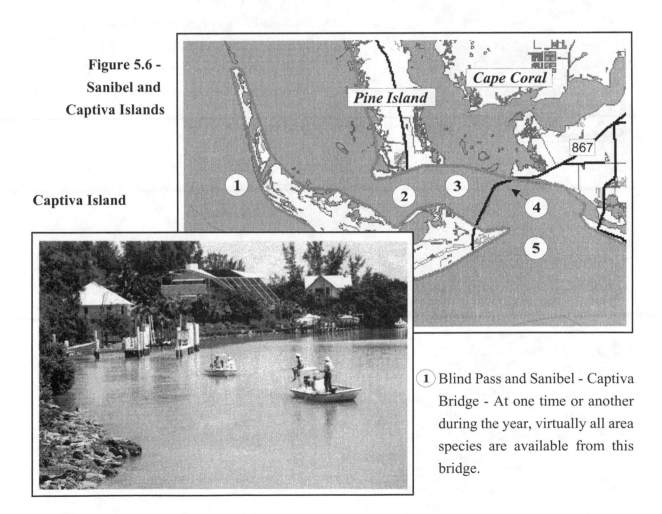

Figure 5.6 -
Sanibel and
Captiva Islands

Captiva Island

① Blind Pass and Sanibel - Captiva Bridge - At one time or another during the year, virtually all area species are available from this bridge.

② Tarpon Bay (Sanibel Is) - A shallow (5 ft.), seagrass rich, bay that is a relatively new management addition to the surrounding world famous J. N. Ding Darling National Wildlife Refuge. There's a marina on the bay which has a ramp for small boats and offers bait, tackle, and rental canoes and kayaks. It's open seven days a week. Count on great fishing for Specs, Reds, Snook, Mangrove Snapper, Barracuda, Jack Cravalle, and Ladyfish. It is also a great spot for winter Snook.

③ San Carlos Bay - Very fishy flats run along the north shore of the bay. Superior wade fishing. Park at the foot of the Sanibel Causeway. All of the following are possible at one time of the year or another: Flounder, Specs, Reds, Spanish, Cobia, Grouper, Sharks, and Jack Cravalle.

④ Sanibel Causeway - Marvelously productive area year round. The entire SW Florida cast of characters except for Offshore species can be caught along/off the causeway.

⑤ Point Ybel (Lighthouse Pt) on Sanibel Island - Giant Reds wander the area between August and October. Pompano, Specs, Whiting, Snook and Tarpon are year round possibilities. There's an excellent boat ramp next door at the Sanibel Pier.

Lighthouse Point

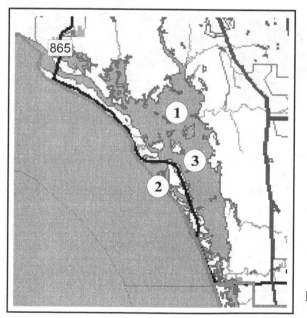

Convenient Boat Ramps

- Cocohatchee River Park on Vanderbilt Dr in North Naples.
- Carl Johnson County Park adjacent to Lover's Key.
- Conklin Pt On Vanderbilt Dr in North Naples.
- Delnor Wiggins Pass Recreation Area.

Figure 5.7 - Estero Island Area

(1) Estero Bay - Bounded on the west by Estero Island and accessed by New, Big Carlos, Matanzas, and Big Hickory Passes, this bay is fertility in action. A number of rivers and creeks on the mainland provide optimum habitat for juveniles of many species. The bay itself is comprised of fertile grass beds, oyster bars, sandy shoals, and random deep channels. At various times of the year, expect to find plenty of Reds, Snook, Jewfish, Specs, Sharks, etc., etc.

Estero Bay Action

- June is usually a great month for sight casting for Snook and Reds around the bay's mangrove islands. Water clarity is usually good till mid-summer rains begin.

- In the fall, check oyster bars and sandy shoals for large schools of even larger bull Reds.

(2) New/Big Carlos Passes - The north point of New Pass and the south beach of Big Carlos consistently produce some of the biggest Snook on Florida's West Coast.

(3) Lover's Key State Recreation Area - Its a magic place for a fisherman. It's located on the south shore of Big Carlos Pass and offers 434 acres of canals, tidal lagoons fringed with mangroves, and access to Estero Bay. Most of the time, the fishing for Trout, Redfish, Snook, and Tarpon can be quite spectacular. There's even a boat ramp next door at the Carl Johnson County Park.

Matanzas Pass Area

Naples Bay

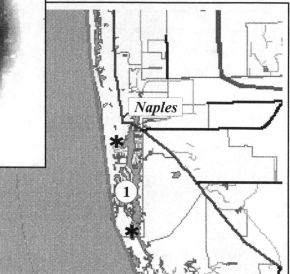

Figure 5.8 - Naples Area

Convenient Boat Ramps (✱)

- Imperial Boat Ramp - Hwy 41 just south of the Imperial River.
- Bayview Park - Danford St off Thomasson Dr.
- Cocohatchee River Park - Vanderbilt Dr just south of Wiggins Pass Rd.
- Naples Landing - East end of Broad Ave.

① Naples Bay - The secret of consistent success here is - - fish man-made structures like boat docks, seawalls, jetties, riprap, deeper dredge holes, and channels. In mid-winter, try the rocky points and seawalls for Snook, Reds, and Specs. In the spring and summer, fine Tarpon fishing exists in the residential canals that border a portion of the bay.

SURF

There are roughly 85 miles of potentially fishable surf from just south of Englewood down to Naples. While much of this is developed beachfront, there are stretches like Useppa Island that are uninhabited and accessible only by boat. Virgin territory in a relative sense to be sure. Even in the developed areas, access to the water shouldn't be a major problem. If you're staying on the beach, great, you've got fishing right out your back door. If you're not, it's still not a problem. There are a number of fine beachfront parks along the coast - - and many additional public beach accesses in between. We'll locate some of these now.

① Don Pedro Island State Recreation Area (Cape Haze) - Located between Knight Island and Little Gasparilla Island, the recreation area is only accessible by private boat or via a ferry from Placida.

② Gasparilla Island State Recreation Area (Boca Grande) - Access to the island is via the Boca Grande Causeway (private toll) at Hwy 775 and Placida. The state park is on the southern tip of the island, adjacent to the world famous Boca Grande Pass. The Boca Grande Public Beach is about a mile north of the park on Gulf Blvd.

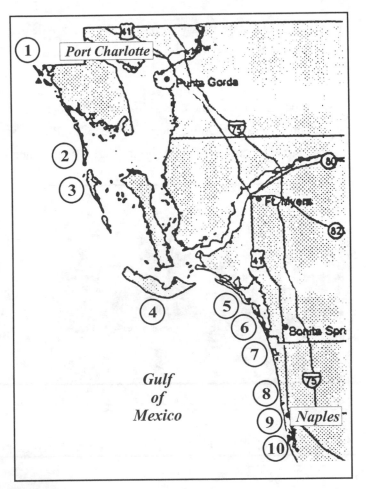

Figure 5.9 - Beach Accesses
Port Charlotte to Naples

Don Pedro Island

Cayo Costa

(3) Cayo Costa State Park (Boca Grande) - The park is located directly south of Boca Grande, across Boca Grande Pass. It occupies most of an island and is only accessible by private boat or passenger ferry.

(4) Sanibel/Captiva Islands - Parking for surf fishermen is available at four different places on Sanibel: Lighthouse and Fishing Pier; Gulfside City Park; Tarpon Bay Road Parking Lot; and Bowman's Beach. The cost is $.75 per hour. Parking at Turner's Beach on Captiva Island is free.

(5) Lover's Key State Recreation Area (Ft. Meyers Beach). Located off Hwy 865 between Ft. Myers Beach and Bonita Beach. Carl Johnson County Park is adjacent to the state recreation area. Little Hickory Island Beach Park is close by - - at the south end of the bridge over Big Hickory Pass.

Lover's Key

(6) Bonita Public Beach - Take exit 18 (Bonita Beach Rd) west off I-75. Cross Hwy 41 and follow the signs.

(7) Delnor-Wiggins Pass State Recreation Area (Naples) - Located five miles west of I-75 on Hwy 846. Vanderbilt Beach is on the south side of the recreation area, and Barefoot Park/Beach on the north side. The park offers great fishing for Reds, Snook, Specs, Snapper, Tarpon, and others. There's a boat ramp and a bunch of very fishy mangrove channels and creeks. Fish the north end of the park adjacent to the pass.

(8) Vanderbilt Beach - North Naples moving south between the Delnor Wiggins recreation area and Vanderbilt Drive. Use the park's observation tower to spot the rock structure along the beach. There's a boat ramp and additional parking in the lot next to the Ritz Carlton. The Naples Municipal Beach is just south of Vanderbilt on Gulfshore Blvd, north of Doctor's Pass.

(9) Loudermilk Park/Beach - Gulfshore Blvd North at Banyan Blvd. Good access but must be fished early or late in the day because the place fills up with volleyballers the rest of the time.

(10) Naples Pier - Just south of Loudermilk Beach. West end of 12th Ave South. If you don't want the hassle of the pier, the surf on either side of it consistently produces good fish, particularly early in the morning.

OK, enough access. Now lets talk about catching something. This stretch of the West Coast offers lots of possibilities year round. Snook and Mangrove Snapper (on close-in rock structure) are prime targets in the spring and summer. They are joined at various times by Flounder, Spanish, and Bluefish. Bigger prey, such as Tarpon, Cobia, and Barracuda, are also distinct possibilities from the beach.

In the winter, a slightly different cast of characters takes over. Sheepshead, Pompano, Reds, and Specs become prime targets. They are frequently joined, however, by Blues, Spanish, Bonito, Black Drum, and the always cooperative Whiting.

In a more specific context, here are some additional points that may be of interest.

- Close-In Rock Structure - There are narrow strips of flat rock formations that essentially parallel the beach - - within casting distance - - between the middle of Gasparilla Island and downtown Boca Grande. Watch for them along other stretches of Gasparilla and Don Pedro Islands, too. Even if you can't see the rocks, assume they are there. In Gasparilla surf, also assume Snook will weigh up to 25 pounds during June and July.

- Point Ybel (Lighthouse Pt) on Sanibel Island - Giant Reds wander by within casting distance in the August - October period.

- Captiva Pass - Good limestone formation just off the beach north of the pass. The Tarpon that hang out there are within casting distance from the beach.

- Sanibel Island's Bowman's Beach - Try sunup September Snook fishing around any structure you can find. While you're on the island in September and October, cast into the drop off just west of the pier. A very large Snook or Red could make fishing interesting.

- Estero and the Hickory Islands - The surf is full of Pompano, Blues, and Spanish during the winter months.

PIERS

In Chapter 1, we identified at least 17 of the 30 or so West Coast gamefish that could be caught off area piers. That's particularly true of the dozen piers between Port Charlotte and Naples. Or, said another way, there isn't a bad pier in the crowd. At any time of the year, you can catch something fun and good to eat off each pier in the area. Lets take a look.

Figure 5.10 - Fishing Piers
Port Charlotte to Naples

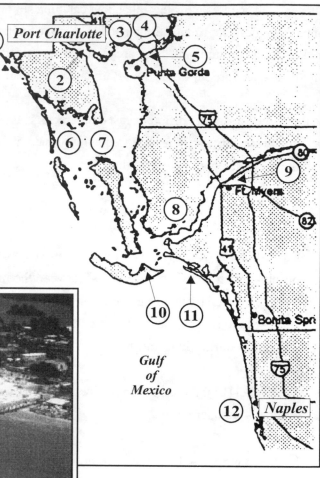

(1) Placida - There are two piers. One, on Coral Creek, is just off Hwy 771 to the north. The other, which provides access to the waters of Placida Harbor, is at the end of a spit of land south of Hwy 771. Good Snook action on both piers in late spring.

Ft. Myers Beach

(2) El Jobean - There are two piers, one each on the NE and SE sides of the Hwy 776 bridge over the Myakka River. Great Snook fishing, particularly in May. Spanish also available during the same period. All kinds of other stuff throughout the year, including Cobia in August.

(3) Port Charlotte Beach - The pier is a part of the Port Charlotte Beach Complex at 4500 Harbor Blvd. It's a 600 footer into Alligator Creek and Charlotte Harbor.

(4) Charlotte Harbor - This one is located on Bayshore Road just west of Hwy 41. It provides good access to the mouth of the Peace River.

(5) Punta Gorda - The city offers two fine piers on the Peace River. The municipal pier (Laishley Park) is located just up river from the Hwy 41 bridges. A brand new pier is now open in Gilchrist Park, just west of the bridges.

(6) Gasparilla Island - There are two piers (North and South) off Hwy 771 at the southern tip of the island. You can fish the waters of Boca Grande Pass from these piers.

(7) Bokeelia Island Seaport Pier - At the end of Hwy 767 on the northern end of Pine Island. Shore access to the mouth of Charlotte Harbor.

(8) Cape Coral - A fine, 620 foot pier that provides great access to the mouth of the Caloosahatchee River. It's located at 5819 Driftwood Parkway.

(9) Ft. Myers - The pier is a part of the city's Centennial Park and is located just east of the Hwy 41 bridge over the Caloosahatchee River.

(10) Sanibel Island Fishing Pier - On the east end of the island, adjacent to the lighthouse. Public parking is available at the beach at the east end of Periwinkle Way. The pier is 120 feet long. Snook, Reds, Sheepshead, Specs, Spanish, Snapper, Cobia, and Tripletail are all possibilities.

Cape Coral

Naples

(11) Ft. Myers Beach - The pier is on Estero Island with access to the full complement of Gulf fish. The pier is 600 feet long and has a bait shop.

(12) Naples Pier - 735 Eighth St South. One thousand feet of great fishing. Built originally as a commercial dock in 1888 but regularly renovated. Free admission but metered parking is tough. Snook, Pompano, Reds, Specs, etc., etc., are regular pier visitors.

INSHORE

As was true farther north, Inshore small boat action between Port Charlotte and Naples is consistently good for both migrating pelagic species and year round bottom dwellers. As Figure 5.11 suggests, there is an excellent system of artificial reefs within easy reach of Inshore fishermen. At least 22 of the area's gamefish can be caught on these reefs, in area passes, or somewhere in between. As you're checking the numbers on each spot, remember that the C suffix indicates to center of the artificial structure.

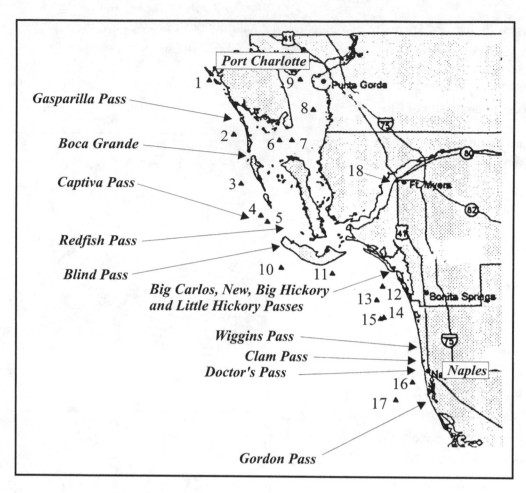

Figure 5.11 - Inshore - Port Charlotte to Naples

Spot #	Name	LORAN Coordinates	Latitude	Longitude	Depth (ft)	Structure
1	Desmond Reef Site/Englewood Fish Haven	14119.1/44228.0 14141.4/44183.2 14122.1/44183.2	26/53.70C 26/54.70C 26/54.70C	82/29.50C 82/21.75C 82/21.75C	50 22 22	Fiberglass boat molds Bridge rubble Bridge rubble
2	Mary's Reef	14128.4/44115.0	26/46.10	82/18.30	32	Concrete rubble
3	Helen's Reef	14112.4/44072.5	26/38.10	82/17.30	32	Barge, concrete rubble, power poles, wreck
4	Redfish Barges Reef	26/33.653 - 82/14.196	26/33.653	82/14.196	24	Two steel barges
5	Redfish Pass Reef		26/32.60	82/13.79	23	Concrete rubble, tires
6	Danger Reef		26/45.55	82/11.18		Wreck
7	Bokeelia Reef	In the bay	26/42.15	82/09.083		400 cu yds concrete culverts

Spot #	Name	LORAN Coordinates	Latitude Longitude	Depth (ft)	Structure
8	Charlotte Harbor Reef	14162.8/44024.7	26/49.887 82/05.543	12	Concrete culverts, catch basins, sewer boxes
		14166.6-8/ 44031.4-7	26/49.887C 82/05.543C	8-11	1027 tons concrete culverts
		14162.8/44024.7	26/49.887 82/05.543	12	1100 tons bridge rubble
9	Hog Is. Fish Haven	14169.4/44064.9	26/54.75C 82/07.617C	6-8	Tires
10	Belton Johnson Reef		26/25.48 82/11.88	30	500 tons culverts
11	Sanibel Reef	14113.1/43900.9	26/24.77 82/02.60	20	Concrete rubble, tires
		14113.3/43906.2	26/24.77 82/02.60	20	Concrete rubble, tires
12	'May' Reef	14122.1/43838.3	26/22.53 81/55.73	20	Bridge rubble
13	G-H(D.J.H.) Reef	14133.8/43850.6	26/20.73 81/57.12	25	450 tons culverts
14	Wiggins Pass 4.6 Mi Reef	14111.1/43824.0	26/17.30C 81/54.85C	28	Barge and crane
15	Edison Bridge Reef	14078.3/43968.7	26/18.45 82/13.36	42	1400 cu yds bridge rubble
16	Naples Pier Reef	14101.1/43765.4	26/07.42C 81/50.48C	20	Concrete rubble, tires
		14100.4/43768.0	26/07.770 81/51.026	20	300 tons concrete
17	Gordon Pass 5 Mile Reef	14089.8/43777.3	26/05.21C 81/53.44C	25	Concrete culverts
18	Ft. Myer's Wharf Reef	14161.9/43868.1	26/38.429C 81/52.482C		4800 tons concrete rubble

Legend - Figure 5.11

Before we head farther out and talk Offshore things, here are a few random bits you might find interesting about Inshore fishing.

- Tarpon - May through July. Johnson Shoal just south of Boca Grande; long bars at Captiva and Redfish Passes; Big Carlos Pass shoals; and really big bar off Sanibel Island's Point Ybel. In the month of June, Tarpon grounds are basically 100 miles long off the beach (Manatee to Lee Counties).

- Gulf of Mexico "Ledges" - One to two foot high rock structure that parallels the coast anywhere from hundreds of yards off the beach to many miles out. Off Naples, ledges have names (i.e., West, Great, Tigers, Monster, etc.). Very productive (Snapper, Grouper, Cobia, Amberjack, Kings). Check a mile or so north of the Boca Grande sea buoy.

- Gordon's Pass - A very fishy place. Snook, Reds, and Tarpon are probably possible year round. South jetty the best.

- Captiva and Redfish Passes - Bull Reds in October is one fun name of the game.

- Snook - May through September. Spawning fish stack up in the following passes:

  - Stump Pass in ski alley during the day and along the north beach at night.
  - Gasparilla Pass just inside on the north side.
  - Captiva Pass grass edges on the north side and the docks on the south side.
  - Redfish Pass - Drift the harbor entrance to the point.
  - San Carlos Pass at the Sanibel Resort docks.
  - Gordon's Pass - The biggest fish are usually around the Gulf markers.

- Gulf Reds - Giant 20 - 30 pounders show up on structure off Naples in November - December. May be from the beach to 10 miles off shore but the most consistent action reported to be three to six miles out. Check out all wrecks, reefs, holes, or other natural structure in the area.

- "Shiners" - A generic name for a whole variety of live bait used for Inshore structure fishing off SW Florida. The following are usually included in this category: Scaled Sardines (a.k.a. white bait, pilchards, big-eye shiners), Thread Herring (a.k.a. threadfins, greenbacks), Spanish Sardines, and Menhaden. Regardless of the name, some or all of these guys can usually be chummed up on a grass flat and then captured with a throw net.

- Winter Specs - Try the area a couple of hundred yards off the La Playa Hotel in North Naples. Drift the area with shrimp tipped jigs in 10 - 20 feet of water. You may also encounter Bluefish and/or Spanish. While you're in the area, check out the "hardbottom" rock piles off the Vanderbilt Inn in Vanderbilt Beach. Sheepshead, Snapper, and perhaps a Grouper are possibilities.

- Electric Trolling Motor - A fundamental piece of equipment for successfully engaging Tarpon along area beaches. Sometimes you won't even be able to get close without one.

- Jewfish (catch and release only) - Here's a recent magazine suggestion for October that sounds like fun. Spots: pilings on the New Pass or Big Carlos Pass bridges, the Sanibel Causeway, or the Boca Grande phosphate dock. Tackle: 100 pound test line, 300 pound test mono leader, very large hook, very heavy rod and reel, and a sinker of a pound or more. Bait: substantial live Jack. Probable outcome: You'll fail to successfully land a 200+ pound Jewfish. Oh well . . .

So much for random bits. Lets move on Offshore a ways and check out the possibilities in deeper water. There are good fish to be caught there year round, weather permitting.

OFFSHORE

Between six and a half and fourteen miles off the beach, you'll find a fine system of artificial reefs. Obviously, they're complemented by non-permitted sites and a variety of isolated but fairly extensive natural bottom features. And there are some other possibilities much farther out. We'll touch on those shortly.

**Figure 5.12 - Offshore
Port Charlotte to Naples**

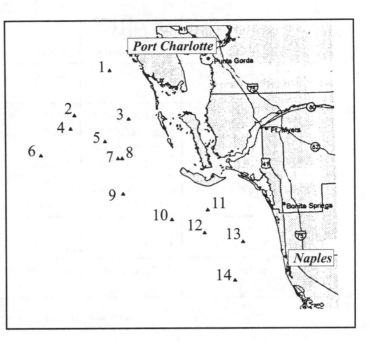

Spot #	Name	LORAN Coordinates	Latitude	Longitude	Depth (ft)	Structure
1	Stump Pass 7 Mi Reef	14126.3/44209.7	26/52.102C	82/26.484C	43	Concrete culverts, boxes
2	Boxcar Reef	14082.6/44239.6	26/42.00	82/36.00	72	48 steel boxcars, concrete culverts, wreck
3	Power Pole - Searun Power Pole-BARCRN	14108.6/44124.5	26/40.88 26/41.87	82/22.25 82/22.47	46	Wreck Concrete rubble, power pole, 65' steel ship, cement mixer
4	Aaron Hendry Reef		26/39.00	82/36.00		Unknown
5	School Bus Reef 2	14086.0/44152.4	26/36.22	82/28.29	70	School bus, culverts
6	Deep Reef	14045.2/44260.0	26/33.27	82/43.47	90	Two piles of hopper cars
7	ARCOA	14083.9/44111.4	26/32.48	82/25.08	57	ARCOA prefab units
8	12 Mile Reef - Culverts 12 Mile Reef - Barge	14085.3/44111.4	26/32.74 26/32.88	82/24.62 82/24.75	60	Culverts Barge, concrete culverts
9	A.R.C. Barge Reef	14067.9/44080.0	26/25.15	82/24.60	60	110' steel barge

Spot #	Name	LORAN Coordinates	Latitude	Longitude	Depth (ft)	Structure
10	Edison Bridge Reef	14078.3/43968.7	26/18.45	82/13.36	42	1400 cu yds bridge rubble
11	Jaycees Reef	14097.9/43912.0	26/20.24	82/05.25	33	Barge with rubble
		14098.5/43912.0	26/20.24	82/05.25	31	225 tons concrete
		14097.9/43913.4	26/20.24	82/05.25	31	300 tons concrete
		14097.2/43912.9	26/20.24	82/05.25	31	310 tons concrete
12	Wiggins Pass 14 Mi Reef	14080.5/43912.2	26/14.010	82/07.736	42	800 tons concrete
		14085.0/43900.0	26/14.86C	82/05.83C	48	Concrete culverts
13	Doctors Pass 5 Mi Reef	14098.5/43818.6	26/10.22C	81/54.34C	28	Concrete culverts
		14098.5/43827.6	26/12.681	81/57.271	30	800 tons concrete
14	Gordon Pass 9 Mi Reef	14076.5/43834.0	26/04.04C	81/59.32C	36	92 concrete modules

Legend - Figure 5.12

In addition to the 14 sites we've just visited, there are obviously many more. Six that may be of interest are much farther Offshore - - from 25 to 75 miles or so off the beach.

• The Bayronto - A 400 foot British steamer sunk during a hurricane more than 50 years ago. Depth: 110 feet. LORAN: 14057.1/44374.9, GPS 26/45.80-82/50.84.

• Fantastico - A 200 foot freighter that went down in 1993. Depth: 112 feet. LORAN: 13994.0/44248.0. GPS: 26/03.10-82/57.42.

• Stoney Point - A Hudson River passenger ferry that was scuttled in 1968. Depth: 132 feet. LORAN: 13966.3/44252.7. GPS: 26/10.11-82/54.61.

• Captiva Blue Hole - Depth (at the rim) 80 feet. LORAN: 14033.4/44247.6. GPS: 26/28.92-82/44.22.

• Naples Spring - Seventy feet at the rim and 224 feet to the bottom. LORAN: 14028.5/43864.5. GPS: 25/50.45-82/09.21.

• Baja California - A Norwegian freighter sunk by a German submarine in WWII. LORAN: 13920.7/43961.5. GPS: 25/21.38-82/31.96.

And that's about it on when and where to **CATCH FISH NOW! on Florida's West Coast**. We've covered a lot of ground - - actually water - - between Cedar Key and Naples. Our next task is to put the whole operation in motion and actually focus on catching some fish. That's exactly what we'll do next.

CHAPTER 6

CATCH FISH NOW!

It's time . . . to catch some fish! To this point, we've been talking about "when and where" sorts of things. We've established some annual patterns for each of the 30 gamefish on Florida's West Coast. We've also talked about proven spots and areas to find these guys. Now, it's time to go to work. This chapter will cover each of the 30 fish of interest. Proven tactics and special tips will be presented to help you **CATCH FISH NOW!** The chapter will conclude with a section on natural and artificial baits and some suggestions on the kinds of tackle required to get the job done. OK, enough talk. Let's go fishing.

GAMEFISH

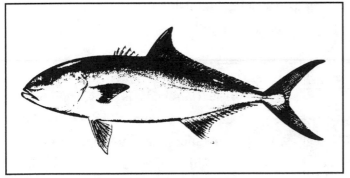

Amberjack (AJ)

The Amberjack (AJ) is a relatively long, slender fish with the pronounced V tail typical to members of the Jack family. The upper part of his body is dark, either brownish, olive, or steely blue. The lower part of his body is lighter, with lavender and golden tints. He may also have an amber band from eye to tail. Although small Amberjack of less than legal size (28 inches to the fork) are frequently caught Inshore, legal fish are out in blue water Offshore around structure. In the case of AJ's, structure can either be something - - or its absence. Deep wrecks and artificial/natural reefs are all potentially productive. But, from Tampa south, so, too, are the blue holes and fresh water springs that occur well Offshore. These holes in the bottom also become very fishy at times.

PROVEN TACTICS. On the West Coast, fish to 75 pounds or so can be caught over structure using two different approaches. First, try anchoring or drifting live bait. The Amberjack will happily consume Mullet, Grunts, Pinfish, or what have you. Use a heavy duty fish finder rig consisting of a 3 to 8 oz egg sinker running free on your line, a 100 lb test barrel swivel, a 3 ft piece of 80 lb test mono, and a 5/0 single bronze hook. Lower your bait down about three fourths of the way to the bottom . . . and hold on! Second, and after your fishfinder has confirmed the presence of AJ's, slow trolling might also work if the fish are less than 50 feet down. Use downriggers/planers and spoons, very large grubs/twister tails, natural rigged baits, or big lipped deep diving plugs.

YOUR WINNING EDGE . . .

✔ If the structure you're fishing has relief off the bottom, try the downstream side if there's a current running. AJ's like to ambush bait from the calm water of the eddy that's been created.

✔ Try an appropriately sized "tuna" or "circle" hook. Its quick "self-set" on the strike increases the odds of a successful hook up.

✔ Chum Mr. Amberjack up to you while you're anchored or drifting. Ground chum will draw baitfish. They and chunks of chum will keep the AJ's interested.

✔ If you're deep jigging, be sure to sweeten your lure with a fresh fish or Squid strip.

The Amberjack has an intense curiosity and very little fear of man. When you hook one, more than likely the entire school will follow the fighting fish right up to the boat. The other fish will hit new baits tossed to them, and will continue to do so as long as one struggling fish remains in the water. The Amberjack is great eating. The Florida record for Amberjack is 142 lbs.

Barracuda

The Barracuda is long, slim-bodied and has a pointed head. Its body coloration is dull to bright silver with a whitish tinge. There are usually a few irregular black blotches scattered along its length. Prominently, its very large mouth is full of very large, pointed teeth. Young Barracuda to about three pounds hang out close to shore and may be caught in shallow water in harbors and coastal lagoons. The big guys to over 100 pounds are found in deeper water Offshore, usually over bottom structure. They are aggressive, carnivorous fish that will attack almost anything that moves. They aren't particularly good eating but are a ball to catch. The Florida record is 67 pounds.

PROVEN TACTICS. Inshore, on flats, along channel edges, and around mangroves, Barracuda are a plug casters delight. They particularly like minnow imitations, but will also hit tube lures, jigs, and shallow-running spoons. Regardless of what you use, a wire leader is a must. Offshore, almost every Gulf wreck and most reefs hold one or more Cudas of substantially greater size. These guys can be caught using either lures or live bait. In the case of artificials, and while many different types will work, tube lures are usually the most effective. Regardless of what you try, speed and erratic violent action is the key to success. Live baiting Barracuda is straightforward. One popular terminal rig consists of a 5/0 or larger hook "haywired" to a short (5-10") piece of 40 or so pound coffee colored single strand wire. The wire is attached to a three foot piece of 60 pound test mono using an appropriately sized barrel swivel. As bottom fishermen know, choice of bait isn't difficult. Basically, carry out what you can get. Blue Runners, Mullet, Pinfish, etc., are all usually effective. If you're really serious, try a Spanish or King Mackerel.

YOUR WINNING EDGE . . .

✔ Replace the treble hooks on your Cuda lures with singles. That will be a big help in unhooking your fish under potentially terrifying circumstances.

✔ Orange and chartreuse seem to be the most effective colors for tube lures.

✔ If, for some reason, you're just blindly trolling lures or natural bait and hook up with a Barracuda - - STOP! Carefully check the bottom with your machine. More than likely, you passed over some structure holding at least Barracuda, and perhaps other fish of interest.

On a final note, don't overlook the fact that Barracuda are year round Offshore and Inshore West Coast residents. Fishing area flats in December or January for Cudas could be a fun alternative . . . to a football game on TV.

The Black Drum has a short, deep body with a high-arched back. Its mouth is low and horizontal with the upper jaw projecting beyond the lower. In life, the Black Drum's body is silvery with a brassy sheen, which turns to dark gray after death. Its fins are blackish in color. Unlike its cousin, the Redfish, it does not have a black spot at the base of its tail. Black Drum have been caught on the West Coast to over 50 pounds. Fish of 10 pounds or less are great eating. Fish larger than that should be released. Look for these guys year round in West Coast waters, particularly off piers, bridges and other spots with pilings and other underwater structure. The Florida record for Black Drum is 93 pounds and the world all-tackle record - - 113 pounds 1 ounce.

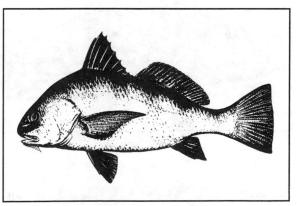

Black Drum

PROVEN TACTICS. Since the Drum is exclusively a bottom feeder, a slip rig is the way to go. It's simple. Select an egg sinker just heavy enough to hold your chosen bait on the bottom. Slip it and a plastic bead up your line and tie on a barrel swivel. Then tie on about three feet of 30# test mono and a 1/0 to 3/0 extra-strength, short shank hook. You're in business. Popular West Coast Black Drum baits include Blue Crab pieces, Fiddler Crabs, Clams, Sand Fleas, and live/fresh dead Shrimp.

YOUR WINNING EDGE . . .

✔ Go for a monster. Fish a known hotspot for the really big guys. Increase your line strength to at least 50#, your leader to 80 pound test, and hook size to at least 7/0. Use a whole, palm sized Blue Crab for bait. Chum the area you're going to fish with Clam/Oyster pieces and/or crab cleanings. Hold on to your rod at all times.

✔ Try a "fish finder" gizmo for attaching your weight, in lieu of an egg sinker. These little Teflon coated plastic sleeves with sinker attachment clips can do two things for you. Your line will slip through them very smoothly so you'll feel any fooling around with your bait. And you'll also appreciate the convenience of being able to adjust sinker weight for changing conditions - - without having to cut your line.

✔ Just for the heck of it, try a lure. We've caught a reasonable number of perfect eating size Black Drum on small silver spoons and plastic grub and twister tails.

And that's Black Drum. If you're looking for real "heft" in your Bay, Surf, Pier, or Inshore fishing, try one - - you'll like it.

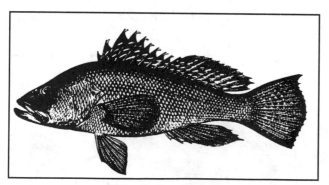

Black Sea Bass

This tasty eating fish is dark brown or black in color with a dorsal fin that has rows and stripes of white on black. Large males have iridescent blue and ebony marking and a fatty hump just in front of their dorsal fins. There is usually a blue pattern around the eyes of both the male and female. Black Sea Bass are common to about a pound and a half (13 inches) and the Florida record for this guy is five pounds, one ounce.

Black Sea Bass are a structure loving fish that can be found, year round, in West Coast Bay, Inshore, and Offshore water. Despite its diminutive size, this guy is an aggressive feeder with a giant appetite. Black Sea Bass are a ball to catch on ultra-light tackle.

116

PROVEN TACTICS. Black Sea Bass will cooperate on either natural or artificial baits. Depending on the depth of water you're fishing, use a slip rig or splitshot above a 10# test leader and #2 hook - - to feed him small live fish, Shrimp, Squid strips, or what have you. A variety of artificials work equally well. Small spoons, almost any color jig, plastic grub, or twister tail, and probably many of the new soft plastic Shrimp and Crabs should all get the job done.

Given the aggressiveness of this fish, tandem rigs are particularly effective. Just tie a three-way swivel to the end of your line and two different length leaders to the other two swivel eyes. Finish the rig off with a couple of jigs of your choosing. An egg sinker above the swivel may be necessary to stay close to the bottom if you're in deeper waters. A small Squid strip on each jig enhances the chances of regular "doubles." Work your bait slowly in short hops for the best results.

YOUR WINNING EDGE . . .

✔ In shallower water, troll over known areas of bottom structure pulling a small planer. If there are any Black Sea Bass around, they'll come off the bottom to hit a small spoon or minnow imitation attached to the planer.

✔ In deeper Offshore water, try deep jigging. Use a three to four ounce diamond jig in a chrome finish. Tie the jig directly to the end of your line, lower away, and experiment at different heights above the bottom structure.

Despite their size, Sea Bass will bite in the middle of winter when nothing else will. And when its fillets are dusted in flour, fried in equal parts of butter and peanut oil, and seasoned with Dale's steak seasoning - - WOW!

This member of the Mackerel family is one of the smallest tuna. It has a typical tuna shape with generally dark coloring over its entire body. It has finlets behind the second dorsal and anal fins which are uniformly black, hence its name. Blackfins off the West Coast may reach 35 pounds, but most are less than 15 pounds. Regardless of size, they are delicious eating. The all tackle world record for Blackfins is 42 pounds.

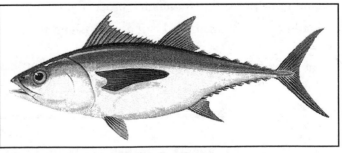

Blackfin Tuna

PROVEN TACTICS. One effective way to catch Blackfins is drifting or slow trolling live bait. The rig for this is simple. Tie a barrel swivel to the end of your line. Then tie on a 3 ft piece of 50 lb test mono with a 2/0 or so treble hook. Although you're going to lose a few rigs and baits if sharp-toothed King Mackerel are in the area, mono is still the way to go! Blackfin are very shy of wire leaders. Vary the depth you are fishing with different sized rubber core sinkers attached to your line above the swivel. Pinfish are probably the best bait, but Blackfins will also take Sardines, small Mullets, Pilchards, and Cigar Minnows.

Offshore, if you are in an area where Blackfin have been reported, go fast! Pull rigged Ballyhoo at sufficient speed (up to 12 knots) to skip them along the surface. This approach is a proven tuna-getter. Lures are also used effectively Offshore. Clark Spoons, Softheads in a variety of colors, California and No Alibi feathers, and Creek Chub Pike jointed wooden plugs have worked well. They should be pulled 100 - 300 feet behind the boat. If no surface action develops, run your lures deep behind #2 or #3 planers.

YOUR WINNING EDGE . . .

✔ Your first and probably best indicator of feeding Blackfins will be . . . feeding birds. Gaggles of birds follow Blackfin schools and patiently wait for surface feeding action to take place. When it does, they join in.

✔ There are several different brands of appropriately sized live bait hooks with enameled finishes available. They increase the probability of successful hook-ups.

✔ If you're in an area that you suspect may hold Blackfins, but standard trolling techniques haven't produced results, try this. Put a couple of feathers out 100 yards behind your boat. From time to time, stop the boat, let the feathers sink a while, then take off and accelerate back up to trolling speed. If there are fish around, you'll get them.

✔ Don't overlook the frequently productive tactic of chumming with live Pilchards, Ballyhoo, Sardines, or chunked dead bait over Offshore structure.

✔ Use light colored (i.e., lime green, pink, etc.) lures mid-day and darker shades toward dawn and dusk.

At various times, this popular gamefish may be found along all area beaches, around jetties, off piers, and over natural structure in area bays. It has a moderately stout body and a belly that is flat sided but blunt edged on the ventral surface. The Bluefish has a slightly pointed snout and a large oblique mouth with a projecting lower jaw. It has prominent, very sharp canine teeth. Its coloration is generally blue-green above, shading to silvery-white on the belly. Bluefish in this area range in size from 7 - 9 inch "snappers" to an occasional 20 pound plus "monster." Regardless of size, they have a well earned reputation for savagery when on a feeding rampage, maiming or killing everything in their paths, including their

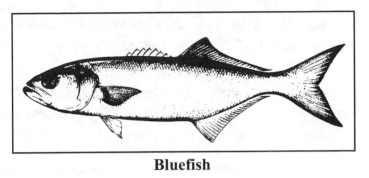

Bluefish

own kind. Never put your fingers in a Bluefish's mouth, no matter how dead he may appear! The current Florida record for Bluefish is over 22 pounds.

PROVEN TACTICS. There are two basic ways to catch Bluefish. Each can be effective under a variety of conditions. If Bluefish are known to be working the surf, bait fishing is always a good approach. Chunks or strips of cut bait fished on the bottom using a two-hook spreader or fish-finder rig can be productive. Cut Mullet has consistently proven to be the best bait, followed closely by cut Cigar Minnows. Heavy wire two hook spreaders (which can be purchased at any tackle store) should be configured with a one to three ounce pyramid sinker on the bottom, 1/0 or 2/0 hooks attached directly to the two spreader clips, with your line tied to the barrel swivel at the top. If you're surf fishing, your rig should be cast out as far as possible, preferably beyond the second bar. A fish finder rig is an effective alternative to a two-hook spreader and allows your bait to move around the area you are fishing. It is nothing more than an egg sinker (again, one to three ounces) sliding freely on your line, which is tied to one side of a barrel swivel. Up to 30 inches of wire leader with a 1/0 or 2/0 hook is attached to the other side of the barrel swivel. Plastic coated, store bought leaders are okay.

Lures are another fun and effective way to catch Bluefish. As a matter of fact, a whole variety of spoons, jigs, and plugs (including topwater) work well. The key with lures is to first locate the fish. Watch for feeding birds and/or bait fish trying to fly. If you happen to be in the neighborhood, the mouths of West Coast passes on the first of the incoming and last of the outgoing tides may prove productive.

YOUR WINNING EDGE . . .

✔ Whether you're using natural or artificial bait, always use some kind of wire leader.

✔ For pure blood curdling excitement, try ultralight tackle and live bait. Pinfish, Glass Minnows, fingerling Mullet, and Bull Minnows (Killifish) all work well.

✔ Fish the surf at night if jumbo Blues have been reported in the area. Use a partially water-filled, large, clear casting float, coffee colored single strand wire leader, and at least a 1/0 treble hook. A whole frozen Sardine or Cigar Minnow is the bait of choice. Hook him through the eye socket and fire away. Hold on to your rod at all times.

Bluefish can be/are good to eat if treated properly. Keep them cool, clean them as soon as possible, and remove the dark strips along each fillet. We particularly like smoked Bluefish that had previously been marinated in saltwater and brown sugar.

Blue Marlin

The Blue Marlin is the largest of the Atlantic Marlin family. It is common to 11 feet in length and is known to exceed 2,000 pounds in weight. All trophy size fish are females; males seldom grow much over 300 pounds. Not surprisingly, a Blue's body is cobalt blue, shading to silvery white underneath. Although he/she is definitely good to eat, the correct name of the game is catch and release. The Florida record for Blue Marlin is just a tad over 980 pounds.

Yes, there really are Blue Marlin off Florida's West Coast. Sadly, they are way off. Having said that, some West Coast big game anglers make the long, 100+ mile run out and are rewarded for their efforts.

PROVEN TACTICS. Both rigged natural baits and a variety of lures can be effective for Blue Marlin. Choosing between the two, however, often comes down to a question of speed. Specifically, because potential hotspots are separated by substantial distances, a brisk (minimum of 8 - 9 knots) trolling speed is required to cover as much potentially productive water as possible. Natural baits just do not hold up long or well, moving this fast or faster. The choice of lures usually focuses on flat or slant-face plastics in medium and large sizes. Other observations by West Coast Offshore big-game fishermen provide additional useful insights.

- Lure size - One school of thought says big only. Softhead, C&H or Snider lures rigged with 12/0 or 14/0 Mustad hooks or regular steel are preferred. Another school says think small. Lures with short heads, measuring no more than seven to twelve inches, including skirt, are considered the best. Popular head styles are those that produce plenty of splash and smoke (bubbles), even at moderate trolling speeds. Using this approach, Reto's Rigs, Boone's Airheads, R&S small Teardrops with their skirts trimmed, standard softhead Hookers, and rubber squids are all lures that can work well.

- Lure Color - There has been much debate about the ability of fish to see color. Two basic principles work well. Dark colors can be seen as a silhouette against the mirror-like ocean surface by a fish rising from deep below the bait. Light colors can be seen by a fish swimming on the surface and viewing the lure against the dark blue ocean background. Of course, you can also choose to imitate the color of the baitfish that may be present. Try blue and silver to simulate flying fish, or green and yellow to mimic Dolphin.

- Live Bait - Great approach if Blues are known to be in the area. A trolling speed of 1 - 2 knots is about right. Good baits include: Black Jacks, Goggle Eyes, Big Eye Scads, Blackfin Tuna and Bonito. When Blackfin are schooling on the surface, catch one, put him down 50 feet or so on a downrigger - - and hold on!

- Lure Spread - One popular trolling spread consists of five lures, two on flatlines, two from outriggers, and one shotgun down the center. The darkest bait is run on the shotgun about 250 feet behind the long rigger, at about the fifth wave behind the transom. The close flatline is usually the largest lure in the spread and is often a lighter color.

So much for observations - - and the Blue Marlin. They are out there and they are big. If you have the time, money, equipment, and patience, have at it and good luck!

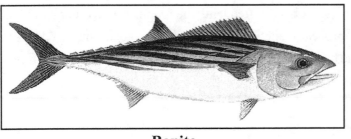

Bonito

The Bonito is a mackerel-shaped fish that is a blueish-steel color on the upper body, shading off to silvery sides and a white belly. He has dark stripes running diagonally down and forward across his upper body. Bonito average 4 to 15 lbs in this area. They are often an unwanted by-product of trolling for King Mackerel. Bonito is a valued food fish in the Eastern Atlantic and there is an extensive commercial fishery for it there. Along Florida's West Coast, however, they are not usually brought home for the dinner table.

PROVEN TACTICS. Bonito are a ball to catch, because they strike aggressively, fight furiously, and don't give up. They'll hit on almost anything you throw in the water for King and Spanish Mackerel, Inshore and Offshore Redfish, and even Blackfin Tuna. They've saved many a fishing trip, simply because they would often oblige - - when nothing else would. And there are frequently lots of them around. Half mile square schools are not unusual at times.

No "**WINNING EDGE**" suggestions are warranted for Bonito. If there are any around, they'll cooperate with whatever you're doing. And, by the way, if you're inclined to do some Shark fishing, save any Bonito you catch. They are primo bait for large Sharks.

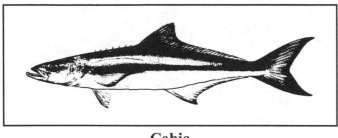

Cobia

From a distance, this fish looks vaguely like a large Catfish and/or a Shark. It has a relatively wide, horizontally aligned mouth and a forked tail. Its upper body is dark brown, its sides somewhat lighter, and its belly a very pale brown. Younger fish have a black lateral band extending from their noses across their eyes back to the base of their tails. A Cobia's fins are mostly black. Spring run Cobia average between 20 - 50 pounds, but fish up to 137 pounds have been caught in Florida waters. A potential new world record of 154 pounds is pending. Cobia is absolutely delicious to eat.

Cobia are (sort of) a migratory species. After wintering in the Keys, they move up Florida's West Coast in the spring and summer. Most/many continue on around the bend toward the Texas Gulf Coast. Others, however, apparently get sidetracked and drop out of the migratory movement, taking up residence in area bays and Inshore waters. They are powerfully attracted to structure in its broadest sense. Pilings, bridges, channel markers, buoys, wrecks, and any kind of floating objects are all potential Cobia hotspots. So, too, are other sea creatures. Cobia can frequently be found around other large fish, rays of all sorts, sea turtles, and will even approach an anchored boat. During many months of the year, Cobia can be caught off West Coast piers and bridges, on deep and shallow flats, and in area bays, rivers, and power plant warm water discharge canals.

PROVEN TACTICS. Besides being tremendous fighters, Cobia are also world class eaters and can be taken on both live bait and artificial lures. They can be caught by nearly every technique, including chumming, trolling, and the hands-down favorite, sight casting. Effective live baits include Silver Trout, Blue Crabs, Pinfish, Eels (if you can find them), Mullet, and other large what-have-you's. Hair or feather jigs, in 1-1/2 oz to 3 oz sizes and every conceivable color, are probably the most popular lures. Chartreuse, chartreuse and yellow, purple, and white have been particularly good colors over the years. Pieces of a whole plastic worm or twister tails hooked on the jig have enhanced fishing success over the last several seasons. A squid head with the tentacles still attached is even better. Tube and Dingaling lures, a variety of artificial eels, and all kinds of large plugs, have also worked well. Regardless of whether you fish live bait or lures, you must use a 30 inch or so piece of 50 lb test mono and a barrel swivel for attachment.

YOUR WINNING EDGE . . .

✔ A Cobia of any size is a powerful fish who has a very bad attitude when it's time to be landed. The preferred approach for minimizing potential damage and destruction is to gaff the fish through the back. Then, in one motion, bring him on-board and straight into your fish box. If that's not possible, then your one motion should be a hit to the head with a substantial club. You'll be sorry if you don't!

✔ In season, anticipate the presence of Cobia on deeper water Offshore natural reefs and ledges. Try live-baiting with Squirrelfish if you suspect Cobia may be around.

✔ If you happen on a Cobia but he/she ignores your offering, don't give up. Keep trying different baits. I've actually had "full" fish regurgitate the contents of their stomachs in order to eat a favorite bait that just couldn't be ignored.

✔ Experiment with non-traditional lures. If you've got a lure from somewhere else that consistently caught something else - - try it. For example, I've had great success throwing a proven Chesapeake Bay Bluefish catcher called a "ragmop." There are obviously lots of other possibilities.

Cobia really are great to eat. Unlike many fish that get tough or stringy as they get larger, Cobia of all sizes are equally superb. And you'll like it - - grilled, broiled, fried, baked, or smoked!

In the water, Dolphin are usually a vivid greenish-blue with dark vertical bands that may appear and disappear. When the fish is hooked, his color fluctuates rapidly between blue, green, and yellow. After death, these colors fade rapidly to a uniform yellowish shade. Dolphin typically have relatively blunt heads and

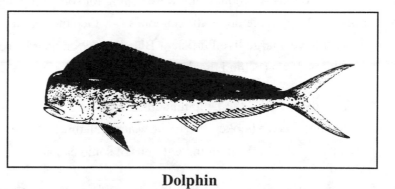

Dolphin

bodies that taper back to a very pronounced fork tail. The Florida record for Dolphin is 77 pounds, 12 ounces, and its fighting ability is legendary. Swimming speeds have been clocked in excess of 50 knots. Dolphin are superior eating, just as their cousins are in Hawaii (Mahi-Mahi) and Mexico (Durado).

PROVEN TACTICS. A Dolphin strikes explosively, fights frantically, and performs beautifully in the air. From time to time, "schoolies" congregate by the hundreds or thousands along tide lines or weed lines Offshore. When this happens, the name of the game is to troll Baby Dusters with Squid strips or small feathers along these lines. When hookups occur, stop the boat, break out the light spinning tackle, and start throwing small jigs, spoons, etc. Catching two to ten pound schoolies on light tackle is a never to be forgotten experience. They are absolutely superior fighters with full bags of acrobatic tricks.

Fishing for big Dolphin farther Offshore is unlike the pursuit of other pelagic species in this area. As others have pointed out, it's more like hunting than fishing. The secret is not blind trolling. Rather, it's a case of high speed running while looking for indications of fish or spots/things that may hold them. Circling frigate birds are the best indication; weed lines are good spots, and any kind of flotsam is a kind of thing likely to have Dolphin close by.

Big Dolphin will hit just about any kind of lure or bait, including those intended for Marlin. Feather jigs, rigged Ballyhoo and strip baits, Moldcraft Hookers, Dolphin Juniors and Seniors, and Jelly Bellies all work well for bull and cow Dolphin. Although color doesn't seem to matter all that much, many fishermen swear by greens, yellows, whites, and orange/yellows. With regard to natural bait, big live baits are the best. On Florida's West Coast, Blue Runners are usually the easiest to catch and they are super for big Dolphin. Ten inches or longer is about the right size. Frozen, rigged Ballyhoo, trolled either naked or with a plastic skirt is another favorite.

YOUR WINNING EDGE . . .

✔ At one time or another, you may encounter a weed line loaded with schoolie-sized Dolphin of three to five pounds. Although you were hoping for something bigger, don't despair. Frequently, much bigger Dolphin are under the schoolies - - which they eat from time to time. If you planned ahead, you'll have a large live Pinfish or Blue Runner on board. Toss it outside the schoolies, hooked so it swims down (behind the dorsal fin). Stand by for action!

✔ Take advantage of the Dolphin's intense desire for "togetherness." When you get into a bunch of schoolies, keep a hooked fish in the water at all times. More often than not, this will keep the school with you. A little chumming with bits of squid can also aid the process.

✔ Try a whole, rigged, 8" - 10", frozen Squid dressed with an Octopus skirt for Offshore trolling in lieu of, or as a complement to, usual rigged species. Squid are extremely durable and a favorite of lots of other big guys besides Dolphin.

✔ If you're Offshore trolling a spread for big Dolphin and others, include down-rigger baits, too. The probability of a Bull deep is higher than on the surface.

The bottom line on Dolphin is - - think conservation. When you get into them, it's easy to fill a boat. Don't! Think hard about how many you can eat and let the rest go.

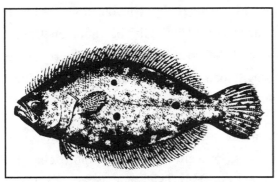

Flounder

There are a number of different kinds of Flounder in West Coast waters year round. All share some common characteristics. These include a broad, flat body with both eyes on one side of the head. Their bottom sides are generally whitish in color and their top sides (where their eyes are) are grey-brown. Flounder caught in the surf tend to have very light coloration on their top sides to more closely match the white sand bottom they live on. Size ranges between 10 - 20 inches in length with "doormats" over 25 inches caught occasionally. Flounder are outstanding eating. The Florida record for these guys is 20 pounds 9 ounces.

PROVEN TACTICS. Flounder can be caught almost anywhere except, perhaps, way Offshore. The preferred approach in bait fishing is a fishfinder rig with a ½ oz to 1½ oz egg sinker and 24 inches of 12 - 15 lb test line as a leader. Small (#2 - #4) treble or standard hooks are about right. Small fingerling Mullet, Pinfish, or Croakers, which you have to catch yourself, or Bull Minnows that sometimes can be obtained at a bait shop, are the preferred baits. There are times, however, when other baits, such as fresh dead Shrimp, Sandfleas, cut bait strips, and Fiddler Crabs will also take Flounder. Live Shrimp, of course, is always an effective, albeit expensive, choice.

Using lures for Flounder can be a lot of fun, particularly on ultra light tackle. In this area, all of the following will catch fish:

- Plastic grubs - white, white with a hot pink tail, chartreuse, dark green with a fire tail, and rootbeer, to name only a few of many effective possiblities.
- Plastic twister tail jigs - white, chartreuse, dark green with a fire tail, and metal flake clear/grey. Experiment with white, red or chartreuse jig heads with the various tail colors.
- Small (1/2 oz) gold spoons.
- Small jigs - white, yellow, or hot pink skirts.
- Small, sinking gold or silver Rapalas, Rebels, or the like.

One recent particularly effective technique has been a white or hot pink jig sweetened with either a small strip of Flounder belly or small live fish.

YOUR WINNING EDGE . . .

✔ If you plan to drift the edges of channels with live bait, you might want to try the following Flounder rig. Tie a snap swivel on one end of a 2 ft piece of 15 - 20 lb test mono. Now feed on a small day glow orange bead, a small barrel swivel, and another orange bead, in that order. Then, tie another barrel swivel to the other end of your 24 inches of mono. Finish the rig by tying on another 24 inch piece of mono to the barrel swivel between the beads. Then tie on a 1/0 English bait hook on the end of that. As far as weight goes, use a sufficiently heavy bell shaped sinker to bounce the rig along the bottom. For what it's worth, the real Flounder purists paint their bell shaped sinkers either yellow or orange. They claim it has a stimulating effect on the fishes' feeding behavior.

✔ In a variation on the theme, another popular way to catch Flounder is with a gig. The usually clear shallow water and sandy bottoms in many parts of the West Coast are ideal for this approach. The scenario goes like this. During the day, Flounder lie off the shore in deeper water. At night, however, they come into the shallows (1-3 feet) to chase minnows. They become visible and vulnerable - - if you happen to be quietly drifting through the area in a shallow draft boat. The only equipment you will need is a gig head mounted on some kind of a handle, and a light source. There are commercially available floating 12V lights or you can make your own with a 12V sealed beam headlight. Flounder are usually available for gigging from early summer to mid-fall.

✔ Try a jig-head and live bait combo if you want to cover a lot of water fast.

There are lots of great eating fish available on Florida's West Coast. But until you've had Flounder fillets stuffed with Crab meat, you really haven't had the ultimate in epicurean delights.

Of the 50 or so members of the Grouper clan that live in Florida waters, about 10 can be caught somewhere off Florida's West Coast. Three of the most common of these are spotlighted below.

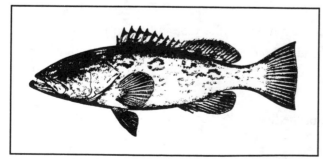

Gag Grouper

The Gag Grouper is brownish gray in color with dark worm-like markings on its sides. Its tail is slightly concave and its anal and caudal fins have a white margin on them. The world record of 71 pounds, 3 ounces for a Gag was set in Florida waters. This fish is common to 25 pounds on Offshore rocks and reefs.

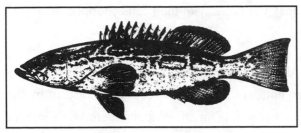
Black Grouper

The Black Grouper has olive or grey body coloration with black blotches and brassy spots. Black Grouper are common to 40 pounds and sometimes are caught over 100 pounds. There is no Florida record, however, because this fish is frequently confused with the Gag, which is often mistakenly called a "black grouper." You'll find these guys Offshore on rocky bottoms and reefs, usually in more than 60 feet of water.

The Red Grouper is a squatty shaped fish that is generally olive-grey in color with a slight salmon cast to it. Its jaws are pale olive with a slight reddish cast to them. It has dark bars on its head and body and, on some fish, there are also scattered white spots. The Florida record for this guy is 39 pounds, 8 ounces. It's common to 15 pounds, and hangs out on Inshore structure.

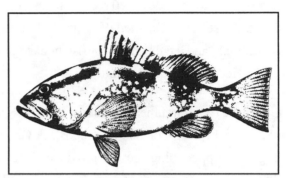
Red Grouper

Grouper are clearly one of the West Coast's premier gamefish - - for a whole bunch of reasons. Some grow huge, all are strong and tenacious fighters, and many frequently do the unexpected. As bottom dwellers, they'll come to the surface to feed and have even been known to jump. Although they exist on natural forage, Groupers have a keen eye for a well presented artificial bait. All this, and they are unequivocally world-class in the eating department.

PROVEN TACTICS. There are probably as many ways to catch Grouper as there are kinds of places to find them. But there are some fundamental approaches that work, whether you're fishing the edges of Tampa Bay ship channels, natural ledges far Offshore of Cedar Key, or in the Gulf passes up and down the coast. If you're going to be fishing natural bait, a slip rig is the way to go. Use a large enough egg sinker to just get your bait on the bottom. A 5/0 hook, six to eight feet of 80 lb test mono leader, and live bait finish the rig. While Grouper will take dead bait like butterflied Mingo Snappers, live bait usually has more appeal. Pinfish, Cigar Minnows, Squirrel fish, and Sand Perch are routinely used in this area, with the latter being preferred due to its shininess in the water. Grouper usually feed by sight.

Drifting/slow trolling over deep water structure is a variation on the natural bait theme. It can be productive, particularly if you have a downrigger. In this approach, hook a big Pinfish (or other live bait of choice) just ahead of the dorsal fin with a 5/0 treble hook attached to an 80 lb test leader. Use a 15 or 20 ft drop back from the downrigger weight. Lower your bait to about five feet above the structure and then bump your boat in and out of gear to just barely maintain forward motion. Other good live baits include Blue Runners and Porgys - - and two pound Jack Cravalles with their tails chopped off if you are looking for giant Warsaws or Jewfish.

Another variation on the theme uses lighter, 20 pound class tackle and targets Red Grouper in relatively shallow water sandy depressions and/or areas of hard bottom. Anchor upstream from or drift by the bottom feature. In either case, chum a bit. Then toss a live bait (Pinfish, Whitebait, etc.) on a slip rig into the area. Squid, Pinfish, Jack, or Mullet cut bait can also be used effectively.

A final and much heavier approach is popular for working ship channel edges and area passes. One favorite set-up includes a 4/0 reel, 50 lb test mono, and a stout 5½ foot trolling rod. Depending on water depth, the set-up is finished off with a #2 through #5 planer, 20 feet of 100 pound test mono, a 5/0 3x treble hook, and a palm sized Pinfish hooked just ahead of the dorsal fin. Troll just fast enough to keep your bait 4-10 feet off the bottom.

Under the right circumstances and at suitable spots, Grouper can also be caught effectively on all kinds of artificial lures. For fish like the Black Grouper, trolling speeds up to six knots are about right and large, big lipped, plugs get the job done. Deep jiggers rely on drifting and fishing different depths. In this approach, two to four ounce bucktail or plastic tail lead head jigs in a variety of colors are used. Trolling with planers for depths down to 30 feet is usually effective. Below that, however, downriggers are the way to go. Sometimes, when you want to pull a spread of baits, a combination of downriggers and planers will provide the required flexibility. Please see the lure summary at the end of this chapter for a comprehensive listing of effective Grouper lures.

YOUR WINNING EDGE . . .

✔ If you're going to be fishing for Grouper in deeper Offshore waters, you might want to consider using Dacron line. Dacron doesn't stretch the way monofilament does and can be a big help in instantly popping a big fish off the bottom. A good compromise is to use the lower visibility mono for a leader attached to your Dacron line.

✔ If you're drifting live baits in relatively shallow water, thread a soft plastic twister tail up your hook before adding a bait. The result appears to be your bait trying to eat a smaller fish.

✔ Try fishing at night using stink baits. Three popular aromatic offerings include: a strip or fillet of Bonito, three dead herring with the middle bait squashed for more scent, and a Squid pie which alternates three herring and two chunks of Squid on a 7/0 hook.

✔ When a Grouper carries your bait back into his hole, don't give up. Try these simple steps. First, just keep the pressure on him. Once in a while, you can pull him out. After that fails, give him slack for just a few seconds. Then hit him hard. Sometimes he'll be fooled, relax, and you've got him.

If you're still stuck, give him some slack again, put your rod in a holder, and do something else for awhile. If your Grouper is really stupid or just not paying attention, he may just come out of his hole by himself. Otherwise, break your line and start over.

✔ Don't buy a several hundred dollar downrigger. Make your own for $25. Buy a five pound downrigger ball and release clip and 100 feet of stout nylon line. Mark the line in five foot increments using nail polish. You're in business. The same cost effective approach can be used with planers with the simple addition of a release clip.

So much for Family Serranidae. If you aren't currently a confirmed "Grouper Digger," consider changing your ways. Can you even imagine the thrill of landing a 486 pound Warsaw. . .

The Jack Cravalle has a light olive back, greyish gold sides, and a yellowish belly. He is blunt-nosed and has a broad forked tail. There is a distinct black spot on each of his gill covers. The average weight of a Jack Cravalle is three to five pounds. But in August and September, schools of 30 - 40 pound fish frequent large sections of West Coast Bay and Inshore waters. The Florida record for the Jack Cravalle is 51 pounds.

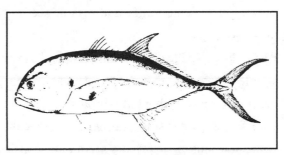

Jack Cravalle

PROVEN TACTICS. There are two basic ways to catch big Jack Cravalle. Live bait fishing using large (9-12 in) Mullet is always a productive approach. Use a 2 to 3 ft leader of 30 - 40 test mono, a barrel swivel, and a 5/0 to 7/0 hook. A Mullet can be hooked in a variety of locations, depending on what you want it to do. If you're fishing where there is a substantial current, hook him through the nose or just ahead of the dorsal fin. If you want him to swim down, hook him just behind the dorsal fin. And hook him just behind the anal fin towards the tail if you want him to swim away from you. Other good live baits include whatever is schooling where you (and the Jacks) are. You can be assured that's why the Jacks are there.

Lures are another effective approach for Jack Cravalle. They will hit almost any kind of top water plug, bucktail jig, plastic grub, or spoon. Surface chuggers probably provide the ultimate in catching excitement for this correctly named "bulldog of the sea." I've had great success for Jacks to 48 pounds using a Zara Spook or the largest Cordell Spot in a black and silver finish. Regardless of whether you choose bait or lures, your reel should be loaded with at least 200 yards of at least 20 lb test line. Allow about an hour to bring in a 30 pounder and use a net to land the fish. Jack Cravalle are not good eating, so should be released to fight again.

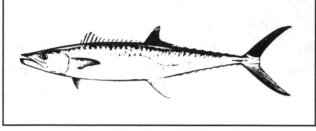

King Mackerel ("King")

A King Mackerel is a relatively long, slender fish with a mouth full of very impressive teeth. He has an iridescent bluish green back with shades to silver on his sides and white on his belly. Juvenile Kings frequently have spots on their sides like Spanish Mackerel. But these rapidly disappear as the fish mature. Spring schoolie Kings average 8 to 20 pounds. However, later in the season, 30 - 50 pounders are possible. The Florida King record currently stands at 90 pounds. Kings are good to eat. Our favorite is grilled, after being marinated in a mixture of soy sauce, butter, lemon juice and sesame seeds.

PROVEN TACTICS.   King Mackerel can be caught in a variety of ways. One common and relatively simple approach is to troll Dusters with frozen Cigar Minnows. A Duster is nothing more than an ounce or so lead head with a hole through it. The head is usually painted white and is usually trimmed with a 3 - 5 inch Mylar skirt. Although skirts come in a variety of single and multiple colors, green, blue, white and pink prism colors seem to be consistently the best.

A Duster may be rigged in one of two ways. The only difference between the ways is the hook arrangement. In one arrangement, a commercially available "Mino-Troll" rig is used. It provides both a mechanism for attaching a frozen Cigar Minnow to the Duster and a hook for catching fish. A 30 inch piece of 40 pound test or stronger single strand wire leader is run through the hole in the Duster head and then attached to the Mino-Troll with a haywire twist.

The other way to rig a Duster is to build a Cigar Minnow holder into the leader itself. In this case, your wire goes through the head of the Duster and is haywire twisted onto the eye of a 7/0 conventional or 3/0 treble hook. When you put the wire through the eye of the hook, pull it through far enough so that when the twist is complete, there are about three inches of excess wire remaining. Now, bend that tag end of wire up and away from the twist at a 45-degree angle. Halfway out, bend the remaining inch and a half back down to your leader. Finish the rig by bending a small U shape on the end. In actual use, the little U shaped wire is pushed up through the Cigar Minnow's head, starting under the jaw and exiting between the eyes. Pre-poking the hole in the Minnow's head with a nail, ice pick, or awl helps the process considerably. It is then bent down the outside of the minnow's nose and clipped to the leader. It sounds complicated, but it really isn't.

Another way to catch Kings is with live bait. Talk about excitement! First, you have to catch your bait. This is most effectively done with light spinning tackle and bait catcher, gold hook, or similar rigs - - or with a throw net. Once bait (Cigar Minnows, White bait, small Hardtails, Mullet, etc.) has been caught, you have to keep it alive. This can be in a live well, portable bait tank with recirculating pump or aerator, or in a large trash can with manually recirculated water. A rig for live bait is simple - - a barrel swivel, a piece of wire leader, and a treble hook sized for the bait you've caught. Hook your bait through the eye socket and troll slowly or just drift. But before you do that, check directly under your boat. King Mackerel are similar to Cobia in their fascination with floating objects. Therefore, at the start of, and periodically during your fishing, put a rubber core sinker on your line, and lower your live bait straight down.

Before leaving the subject of natural baits - - dead, alive, or whatever - - we've got to talk stingers. Kings are notorious for short strikes. They'll take the back half of whatever you've got. Don't let them do it. Haywire twist another piece of wire leader onto the eye of your first hook. Attach a second, slightly smaller hook a few inches (function of bait size) down the new piece of wire. The second hook can then be nicked into the bait or left free.

Lures are certainly a viable alternative to natural bait for Kings. They work well. The toughest thing about using artificials is choosing which one to use. Generically, there are whole families of spoons, jigs, deep diving and surface running jointed and one piece plugs, and feathers that all produce fish at one time or another. Regardless of what you choose and how big or what color it is, you've still got to use a wire leader. And, whether you're using bait or artificials, keep your planers and/or downriggers at the ready. When the fish go deep, you must, too. Please see the lure summary at the end of this chapter for specific suggestions on proven artificials for Kings.

YOUR WINNING EDGE . . .

✔ If you're trolling any kind of whole dead bait like Cigar Minnows, you can't let it spin. Your bait must appear to be swimming. If it doesn't, massage and wiggle it to break more bones or smack it against the water for the same reason.

✔ Try to catch and use the predominant live bait in your area. Big Kings did not get big being stupid. You must present an appropriate bait.

✔ If you're after Kings that are working a bait fish school, circle slowly in a clockwise direction. That's the direction bait usually moves, and you can present your bait as a part of the movement. But your bait will look different - - and that's why you'll get bit!

✔ Don't overlook the value of chumming with "slightly injured" live bait when drifting structure.

✔ Always set your drag loose for Mr. King. He usually strikes from the side of a bait, so you have to let him eat and run before setting the hook.

✔ If you want to anchor on some potentially productive structure, be prepared to chum. As a minimum, you'll want to put down a block of frozen stuff and then regularly augment the chum line with crippled live baits.

✔ Don't forget that the area around Stone Crab trap buoys is a good place to check for Kings. The traps are usually on ledges and hard bottom - - which hold bait - - which is of interest to a Kingfish.

✔ It is alleged that Kings travel in one of three ways: a mating pair only; a few big fish with a bunch of smaller schoolies; and schools of big fish.

✔ If you're deep jigging, sweeten up your bait. Use a soft plastic tail, pork rind, or natural strip trailer. Really, why not?

✔ When out trolling a new area for the first time, keep an eye out for birds. Diving and wheeling pelicans and gulls can lead you to bait that's being hassled by Kings and/or others.

✔ As one wise expert confided, your rod holder is the best fisherman on the boat. It never jerks the rod or tightens the drag. It simply holds on and lets the rod and reel do their jobs. You take over after the fish is hooked.

✔ Try a teaser while trolling lures. Plastic squid, birds, or flying fish are all effective. And don't forget to keep your speed up. Depending on lure type and running depth, six to eight knots isn't too fast.

✔ Pier fishing for Kings is about the same as from a boat. Live bait is best. Catch it on the pier, transfer it to heavier tackle, and fire away. Lures work well, too.

A King Mackerel deserves his name and has earned his reputation. He's arguably as fast as a Wahoo, skyrockets live bait like a Sailfish, makes powerful long runs like a Tarpon, and tastes great off the grill. He's a "must catch" on any fisherman's list.

━━━━━━━━━━━━━━━━━━━━━━━━━━━━━━━━━

A Permit's body is a basic gray color. The upper half has a dark or iridescent blue tint which shades to silvery sides. There are usually golden tints along the stomach area. Permit grow much larger than Pompano. The Florida record is 51 pounds 8 ounces. Fish to 25 pounds are not uncommon. Look for Mr. Permit on Offshore wrecks and other structure and Inshore on grass and sand flats and in deeper channels. Permit are good to eat.

PROVEN TACTICS. Permit are easy to fish for but, frequently, tough to catch. They're easy to fish for because their choice of food is very limited. Small live crabs and Shrimp are about it in the natural bait department. Quarter ounce or so yellow or white jigs just about runs the list of artificials. Permit are tough to catch because they're hard to see in the water, their hit on bait can be surprisingly soft, they're big, immensely powerful, and know how to use their body shape in a fight.

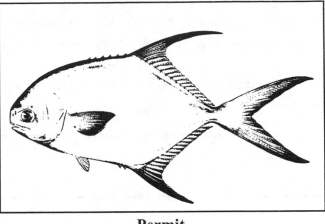
Permit

A slip rig is a relatively standard approach to fish wrecks, reefs, Offshore springs and around bridges. Use an egg sinker heavy enough to get your bait to the bottom, a barrel swivel, a couple of feet of 30 - 40 pound test mono for leader, and a #1, 1/0, or 2/0 hook depending on the size crab you're using for bait. Just leave off the sinker for flats fishing. When you're fishing wrecks, reefs, and springs Offshore, be prepared to fly-line your bait instead of heading for the bottom. Permit will often be up in the water column or hanging around on the surface over bottom structure. Jigs can be fished effectively in all venues. Try yellow or white skirts or jig heads tipped with a live Shrimp or a plastic grub tail.

YOUR WINNING EDGE . . .

✔ Regardless of where you fish, make chumming an integral part of the process. If you're fishing a bridge, scrape barnacles off the pilings. On open water spots, including flats, ground up crabs, including Sand Fleas and frozen Shrimp, get the job done. If you're feeling really extravagant and conditions warrant, toss in a few live Shrimp or crabs.

✔ In the winter, don't overlook the warm water discharge canals of most West Coast power plants. Permit often school there and will usually cooperate on 1/4 ounce jigs tipped with a grubtail or whole live Shrimp.

✔ If you're using small Blue Crabs for bait, don't dull the point on your hook. Take a battery powered electric drill with you and drill a tiny hole in the corner of the crab's shell.

✔ Fiddler Crabs are a good alternative to Blue Crabs. Downsize your hook accordingly and insert the hook where the second leg from the back attaches. Rotate the point of your hook horizontally out the flap on the rear.

✔ On the flats, slow moving, tailing, and feeding fish are great targets for jigs. Fast moving fish pushing wakes probably won't give you the time of day.

✔ According to one expert, the ideal Offshore structure has bottom relief of 15 feet or so and Barracuda present. It seems Barracuda and Permit like the same kind of habitat.

And that's Mr. Permit - - a world class fighter and a gourmet's delight that can also be an intellectual challenge.

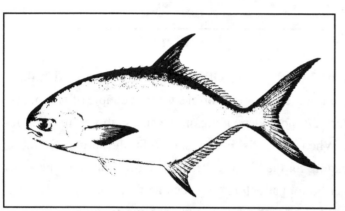

Pompano

The Common Pompano is a wide-sided, relatively narrow fish. Its back and upper sides are grayish-silvery blue and its belly is yellow tinted. Its upper fins are dark in color and its lower fins have a yellowish or light orange cast to them. There is a blue patch just above its eyes, and its yellowish tail is deeply forked. On the average, Pompano weigh between 1½ to 3 lbs. However, fish in the 5 - 6 lb range have been caught at various spots in the area. The Florida record for Pompano is eight pounds, one ounce.

Pompano is prized by gourmets as being without peer from either fresh or saltwater. Its flesh is firm and rich. It brings the highest price at the fish market of any fish caught in Florida waters. In addition to superior eating, it is also an outstanding gamefish on light tackle. It strikes hard, runs fast, uses its flat-sided body to execute sudden reversals, and frequently jumps, carrying sinkers and rigs or lures with it. In short, it is a truly world-class fish.

PROVEN TACTICS. As with the Permit, tactics for Pompano aren't very sophisticated or exotic. A very short bait list (Crabs and Shrimp) and small jigs about does it for these guys. Bait fishing rigs are straightforward, whether you're fishing in the surf, around or off area bridges or piers, or on the flats. One rig is often called a two hook spreader. Start with about three feet of 20 pound test mono. Tie a snap swivel on one end and a barrel swivel on the other. Then tie a pair of dropper loops about equidistant on the mono. Then slip the dropper loops through the eyes of a pair of #1 hooks and pull them back through. You're in business. If you're not into loop tying, most tackle shops would be delighted to sell you a two hook spreader.

Another good bait rig goes like this. Start with about two feet of mono. Tie a barrel swivel on one end. Then tie on a hook at the other end. A second hook goes on a dropper loop tied in the middle of the mono. Slip an egg sinker on your line and then tie it to the barrel swivel. Once again, you're in business.

DROPPER LOOP

1. First, form a loop in the line. Hold the loop with your thumb and forefinger where the line crosses.

2. With your forefinger, keep a loose wind in the center as you take 8 - 10 wraps in each direction.

3. Now pull the top of your original loop through the loose wind in the middle.

4. Finally, using your teeth or with the help of someone else, simultaneously pull the emerging drop loop and the line on either side of it.

5. Set the knot by pulling both ends till everything is tight and the dropper loop stands out. Repeat the process about 12 inches down the mono to create a "two hook spreader."

Sandfleas are the preferred natural bait for Pompano. They can either be caught live along West Coast beaches or bought frozen from local tackle stores. Hooking a Sandflea is easy. Run the hook through the V-shaped flap on the flea's belly and rotate it on around so that the barb of the hook just protrudes from the top of the shell. Fresh dead Shrimp, available at local fish markets, is a good second choice bait for Pompano.

Jig fishing is rapidly becoming a popular second approach to catching Pompano. In this area, 3/8 to 5/8 oz white or beige colored jig heads with white, yellow, orange, hot pink, or pearl skirts have been the most successful. If you're surf fishing, the jig should be worked through and along the troughs between the sand bars paralleling the beach. While you are doing that, keep your eyes open for schools of Mullet or Whiting. West Coast surf fishermen have found that Pompano, while not mingling, will follow along closely behind these schools.

YOUR WINNING EDGE . . .

✔ Squid strips, Fiddler Crabs, and soft plastic crabs rigged Texas style with a slip lead will all (occasionally) catch very large Pompano.

✔ If you're using jigs, sweeten your hook with a small flea.

✔ To catch Sandfleas on the beach, watch for clusters of tiny V's in the sand as waves recede into the Gulf. The V's are caused by the antennas on the Sandflea's head and mark the spot where you should dig. Digging can be either with your hands, using half a minnow trap, or a Sandflea rake.

✔ Sandfleas can be preserved indefinitely even with repeated freeze/thaw cycles - - if you'll blanch them first. Drop live fleas into boiling water for not more than five seconds. That's it.

✔ If you're going to be fishing around pilings, use the Permit trick and scrape off barnacles for chum.

Are Pompano worth the trouble? Your first bite of Pompano en Papillote (parchment) will answer that question.

The Redfish, which is also called Red Drum or Channel Bass by many, is somewhat similar to the Black Drum in shape. His coloration, however, is distinctly different. A Red's body is a copperish iridescent color shading to copperish-red toward the back. As the fish matures, he becomes reddish-bronze all over. All Redfish usually have

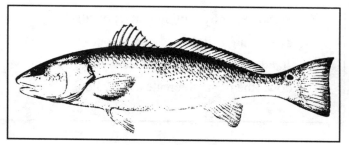

Redfish ("Red")

one or more black spots at the base of their tails. The Florida record for Redfish is 51 pounds, 8 ounces. Thanks largely to various catch restrictions, there are now lots of Redfish in West Coast waters. At one time or another, you can find them in area rivers, creeks, bays, the surf, around piers, and on both Inshore and Offshore structure.

PROVEN TACTICS. The Redfish is a bottom feeder who has a voracious appetite for all sorts of things like Shrimp, Blue Crabs, Sandfleas, fingerling Mullet, Pinfish, Sardines, etc., etc. One of three terminal rigs, tailored to your bait and where you'll be fishing, will get the job done. At the fundamental level, tie an appropriately sized hook on one end of a two foot piece of 30 pound test mono. Tie a barrel swivel on the other end. If you slip an egg sinker up your line and then tie on the hook and leader, you're ready to fish deeper water wherever it might be - - and the surf. If you leave off the egg sinker but add a popping cork up your line, you're ready for intermediate depths like channels, some grass flats, and around structure. And, without either a sinker or a float, you're set to flyline in the shallowest water.

Reds will also hit a variety of lures. These include spoons (usually gold), deep diving plugs, metal squids, and plastic grubs and twister tails in many different sizes and colors. Particularly hot lures for big fish have included large Cordell Spots in blue and silver, and black and silver, gold and firetiger Rat-

L-Traps, and white nylon jigs with about a 4 inch piece of chartreuse plastic worm as a trailer. Another productive approach to catching Reds in some of their shallow water habitats is with floating/diving crankbaits. This type of lure is particularly effective where there is a hard, rough bottom in one to five feet of water, that slopes off to a deeper open channel. While top water or subsurface plugs can be used in such spots, floater/divers are the only lures that can get down to the fish without getting hung up. Check your freshwater tackle box. You are looking for plugs that have relatively compact bodies, 2½ to 3½ inches long and a big lip. When used, the plug should dive at a relatively steep angle, not get much deeper than five to six feet, and most importantly, achieve a wide, wobbling action on a slow retrieve. One productive lure of this type has been the Mann's Crawdad in the quarter ounce size.

YOUR WINNING EDGE . . .

✔ When your lure isn't working, sweeten it with something yummy like Shrimp. If that doesn't work, switch to live bait. If that doesn't work either, chum, too. Live Sardines work great on most flats.

✔ Sometimes Reds working on a flat can get really spooky. If you suspect that's the case, park your boat and wade. A stealthy approach and long casts are the key.

✔ When you are stalking tailing Reds, cast well beyond them but don't immediately retrieve your lure/bait. Wait till their tails go down, indicating their noses are not stuck in the bottom. Then retrieve. The odds are much better of being seen (and caten) when Reds are nose-up.

✔ If you're on the flats, watch carefully for schools of Mullet or passing Rays. Check around both of these for Reds. As opportunistic feeders, Reds love to have someone else stir up the bottom and any food that might be present.

✔ Legal size (18 - 27 inches) Redfish are great eating, with flesh that is ideally suited for blackening, using commercially available Cajun seasonings. It is a taste treat you really must try.

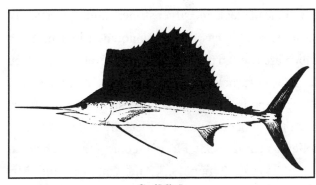

Sailfish

The Atlantic Sailfish has one not surprising physical characteristic, an enormous dorsal fin. It is much higher than the greatest depth of its body and extends from its head to more than halfway down its body. The Sail's body is long and slender and dark steely blue on top and white on the bottom. His huge dorsal fin is bright cobalt blue and may be sprinkled with round black spots. The Sail's spear is long and slender and often slightly curved. An Atlantic Sailfish has an average weight of around 40 pounds. The Florida record for Sailfish, however, is 116 pounds. And, yes, there are fine Atlantic Sailfish in West Coast Offshore blue waters.

PROVEN TACTICS. Well rigged natural baits are often productive for Sails. Ballyhoo, Mullet, and Bonito strips are all used by local fishermen. Of these, Bonito strips frequently get the nod because their durability permits faster trolling speeds. If you are willing to go to the trouble of rigging Ballyhoo, it will usually pay off in fish. One popular terminal rig consists of a 5 or 6 foot length of 65 - 80 lb wire with a loop on one end and a good snap swivel at the other. The Ballyhoo is rigged to a 7/0 or 8/0 needle eye hook, with a 3/4 inch wire spike left on the wire wrap. This is used to pin the Ballyhoo's head. One end of a small rubber band is slipped over the spike, then stretched around the head of the Ballyhoo and also hooked over the end of the spike. A 12 inch piece of wire with a loop on one end is attached to the eye of the hook with a haywire twist. The bait, and others pre-rigged like it, can then be quickly attached to the snap swivel mentioned above.

Although a well-rigged natural bait is effective by itself, there are times when a skirt or Sea Witch lure can help. Traditionally effective Sea Witch colors include blue and white, pink and blue, and red and black. A good rule of thumb is usually bright colors on bright days, darker color combinations on darker days and early and late in the day.

Many fishermen looking for Sails try to pull as many lines as possible behind their boats. One or more of these lines are used for teasers. These can range from daisy chains of hookless small Mullet or plastic squid to single large hookless Ladyfish, Mullet, or horse Ballyhoo. Another choice is a large, thrashing mirrored plug. There are a number of lures that have also caught Sails locally. They include Moldcraft's Softhead Hookers and Birds, Tony Accetta Jelly Bellies, Arbogast's Reto' Rigs, and Boone's Airheads.

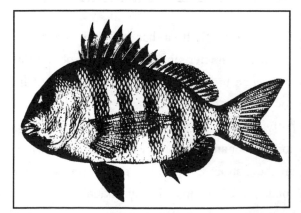

Sheepshead

The Sheepshead is a squatty shaped fish with pronounced black and silver stripes running vertically on its sides. It has strong, unnotched incisor teeth which are used to pick mollusks and crabs and scrape barnacles off rocks. The average weight of local area Sheepshead is 2 - 3 pounds, but fish to 10 pounds are not totally uncommon. Its fillets are pure white and delicious eating. The Florida record for Sheepshead is 15 pounds, 2 ounces. And you can find Mr. Sheepshead almost everywhere in West Coast waters.

Anywhere there are pilings (piers, bridges, docks), oyster bars, grass flats, the surf, and artificial/natural reefs - - look for Sheepshead.

PROVEN TACTICS. Sheepshead are almost exclusively caught on bait. Although once in a great while one will take a small fly or jig, real food is the preferred approach. Effective baits include live and fresh dead Shrimp, Fiddler Crabs, Hermit Crabs, Tube Worms, and Sandfleas. From a cost, durability, and performance standpoint, Fiddlers usually get the nod. Hooking Fiddler Crabs can be sporty. They do have claws which can give you a good pinch. To solve this problem, many fishermen use pliers to break off the big claw prior to baiting up. Putting a Fiddler on your hook is easy. Hold him between your thumb and forefinger, right side up. Insert the hook point into the socket where the second leg from the back joins the body. Rotate the hook around and bring the hook point and barb out the back of the body shell. This method does not hurt the crab and he will remain alive and kicking. The two hook spreader and slip rigs suggested earlier for Permit and Pompano are also ideally suited for catching Sheepshead. You might want to use a smaller hook size (#1 or #2), however, depending on the size of bait. Whatever size hook you end up with, make sure it is substantial. Sheepshead can destroy flimsy wire hooks.

YOUR WINNING EDGE . . .

✔ Frequently, when you least expect it, Sheepshead wander by. If you are unprepared (i.e., no live or dead Shrimp, Fiddler Crabs, etc.) you are usually out of luck. However, if you just happen to have a soft plastic crab in your tackle box, try it. Rig it Texas style, with a slip sinker and quietly present it to the fish. They really will hit them, regardless of color.

✔ If you're using live Shrimp for bait, hook it through the tail rather than the head. Because a Sheepshead usually takes the head off the Shrimp first (and you probably won't feel him do it), when he finishes off his meal, your hook in the tail will get him.

✔ To get the fish in a proper mood (hungry), take a scraper of some kind with you when you fish around pilings. Scrape off the barnacles and oysters for a very effective natural chum.

✔ Chum works equally well on the flats. Stake out or anchor your boat upcurrent from a fishy spot (oyster bar, channel edge, etc.). Toss in bits of oyster, clams, shrimp, or crab. Then flyline your bait into the area. You may have to add a split shot above your leader.

A final word on hooking Sheepshead might help. According to the conventional wisdom as articulated by the "good old boys," the secret to catching Sheepshead . . . is to set the hook just before the fish bites. I wish I could tell you how to do that.

As was true with the Grouper family, there are a number of different kinds of Snapper present in West Coast waters at various times of the year. Probably the most common and in descending order of their numbers are Mangrove, Yellowtail, Lane, Red, and Mutton.

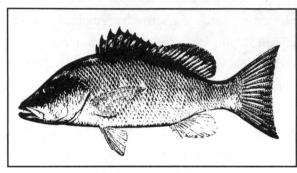
Mangrove Snapper

Although usually called Mangrove or Black, this guy's correct name is Gray Snapper. Regardless of what he's called, he is everywhere in West Coast waters - - from up rivers and creeks to way Offshore on the Florida Middlegrounds - - and everywhere in between. This fish's body is bronze-green on top, shading in to brassy-red on its sides and light grey on its belly. It has a dark streak which runs from its nose across its eyes and then fades toward the dorsal fin. Some of the scales on the fish's sides have random darker markings. Although Gray Snappers have been caught to over 10 pounds, 1 or 2 pounds is considered a good fish. The Florida record is 17 pounds. Superior eating.

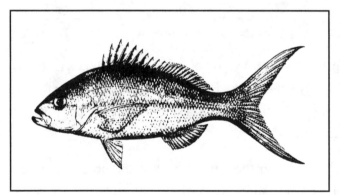
Yellowtail Snapper

The Yellowtail has an olive to bluish back with yellow spots. A yellow stripe runs from mouth to tail which is also yellow. His belly is silverish, often with faint horizontal stripes. Yellowtail are common to three pounds, and the Florida record is 8 pounds 8 ounces. Superior eating.

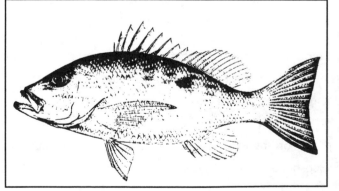
Lane Snapper

This colorful guy is silvery-pink to reddish with short, irregular pink and yellow lines on his sides. Lanes usually weigh less than a pound, but the Florida record is 6 pounds 6 ounces. Superior eating.

The Red Snapper is a medium sized fish that is relatively common up to 35 pounds and 30 inches in length. An averaged sized West Coast Red is considerably smaller. Not surprisingly, he is rosy-red on his upper body, shading to lighter red on his lower sides and belly. His fins and eyes are also shades of red. The Red Snapper is usually found in schools which frequent an area with a hard bottom and adjacent structure of some sort. The world record Red Snapper weighed 46 pounds, 8 ounces, and was caught on Florida waters. Superior eating.

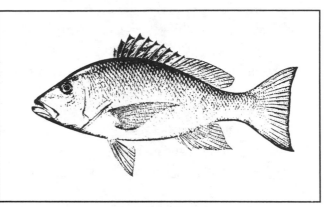

Red Snapper

The Mutton Snapper is olive green on its back and upper sides with all its fins below the lateral line usually having a reddish tinge. The Mutton almost always has a bright blue line below each eye. Up to 15 pounds is a common weight, but the Florida record is a most impressive 27 pounds, 6 ounces. Superior eating.

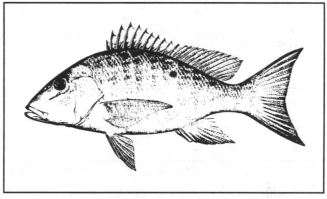

Mutton Snapper

PROVEN TACTICS. All of these Snappers share some common traits. All are aggressive and smart, can be caught on both natural and artificial baits, and are at the top of the world-class eating index. These fish do have some significant differences, however, including size, preferred habitat, and eating habits. With these differences in mind, we can focus on a few of the many potentially effective ways to catch each of them.

- Mangrove - This guy is extremely difficult to catch. The bigger fish are very reluctant to hit anything that doesn't look entirely natural. Once hooked, they are also most adept at cutting lines on sharp edges anywhere in the area. A rig for this guy is simple. Tie an appropriately sized bronze hook to the end of the line. Attach a split shot or rubber core sinker a couple of feet above it. Use live Shrimp (which you can buy) or small live Croakers or other small fish (which you must catch) for bait. You've got to react immediately when you get a hit or risk a cutoff. Sometimes, feeding Mangrove Snapper will just turn off. One way to get them going again is with a judicious application of cat food to the area. Be sure to use the canned stuff with a fish base.

Mr. Mangrove will also take a variety of lures. A Crappie jig with a live Shrimp on it is always popular. Top water plugs around four inches long are a ball along mangrove shorelines. Rapala and Rebel minnows get the job done. Always use a leader and attach your lure with a loop knot.

- Yellowtail - Look for them Inshore on ledges and breaks, live bottom, wrecks, and artificial reefs. Confirm the presence of fish with your meter. Anchor up-current. Toss in a chum bag of good stuff, pieces of Sardine, and perhaps some small live baits. Use a small live fish (Sardine, Shiner, etc.) for bait, 30 pound test leader, #1 - 2/0 hook, and only the minimum weight necessary to get to the fish. Yellowtail really aren't into artificial lures.

- Lane - These guys are shallow water dwellers that can often be caught off area bridges and piers. They'll take live and cut bait and, occasionally, very small artificials. Mangrove and Yellowtail bait rigs work for Lanes too.

- Red - In Inshore and Offshore waters, a good rig for Red Snapper is called, not surprisingly, a Snapper rig. Making one is easy. Using a 6 foot piece of 50 to 80 pound test mono, first make a loop at one end with a double surgeon's knot. Depending on the current, loop on an 8 to 16 oz bank sinker. Next, make two droppers 16 and 32 inches above the sinker (see Pompano writeup). Each dropper should be 10 to 16 inches long. Finally, tie on a barrel swivel 18 inches above the top dropper and attach hooks to the droppers by inserting the loops through the hook eyes, and then doubling the loops back over the shanks of the hooks. Depending on the expected size of the resident fish, a 3/0 to 4/0 bronze hook is about right. Live or fairly substantial cut baits get the job done, but be sure you vary the depth of the baits. Red Snappers will often suspend over the bottom structure.

- Mutton - A strong fighter that is ideally suited for light tackle. Big Muttons are often caught by slow trolling near the bottom with both artificial and natural baits. They can also be chummed to the surface and caught with feathers, jigs, and plugs. Top water plugs will catch Muttons. Look for these guys on a sandy bottom next to a reef.

YOUR WINNING EDGE . . .

✔ For really big Mangroves, fish at night using live Pinfish or Pigfish (Grunts) on a slip rig. Let nature provide live chum by using bright lights on your boat.

✔ Two good dead baits for Red Snapper are whole Squid or Cigar Minnows. Fish these baits three to five cranks off the bottom to avoid ever present junk fish. A filleted Vermillion Snapper is another deadly bait. Save the fillets for your dinner table - - and use the carcass, hooked through the eye socket, to catch other, really big Red Snappers.

✔ Try deep jigging for Muttons well Offshore (80 - 120 feet of water). Use 40 pound test mono or #7 single strand wire leader and the lightest possible jigs (2 - 5 ounces). Improve the odds by tipping your jig with a whole, medium size Ballyhoo, Bonito or Mullet strip, or a 9 - 12 inch white plastic worm that glows in the dark.

✔ Fly lining live Shrimp under docks at night is fun and can be productive for Mangroves. Also try very small Bonito fillets. They really work!

✔ Here's a not-original but clearly tasty recipe for Yellowtail (and others) chum. Mix together four or five blocks of frozen chum, macaroni, steam rolled oats, ground Bonito and Ballyhoo, glass minnows, and Menhaden oil. Yum. As is, it can be tossed overboard for near-surface attraction. Add some sand to it, form it in balls, and you can spice up the water all the way to the bottom.

✔ Fish "white spot" depressions in area bays and Inshore water for Mangroves. Anchor up-current and chum with that yummy stuff described above or fish based cat food. Use an appropriately sized slip rig and fresh Pinfish fillets for bait. Other kinds of Snapper, Grouper, Spanish, and Barracuda may also participate.

A Snook is long-bodied but thick through the middle, with a depressed upper snout and a protruding lower jaw. His/her color is variable according to habitat, but is generally brownish or brown-gold on the back shading to a lighter color on the belly. It has a pronounced black lateral stripe that extends to the tail. West Coast Snook generally follow a standard annual pattern of movement. In the

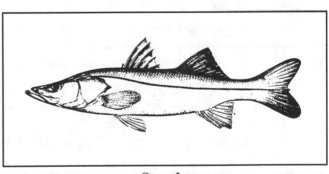

Snook

winter, they'll be up area rivers and creeks and in deeper canals. As the water warms in the spring, they begin to move toward passes into the Gulf. After summer spawning in and around the passes, they'll once again begin a migration inland toward their wintering grounds. Snook is delicious eating. The Florida record is 44 pounds 3 ounces.

PROVEN TACTICS. Snook are world-class gamefish, with the physical attributes, predatory nature, and insatiable appetite necessary to turn you every way but loose. And, they're cooperative, too. As noted above, they essentially inhabit all West Coast waters except, perhaps, Offshore. From Homosassa south, and at one time or another, Snook will also eat about anything you throw them. Live and dead natural baits and a vast array of artificials all find willing fish. Not surprisingly then, a wide variety of fishing tactics and techniques are possible.

- Access to the fish - By boat trolling, drifting, or anchored; wading the flats; from the shore; from bridges, docks, seawalls, jetties, and piers; and from the beach in the surf.

- Live Bait - Pinfish, Mullet, Ladyfish, jumbo Shrimp, Croaker, Greenbacks, Ballyhoo, Grunts, Sand Perch, and Menhaden.

- Cut Bait - Ladyfish, Mullet, and Menhaden are probably the most popular. Whatever you use, it must be fresh. Use it whole but, if you cut off the tail, it will cast better and not spin in the current.

- Generic Rigs - Use a slip rig with about four feet of 80 pound test mono, a 4/0 hook, and an egg sinker for cut bait. For live bait, an 18 inch, 30 pound test leader and a 4/0 hook is a good place to start. Use the same test leader when fishing with artificials.

- The number and type of artificial lures that catch Snook is almost mind-boggling. Some specific suggestions are provided at the end of this chapter.

YOUR WINNING EDGE . . .

✔ If you're surf fishing, try 400 - 500 yards on either side of a pass or inlet. Also be sure to work around any bars that extend out in the Gulf, rock groins along the beach, or other types of shore/near-shore structure. Enhance your probability of success by chumming with live bait.

✔ An interesting way to hook a Mullet and other live bait is just under the skin under his chin about due south of his gill plates. Hooked this way, your bait will swim naturally until you pull on the line. Your pull will flip the bait over and cause him to "flutter" toward the bottom - - and get eaten.

✔ You've got to have good current for good Snook fishing. Three days before and after a full or new moon is good. An unstable (moving) barometer is great, too.

✔ Very large Snook have a thing for large, well-fed, 7-8 inch Pinfish hooked just ahead of the dorsal fin.

✔ When night fishing shadow lines along a bridge or pier, cast just outside the lights' halo. Snook ambush food from the shadows.

✔ Don't overlook the warm water discharge canals at most West Coast power plants. They're usually productive for winter Snook action.

✔ If you're going to fish fresh dead Mullet, crush his head before you toss him in. He'll be more aromatic.

✔ Surf fishing with lures is usually most productive at night or other periods of low light levels. Wade out just a bit and make long casts parallel to the beach.

✔ Try night fishing off a bridge. Use a lead head jig with a live Shrimp hooked up through the head. Throw it up-current and bounce it slowly toward you.

✔ Here's a suggestion on trolling mangrove channels. Pull two lines with red and white or black and silver Rebels, Rapalas, or Bombers on them. The lures, which should be medium-lipped models, should be dropped back 40 - 50 feet. About four knots would be a good speed to get your lures down in the 4 - 6 foot depth range.

✔ If you are a freshwater bass fisherman, take your tackle box Snook fishing. Probably most, if not all, the goodies in it will catch Snook.

Let's close out this brief discussion of Mr. Snook on a very positive note. I recently learned that the Florida Guides Association had adopted a no-kill policy for any Snook over 34 inches. That was done to protect genetically superior breeders which, most believe, have suffered a decline in their numbers. That's an absolutely outstanding policy - - that I intend to follow. Hope you will, too.

A Spanish Mackerel is dark bluish-brown on the top part of its body and silvery on its belly. It has golden spots above and below its lateral lines. It also has a dandy set of small razor like teeth. Spanish average 1½ to 3 pounds, but fish to 10 pounds are caught in West Coast waters. They are particularly good eating when cooked fresh on the grill. The Florida record for

Spanish Mackerel ("Spanish")

Spanish is 12 pounds. Spanish can be caught at one time or another in area bays, off piers and bridges, in the surf, and all over the Gulf - - often from the beach to as far as 25 miles Offshore.

PROVEN TACTICS. Spanish will usually cooperate on either live bait or lures. In the bait department, Sardines or "Whitebait" are always favorites. Live Shrimp are another good, albeit more expensive, choice. Fly lining is the most effective approach, using about 12 inches of mono for leader and about a 1/0 hook. Yes, they will chew through your leader at some point. But even the finest wire just can't compete in the hook-up area.

Lures are an equally effective approach. Spanish are extremely aggressive and will hit just about anything you care to use. Bucktail jigs, plastic grubs, small spoons, and a variety of plugs will all get the job done. Use the same piece of leader as with bait. Chumming is an essential part of wide-open, fish-on-every-cast, Spanish action. As soon as you've got a school cornered, get up-current and hang over a block of ground up chum. If you're not fishing from a boat, consider throwing fish based cat food into your area of operations.

YOUR WINNING EDGE . . .

✔ As noted above, schoolie Spanish Mackerel will tear into almost any small lure when they move into an area. Nylon jigs, feather lures and spoons are all traditionally effective. Regardless of what's used, Spanish can't seem to resist a darting action. You should use a rapid retrieve with regular snaps of your rod tip to make your lure jump and dart through the water.

✔ Recently, three lures have had noteworthy success for Spanish in West Coast waters. The first is the old standby, Gator spoon in ½ oz and ¾ oz sizes. Make sure you use the version with the small fluorescent pink tab on the split ring. The second is the Gotcha in a variety of sizes and colors. The third is the almost unbelievable straw rig. This lure is nothing more than about 30 inches of heavy mono with a barrel swivel on one end and a 2/0 or so treble hook on the other. A two inch piece of McDonald's (yes, of the "Golden Arches") soda straw covers the shank of the treble hook. The rig is fished with a partially water-filled clear plastic casting bubble running free on your line above the barrel swivel. It is cast out as far as possible and then rapidly retrieved with frequent major popping actions with your rod tip. Fishing success with the straw rig has been truly extraordinary.

✔ Another extraordinary lure for blind trolling might be of interest. It's called a Mackerel Tree. The Mackerel Tree is nothing more than a heavy piece of mono with a barrel swivel on one end, four hooks sheathed in bits of brightly colored tubing spaced equidistant down the mono, and a snap swivel on the other end. Many fishermen attach a #1 or #2 Squid or Clark spoon to the snap swivel. The rig is slow trolled where Spanish tend to hang out. Up to three or four nice fish at a time are not uncommon.

✔ Spot feeding Spanish by either gulls working or fish jumping. The experts say avoid diving Pelicans because, in some areas, that means Menhaden is the eatee and catfish are the eators.

✔ One way to give your leader some protection when fly lining bait is to use a long shank hook.

✔ If you're feeling really wild and crazy and happen to be anchored up on Inshore structure catching Spanish, try this. Rig up a rod with a wire leader and a 5/0 hook. Transfer a live Spanish to the heavier tackle and turn him loose. If there are any resident Barracuda, Sharks, Cobia, Tarpon, or Bonito, you'll probably score.

To re-emphasize an earlier point - - fresh Spanish are delicious eating. But they don't freeze all that well. So keep only what you need for dinner tonight. Turn the rest loose to fight another day.

There are Swordfish in the Gulf of Mexico and, occasionally, they are caught in far Offshore West Coast waters. However, entire books have been written about catching this elusive denizen of the deep. So, these comments will be concise. The color of a Swordfish's back varies among black, greyish blue, brown, metallic purple and bronze. Its underbelly is a dirty white. And, not too

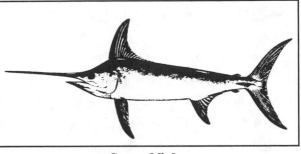
Swordfish

surprisingly, it has a long, flat, sword-like upper jaw. Commercially caught Swordfish used to average 200 pounds but sadly, due to over-harvesting, average catch weights are now substantially less. The Florida record for a Swordfish is 612 pounds, 12 ounces. Swordfish steaks are a gourmet's delight.

PROVEN TACTICS. Trolling is one possible method of catching Swordfish, although West Coast area fish are much more frequently pursued by drift fishing at night with live bait. Squid, Bonito and small Tuna are all good baits. Fresh Squid is much preferred over frozen; hook size must be at least 12/0, and monofilament leaders must test at least 200 lbs. Successful Sword fishermen in this area insure their bait's visibility at the required depths by using battery powered lights and Cyalume glowsticks. The highest probability for Swordfish success is usually at night , at depths between 600 and 1,500 feet.

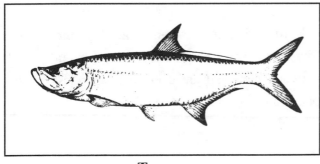
Tarpon

Tarpon are usually dark-blue to greenish-black in the dorsal fin area, shading to bright silver on their sides and bellies. Fish from inland waters sometimes display brownish or brassy colors. West Coast Tarpon get big, with fish over six feet in length and 100 pounds not extraordinary. The Florida record for Tarpon is 243 pounds.

PROVEN TACTICS. Tarpon are every bit as cooperative as a number of other premier West Coast gamefish. At one time or another, they are delighted to eat all sorts of artificial lures, flies, and live/cut baits. They do their cooperating in a variety of places, too: rivers, flats, passes, and along the beach. Action from either ashore or afloat can be equally good.

A menu of live bait for Tarpon usually includes Blue Crabs, Pinfish, Threadfin Herring, Mullet, Squirrelfish, Grunts, Ladyfish, et al. Two basic rigs with only a few variations can accommodate all these baits. One rig is basically just a hook on a leader for fly lining bait. For "baby" Tarpon to 40 pounds or so, mono leaders to 80 pound test are common. They should be roughly four feet long, and have a barrel swivel on one end and a short shank, bronze 4/0 hook on the other. Grown-ups require heavier components: 100 - 150 pound test mono leader, hooks up to 7/0, depending on bait size, and leader lengths up to 10 feet. A variation uses a short length (12 - 15 inches) of 100 pound test cable leader spliced through a leader sleeve to five feet of 40 - 50 pound test monofilament. Another variation incorporates a sliding float. Tie 18 inches of 100# mono to your hook. Then tie six feet of 50 pound mono to the 100. Thread on a long weighted balsa casting float and a plastic stopper bead. Finish off the rig by tying the 50 to your main line, which has a section doubled via a Bimini Twist.

A second basic rig is for bottom fishing with either live or cut bait. It is ideally suited for fishing West Coast passes, including Boca Grande. Tie a 4/0 or 5/0 forged, needle eye hook on one end of a 10 - 12 inch piece of 80 - 100 pound mono. Attach a 5/0 size barrel swivel on the other end and tie on your line. Now, stick one end of a piece of soft copper wire through the hole in an eight ounce egg sinker. Wrap the wire around the sinker just enough to hold it. Stick the other end of the wire through the loop on one end of your barrel swivel - - and wrap the end around your leader loosely. And that's all there is to that. When Mr. Tarpon takes off with your bait, your sinker will be ripped off and it will be just you and the fish. Speaking of bait, we can't leave this rig without mentioning the dead (fresh) stuff. From north to south, Tarpon fishermen offer variety. Mullet heads are popular in the Homosassa area. Farther down the coast, catfish tails are big around Tampa Bay bridges. Other favorites across the area include "pogies," Mullet, Menhaden, and Pinfish. Depending on your target, serving size can be as big as 10 - 12 inches.

Tarpon have very eclectic tastes when it comes to artificial lures. As can be noted in the specific suggestions at the end of this chapter, all sorts of jigs, soft plastics, plugs, and spoons apparently catch fish - - or fishermen wouldn't buy so many of them (would they?). In any event, and regardless of what type you choose, a two foot leader of at least 80 pound mono is mandatory.

YOUR WINNING EDGE . . .

✔ The first rule for keeping a Tarpon on the hook when he jumps is - - bow to the fish. Lower your rod tip and point it at him when he goes airborne. The slack in your line will keep the hook set, your line from breaking, and the lure from flying back at you if it should pull loose.

✔ If you want to try cut bait on the bottom, Mullet is a good choice. Use half a large fillet for bait and chum with tiny bits of the rest of the fish.

✔ Try a soft plastic jerk bait. Throw it in front of a fish and allow it to sink weightless and without any movement. Natural action will make your worm of interest.

✔ Dawn and dusk are good times for artificials. Natural baits do better during the day.

✔ A trolling motor is essential to successfully catch fish along the beach.

✔ Use a battery powered electric drill to put a hole in the "point" of your Blue Crab bait. Save the sharpness of your hook point for the fish.

✔ If you need to gaff a fish for a picture, grab the Tarpon's lower lip with a gloved hand. Pull the gaff down through the lower lip and lift. Return the fish to the water immediately after picture taking.

✔ If you're fishing for giants off a bridge or pier, assume your target is by the pilings under your feet. Calculate drift angles and toss your live bait out and away accordingly. If you figured right, your bait should drift toward the piling in a very natural presentation.

Tarpon of any size are a priceless resource. Enjoy the thrill of a lifetime - - often! But always return your fish to freedom in the best possible condition.

The Gray or Common Triggerfish is a frequent inhabitant of both Inshore and Offshore bottom structure. It attains a respectable size of up to 10 pounds, with average weights of 1 to 2 pounds. It is usually gray in color with random darker markings and has an impressive set of dentures. The Triggerfish is difficult to clean because of its thick, heavy skin. However, the cleaning effort is well worth it, since the Triggerfish is delicious eating. You'll find these guys on the same limestone ledges inhabited by West Coast Groupers and Snappers, as well as on most artificial reefs.

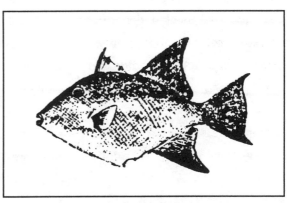

Triggerfish

PROVEN TACTICS. The two hook Snapper rig, described previously, is a good one to use for Triggerfish. Hook size should be reduced, however, to a #1 or #1/0 if Triggers will be the only anticipated catch. Relatively small pieces of frozen Squid or fresh, dead shrimp are the best baits.

For what its worth, the Triggerfish gets that name because of the interaction of its three dorsal spines. The first spine is very large and bony and can be locked upright by the fish, or even by an angler after the fish has died. When locked, the big fin is unmovable. That is a distinct advantage to the Trigger when something large is trying to swallow it. The fin can also be used as a wedge when a predator is attempting to pull the Trigger out of a hole. Other fish don't know the secret but anglers long ago learned that the second dorsal fin - - the "trigger" - - can be easily depressed to unlock the bigger one.

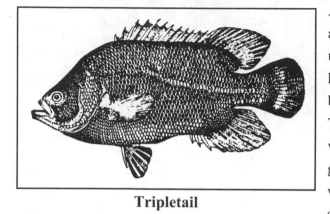

Tripletail

As this picture shows, the Tripletail is appropriately named. The combination of his upper and lower fins and his tail appear to give him three tails. Coloring varies widely, with black, brown and yellow predominant colors. The Tripletail attains a length up to three feet and can weigh over 30 pounds. It is a good eating and great fighting fish. You'll find these guys around wrecks, sunken debris, Stone Crab trap buoys, and channel markers. And you may see them practicing their very own stupid pet trick. For unknown reasons, Tripletail will come to the surface and just float . . on their sides. No one knows why. The Florida record is 32 pounds.

PROVEN TACTICS. Tripletail will hit both live bait and artificials. Shrimp is the hands-down favorite in the live bait department, but Mullet, small Pinfish, and clams will also be accepted once in awhile. One rig for live baiting Shrimp includes the following: an 18 inch, 30# test monofilament leader attached to a barrel swivel; a sliding one ounce egg sinker above the swivel; and a popping cork. The cork is just to help casting and for marking the bait. Don't pop it or you'll scare away Mr. Tripletail.

A Tripletail's choice of artificials is very limited - - bucktail or soft plastic jigs. Hot pink and white bucktails and green twister tail grubs have proven their worth.

YOUR WINNING EDGE . . .

✔ If you suspect a particular channel marker is holding Tripletail, very quietly anchor exactly up-current from it. Very quietly again, cast your live bait or jig right to the marker. Allow the jig to fall straight down against the marker and then, using the current, bounce it in place. In the case of live bait, keep the float right at the marker. In either case, if there's a fish there, you should get it.

There are three kinds of Trout caught in West Coast waters. The first is often called a White Trout although its correct name is Sand Sea Trout. This is a relatively small fish of 10 - 12 inches in length and less than a pound in weight. Its body is pale silver in color without well defined spots. Its upper body has a yellowish tint to it. Because of its feeding habits and food preferences, it's a good fish for young folks to catch. Look for these guys in area bays. They're good to eat.

The second kind of Trout is the Silver Sea Trout. The Silver is the smallest member of the Trout clan, usually weighing a half pound or less. Its back is the color of pale straw, its sides are silvery, its belly white and it has no distinct pigmentation. It comes into area bays during colder months. People, Grouper, Cobia, and others enjoy eating them.

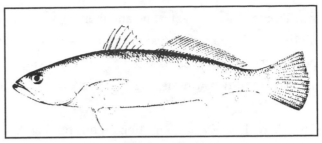

Sand Sea Trout

The king of the Sea Trout is the Spotted Sea Trout. Although he is often incorrectly labeled a Speckled Trout - - and called "Spec" by all his friends - - he does not have an identity problem. This fish has a relatively long, slender body which is dark grey above, with sky blue reflections shading to a silvery color below. The upper part of its body, including the dorsal and caudal fins, is marked with numerous round, black spots. Mature Specs average about four pounds, with lunkers in this area sometimes going over eight. The Florida record for a Spec is 17 pounds 7 ounces. At one time or another during the year, Specs will be up area rivers and creeks, in bays, on flats, in passes, and all over

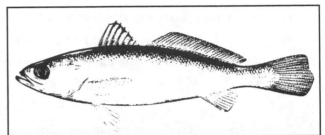

Silver Sea Trout

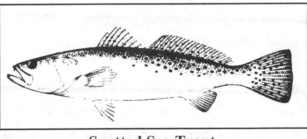

**Spotted Sea Trout
("Spec" or just "Trout")**

mangrove islands. They are delicious eating all kinds of ways - - including as a world-class Trout Almondine. The remainder of this discussion will focus exclusively on Specs.

PROVEN TACTICS: Live bait and artificials work equally well for Trout. In the live bait area, Trout are not picky eaters. Shrimp is a traditional offering that catches large and small fish alike. And in its fresh dead form, Shrimp can also be used to sweeten bucktail jigs, grubs, etc. But Shrimp can be expensive and hard to get at various times during the year. It is also a favorite of lots of other undesirables in West Coast Trout waters. Small fish of various kinds are a good alternative to live Shrimp. Specs are particularly fond of Pinfish, fingerling Mullet, Croakers, and "white bait." Typically, Pilchards, Greenbacks, and Threadfin Herring are included under the white bait umbrella. If you're intent on catching large "gator" Trout, try live fish up to six inches or so.

Rigging to fish live bait is pretty basic. If your line is eight pound test or heavier, you can probably get away with no leader. Tie a 1/0 or 2/0 hook directly to the end of your line for baits up to four inches or so. Trout won't bite your line and their jaws aren't very abrasive. But remember that you'll probably be fishing shared water at some point. A Snook, Tarpon, or whatever, could make fast work of eight pound test. A foot of 20 pound test, attached with a small barrel swivel, provides good insurance. Use 10 pound test if you're fishing four to six pound ultra-light tackle.

There's really only one variation on this rigging theme - - a float or cork of some kind. One approach used on the northern end of the West Coast goes like this. Use what's called a Float-Hi bobber with a fabric tie that allows your line free movement through the float to whatever depth you've chosen. Below the float, string on a ½ oz slip sinker and then tie on a small barrel swivel. Three feet of 20-25# test mono and a hook appropriately sized for your live bait complete the rig. Another, and probably more common approach, is just a plain old popping cork of sufficient size to hold your bait where you want it.

Artificial lures are certainly a viable alternative to live natural baits. As with several other popular gamefish, the numbers and kinds of lures specifically designed to catch Specs are almost mind-boggling. The specific suggestions at the end of this chapter confirm the point. Jigs, grubs, plugs, spoons, and most of what's in your freshwater tackle box will work for Trout. We won't say much more about them except - - a bit of leader isn't a bad idea here, too.

There are some new types of lures on the market that are already proving themselves very effective in West Coast Trout water. Three are worthy of mention here. The first is what Largemouth Bass fishermen have known for years as a "jerkbait." Soft plastic jerkbaits will cast a mile, can be worked fast or slow on the top, middle, or bottom and, because they're nice and squishy, they don't get immediately spit out. Rig a jerkbait Texas style and weedless with a 3/0 or 4/0 worm hook.

The second new type Trout toy is nothing more than a plastic jig (grub) with a float a few inches above it. The float itself is only an inch and a half long. But it makes a commotion in the water which seems to attract Trout. The float also keeps the sinking jig from snagging grass, so it's ideally suited for flats work. Obviously, great variety in plastic tail shape, size, and color is possible on the lead jig head.

The final new lure is called Kalin's Dorky Mullet. No kidding. It's shaped and colored like a relatively small (4 inch) baitfish and is constructed out of salt proof soft plastic. You throw the thing out, it sinks very slowly to a desired depth, and then you retrieve it in slow short jerks to maintain the desired depth. So far, Mr. Dorky Mullet has been deadly on Specs, Reds, and Snook.

YOUR WINNING EDGE . . .

✔ There's no way around it. Go with bigger baits and lures (up to 8") for "gator" Trout.

✔ Make your Zara Spooks more interesting by inserting a modest number of B-B's in them.

✔ Specs are notorious for missing top water lures on their first passes. Help them. Don't move your lure after a missed pass. Just "twitch" it a bit. Also, try attaching a jig, plastic grub, or twister tail to your surface lure via 12 - 18 inches of mono. Tie to the eye of your rear hook.

✔ Try trolling for Trout, particularly in the colder months. Creeks, rivers, and many residential canals can be productive. Soft plastics, spoons, and lipped plugs will all catch fish.

✔ While you're trying things, give lantern fishing on a dark bridge a go. Springtime is a good period. Hang a Coleman gas lantern to within six inches of the water. Natural chum (little fish) will come. Trout and others will, too. Feed them fly lined live Shrimp.

✔ When choosing a top water lure, one West Coast expert believes anything with an orange belly will be effective.

✔ In clear water, reflective chromes are a good color choice for your top water lure. In stained water, green or chartreuse should be tried. On dark days with stained water, go with a frog pattern.

Before leaving Mr. Spec, one caution may be helpful - - if you're a new Trout fisherman. Regardless of whether you are fishing bait or lures for Trout, don't horse a hooked fish. The Trout has a very soft mouth and any undue pressure will cause your hook to pull out. Be gentle but firm.

The Wahoo is a long, slender member of the Mackerel family. It has a long, tubular snout and a mouth full of very wicked teeth. Its body is dark green to steel blue on top, shading to paler silver on its sides. It also usually has narrow grayish yellow bars running vertically on

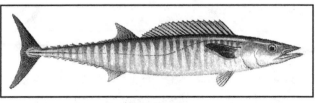

Wahoo

its sides. Wahoo in this area average 15 - 25 pounds, but fish up to 100 pounds are not unheard of. The Wahoo is a tremendous fighter and is reputed to be the fastest fish in the sea. They are delicious eating. The Florida record is currently 139 pounds. You'll find these guys in blue water well Offshore.

PROVEN TACTICS. One of the hot tickets for Wahoo has consistently been large, trolling plugs pulled on downriggers. Offshore lipped favorites include Rapala's CD 18 Magnum series, Bagley's DC-08 Diving Bank-O-B, Rebel's Jaw Breaker and the Mirrolure MR III. Three other unlipped plugs, the Boone Cairns Swimmer, Williamson Lures' Australian Runner and Braid's Flashdancer, also produce good fish. Bait-O-Matic is another family of lures that works very well for Wahoo, as well as for

Dolphin, Marlin and Tuna. The Bait-O-Matic can be used effectively with dead or live bait or without dressing.

Recently, fishermen specifically targeting Wahoo have begun using very specialized tackle and consistent high speed tactics. Seven foot rods and 6/0 or 8/0 reels filled with 316L, 80 pound test stainless wire line are becoming common. Trolling speeds are at least 12 to 15 knots. The wire line is preferred because it slices through the water at fast trolling speeds. It has a quick entry, trolls uniformly, and really sets the hooks because there's no stretch and hardly any belly.

A White Marlin is the smallest member of the Marlin family, with an average weight of 50 - 60 pounds and a maximum of 160 pounds. The upper part of his body is brilliant greenish blue, which changes abruptly to silvery white at about the lateral line. His belly is white. He has light blue or lavender vertical bars on his sides and a bright blue dorsal fin that is spotted with black or purple. White Marlin are common up to about eight feet in length. They are not good to eat. The Florida record for White Marlin is 161 pounds.

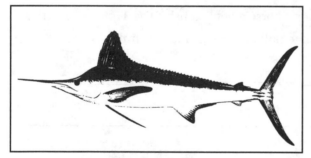

White Marlin

PROVEN TACTICS. The secret to successful White Marlin fishing is finding a temperature break, good water color, and bait - - ideally coincident with some sort of bottom structure. If these conditions are present, the fish usually are, too. But finding them is one thing, getting them to bite is another. White Marlin have a well deserved reputation for "window shopping" before they bite. They will, however, usually strike at almost any kind of bait, including spoons, feathers, whole fish and strip baits. Ballyhoo and Hoochie skirt combinations have proven particularly effective in Offshore West Coast waters. Sevenstrand and/or number 1220 Flying Fish Clones, fished six to nine waves back on an outrigger are a good complement to the skirted baits. Other natural baits, that can be fished either skirted or naked, are swimming Mullet and eels. Most successful White Marlin fishermen also use some form of teaser. Spreader bar natural bait teasers, Hawaiian Eye daisy chains with Ballyhoo, and multi-lure combinations can all contribute to producing a Marlin intent on eating something.

A Whiting is a relatively small (10 - 16 inch) fish that is present in West Coast surf most, if not all, of the year. It's basically silver in color with darker shaded areas running diagonally across its body. As a bottom feeder, its mouth is located under the point of its nose. While relatively small, the Whiting is delicious eating. A giant Whiting might weigh three pounds and a nice average fish about a pound.

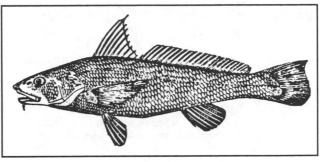
Whiting

PROVEN TACTICS. Whiting are most frequently caught on bait. While they are known to feed on a variety of crabs, shrimp and mollusks, small pieces of fresh dead shrimp are the preferred bait in this area. Both spreader and fish finder rigs work well with hook sizes ranging from one to six.

Another way to catch Whiting is with ultra light spinning tackle and tiny 1/8 oz and 1/4 oz jigs. Four or six lb test line should be used with a 2 ft piece of 20 lb test leader attached on the end via a #12 barrel swivel. Nylon or feather jigs in yellow, white or green all seem to work well. As with Pompano, watch for and cast to these guys in the troughs that parallel the beach. Also, as with Pompano, add a small Sandflea or bit of fresh dead Shrimp to your jig to enhance your success.

The Yellowfin is the most brilliantly colored of the Tunas, with poorly defined golden yellow stripes on its upper sides and a much brighter yellow on its fins. Its lower sides commonly have white spots and vertical streaks. Yellowfins have a traditional Tuna shape and an average weight between 20 and 120 pounds. They're great eating. The Florida record is 230 pounds.

Yellowfin Tuna

PROVEN TACTICS. You never know about Yellowfins in Offshore waters. Sometimes they show up and sometimes they don't. Migrating Yellowfins seem to randomly visit an area, remain for a few days to a week or two to feed, and then vanish.

When Yellowfin are around, daisy chains are an effective way to catch them. Specifically, a group of artificial plastic lures are rigged in series, with a large Tuna hook in the last lure in the chain. Lures strung like this range from standard Marlin lures to soft plastic imitation squids. One variation on this that also works well is to use a stainless steel spreader bar. In this approach, spreader bars are used to trail a pattern of 9 to 11 plastic squids with a hook only in the last lure. The use of birds is another approach to try. A bird, sporting a wing of wood or plastic, is strung in line on the heavy mono leader ahead of the lure. This arrangement simulates a predatory fish chasing a smaller fish that flutters and splashes in front of it. A wide variety of lures can be used behind birds. Regardless of which one you choose, don't overlook the importance of color. The consensus in this area seems to be light and bright. Green, yellow, orange, light blue and hot pink are all popular colors.

OK, that's it for our prey. In the next section, we'll finish off the "how" part of the when-where-how **CATCH FISH NOW!** process. We'll zero in on all the live baits that consistently catch West Coast fish. Then we'll recap and highlight the best of the gazillion artificial lures that are also proven fish catchers. Some suggestions on tackle and a couple of miscellaneous good ideas will close out the chapter.

NATURAL BAITS

By way of introduction, it should be noted that you almost need a scorecard to tell some of the players in the West Coast bait ballgame. Many of the most popular baits have a whole variety of names, some of which are even technically correct. Others aren't. I'll try to clear up some of these identity problems here - - and we'll track them as we progress.

- Glass Minnow - This is not an actual fish species. Rather, it is a generic catch-all name that may include baby Menhaden, Sardines, Threadfin Herring, Sand Perch, etc. On the West Coast, "Glass Minnows" are usually baby Silver and/or Bay Anchovies.

- Menhaden - A specific and distinct member of the Herring family. It is not a "Pilchard."

- Pilchard - A common generic name used (inaccurately) to refer to several different members of the Herring and Sardine families.

- Alewife - Another specific and distinct member of the Herring family. Although it looks like a Menhaden, it isn't one.

- White Bait - A catch-all name that is indiscriminately applied to several different species, including Threadfin Herring and Alewife and other bait fish, very broadly referred to by some as Scaled Sardines and Pilchards.

- Sand Perch - Often incorrectly referred to as Squirrelfish. It isn't one. Mr. Squirrelfish is a separate and distinct species as we'll see at the end of this section.

The next several pages highlight commonly used West Coast live baits. This group, however, isn't an all-inclusive package. There are many other small fish, crab types, and other marine creatures that can and do catch fish. If you have any doubt about something, put it on your hook. You may be delighted with the results. The usual way(s) of getting each bait is highlighted next to each picture. Other alias's are also provided where applicable.

Catch your own with a cast net, Alewife rig, or gold hook rig.

- Great for all area meat eater species - - both for bait and as chum.
- Hook him through the bridge of the nose for both slow trolling and bottom fishing.
- A particular favorite of smoker Kings and gator Trout in the fall.

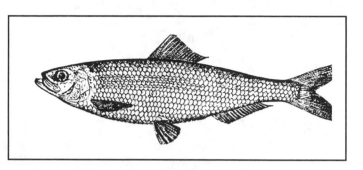

Alewife ("LY")

Balao ("Ballyhoo")

Buy unrigged/rigged frozen Ballyhoo at a bait shop. Catch your own by chumming around reefs and then using a cast net or #10 hooks and tiny bits of shrimp. Hard to find in West Coast waters.

- Superior for Sails, Blackfin, Kings, Barracuda, Wahoo, Dolphin, AJ's, Grouper, and Snapper.
- Neat Rig: Slide a two inch section of soda straw on a piece of 50# mono leader. Tie on a long shank 6/0 hook. Insert hook through the exact center of the bait's lower jaw and out the bottom. Now slip the piece of soda straw over the knot, eye of the hook, and the fish's bill. Slick way to catch a Sail.
- You can also buy a plastic gizmo with hook for fishing Ballyhoo. Bally-Troll and Hoo Nose are two brand names. Rigging a bait is a snap.

Bonito

Catch your own using spoons, jigs, bait, or whatever. They're fun to catch in their own right. Bait shops will often have frozen Bonito for Shark fishermen.

- An important part of a Swordfish's diet. A Blue Marlin usually won't say no either.

- There are a number of ways to rig a Bonito. The easiest is to attach a smaller (3/0 - 4/0) bait hook to a Marlin (11/0) hook with two appropriately sized slip rings. Then hook the bait through the upper lip with the smaller hook.
- Large chunks of Bonito are superior Shark bait due to their oily, bloody, qualities.

You catch your own, usually when you don't want to. Smelly dead Shrimp will get the job done.

- Surprisingly, live Catfish with their three significant spines clipped off are superior for throwing to a Cobia.
- Equally surprising is a Tarpon's interest in Catfish tails fished on the bottom.

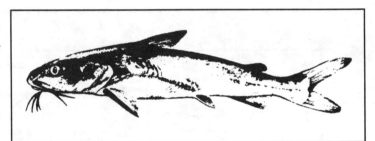
Catfish ("Expletive Deleted")

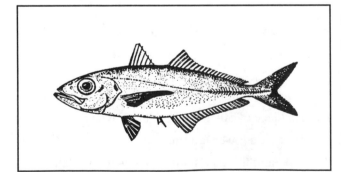
Bigeye Scad ("Goggle-eye Scad," "Goggle-eye Jack")

Catch your own using Sabaki rigs, small jigs, or spoons.

- Excellent bait for Offshore big game - - a particular White Marlin favorite.
- Giant (catch and release) Jewfish think these guys are delicious, too.

Please see the previous Gamefish section for several ways to catch these guys.

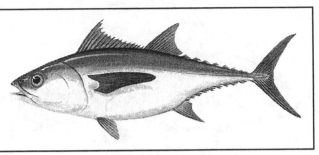

Blackfin Tuna

- A Blackfin is one of the most common items in a Blue Marlin's diet.
- You can always eat your bait if a Marlin doesn't.

Either catch your own using a dip net or trap or buy some live crabs from a seafood store.

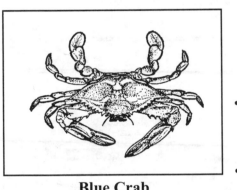

Blue Crab

- Smaller (silver dollar size) crabs are a favorite of Permit, Tarpon, Grouper, Mangrove Snapper, Cobia, and Redfish. To fish this size crab live, insert your hook where the second leg from the back meets the shell - - and rotate the point on out the back.
- On bigger crabs (for bigger fish), use a small hand drill to make a hole by one of the points on either side of the top shell. Rotate your hook through from bottom to top.
- To fish as cut bait (Reds, Pompano, Flounder, Sheepshead, Black Drum), remove the top shell and halve or quarter what's left.

Catch your own, trolling with small jigs, spoons, or Mackerel Trees. Gold hook rigs also work well at the end of a jetty, at the edge of hard bottom, or around markers.

- A great bait for larger fish like Offshore Kings, Cobia, and the entire bluewater crowd.
- Hook him through the bridge of the nose.
- For larger baits (12" and up), consider adding a stinger hook to your rig.
- Runners can be slow trolled effectively either on flat lines or downriggers.

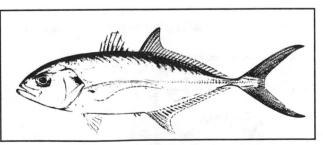

Blue Runner ("Hard Tail")

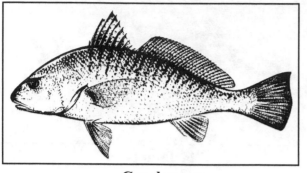
Croaker

Catch your own on the bottom with dead Shrimp for bait and small hooks. You may also get a few when you throw a cast net off a dock or around pilings.

- A superior and consistently effective bait, fly lined for big Trout and Reds, and/or fished on the bottom for Flounder.
- Big Croaker (up to a pound) will also light up a Grouper.

- Hook up through the nose for bottom fishing and just under the skin between the rear dorsal fin and the tail for fly lining.
- Croakers are good to eat.

Some tackle shops stock live eels in season but they're expensive.

- A premier bait for Cobia during their annual migrations.
- It's almost impossible to grab an eel in a bait tank/bucket. So, put them in a cooler on a towel over ice. The ice will make them sluggish and easy to catch. They recover quickly back in the water.

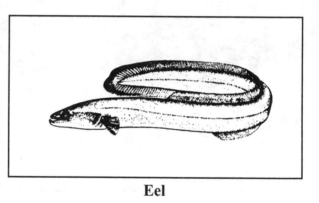
Eel

- Hook an eel through the lips if you want to control its action while throwing to Cobia. For other possibilities (Kings, AJ's, Tarpon, Snook, and Tuna), hook through the eye socket. A multiple hook (stinger) rig works, too.
- A sandy hand makes holding them while baiting up much easier.

Fiddler Crab

Many bait shops sell them live. Catch your own in rotting wood, in rocks and grass at the waterline, or on mud flats.

- Primo Sheepshead and Permit bait. Also effective for Pompano, Reds, Whiting, Black Drum, Mangrove Snapper, and Flounder.

- Hook like a Blue Crab - second leg joint and point rotated out the back.
- Some fishermen believe it's important to break off the male Fiddler's big claw.

Catch your own with small live or cut Shrimp or other cut bait. There are usually lots of them on reefs or rocky areas.

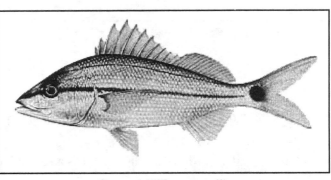
Grunt ("Tomtate")

- Yes, a Grunt does make a "grunt" sound. There are 175 species of them.
- Tomtate is the most prevalent species in West Coast waters.
- Good live for Cobia, Grouper, Amberjack and gator Trout.
- Neat trick: Fillet a good sized (8-10") grunt. Put the whole carcass, hooked through the lips, down on a slip rig for Grouper. You can eat the fillets later. They're delicious.
- Any Grunt you catch, Tomtate or not, will be good live bait.

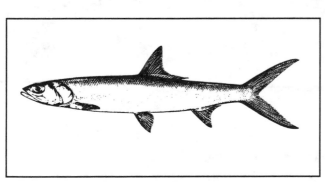
Ladyfish

Catch your own using small jigs, spoons, or imitation minnow plugs. Just off a beach is often productive. You can also chum and use small cut baits. If you're wild and crazy, use live Shrimp to fully enjoy this "poor man's Tarpon."

- A Tarpon won't refuse a Ladyfish; big Snook and Specs love them, and big Ladies are effective for Bull and Blacktip Sharks and Blue Marlin.

- Ideal length is 12" - 18" for Inshore work.
- Hook a Ladyfish in the back behind the dorsal fin to keep it moving around naturally.
- If you're working in a strong current, hook it through the upper lip to keep it aimed right.

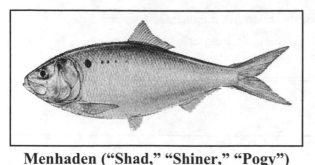

Menhaden ("Shad," "Shiner," "Pogy")

These guys can only be caught with a cast net since they feed on plankton. Watch for schools "ruffling" the water.

- An absolutely superior live, whole dead, or cut bait. Chunked or ground up, the very oily Menhaden is an equally superior chum.

- Menhaden are a "major food group" for almost all species, including Bluefish, Reds, Specs, Swordfish, Tuna, and Kings.
- Hook them through the nose for slow trolling. For bottom fishing, try the nose or just above the anal fin.
- Commercially available Menhaden Oil is an effective chum by itself, an important ingredient in sand or sawdust based chums, and can be sprayed on your lures for a little extra flavor.

Another vegetarian, so a cast net is a must. They can also be caught in a trap, but it's a lot of work. Bait shops usually have frozen Mullet - - sometimes even rigged for Offshore use.

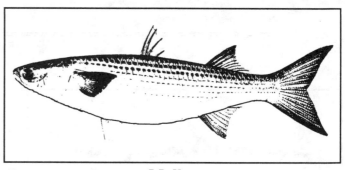

Mullet

- One of the most versatile and effective natural baits.
- In its live form, what a Mullet catches is a function only of its size; i.e., a two inch "fingerling" will catch you a one pound Flounder, while a two foot long "heavy" will entice a 50+ pound "smoker" King.
- Mullet strip baits, particularly when used with a variety of skirts, are great for many Inshore and Offshore species.
- Mullet chunk baits are continuing Tarpon favorites. Use a Mullet head if you're fishing for big Snook on the bottom in a strong current.
- Small (6-8") rigged Mullet are great for the following: Inshore - Tarpon, Snook, Jack Cravalle, and Barracuda; and Offshore - AJ's, Dolphin, Sailfish, Blue Marlin, and Tuna.

Catch them on the bottom with small hooks and cut bait. Gold hook rigs work, too. Some bait shops sell them for about $30 per hundred.

- Another member of the extended Grunt clan.
- Good live bait for bottom fishing. Tarpon and gator Trout are fond of them too.
- Hook them lightly just ahead of the dorsal fin.

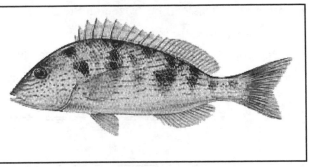

Pigfish

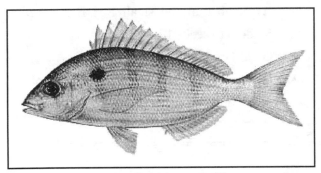

Pinfish ("Choafer")

Some bait shops and marinas have them live. Otherwise, you catch them. Use small hooks, a splitshot, and bits of Shrimp. Traps also work. There are a variety available, including those for freshwater minnows.   Use crab cleanings, catfood, or bread products for bait in your trap.

- A close second to Mullet in the versatility department.

- "Pins" are very hardy and travel well.
- Hook just ahead of the dorsal fin for both fly lining and bottom fishing.
- Pinfish of one size or another are a favorite of about everyone except the exclusive crab eaters.
- They are also a ball for little kids to catch on their Zebcos.

Buy them frozen at many bait shops. You catch your own on the beach. You can buy or make a flea rake that helps. On the beach, watch for tiny V's in the sand as the water recedes into the Gulf. The V's are made by the fleas' antennas. Scoop where you see them, using either your hands, half a minnow trap, or a flea rake.

- Superior for Pompano, good for Permit and Whiting, and will be eaten eagerly by Sheepshead, Black Drum, Reds, and Flounder.

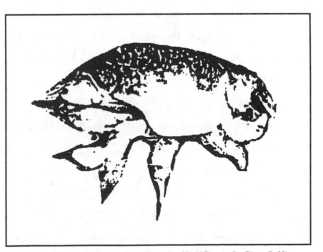

Sandflea ("Mole Crab," "Sand Crab")

- Live Sandfleas can be frozen and reused effectively - - if you dip them in boiling water for five seconds before freezing.
- One good way to hook a flea is up through the V shaped digging flap on his bottom side. Come in from the rear, rotate the hook through his body, and bring the point out aimed to the rear.

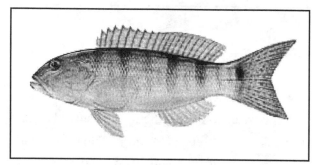
Sand Perch

You catch these guys on almost any sandy bottom using a small hook and any kind of a bottom rig with cut bait.

- A member of the small Sea Bass family. Seldom exceeds 12" in length.
- Great Grouper food.
- Use a slip rig and hook Mr. Perch just ahead of the dorsal fin.

Most bait shops have live Shrimp year round. If you're going to use dead Shrimp, be sure to buy fresh stuff at a seafood market. Frozen Shrimp should only be a last resort.

- Probably the single most commonly used natural bait in Florida waters.
- Live Shrimp will be eaten (one way or another) by everything that swims.
- Most popular place to hook him is where his pointy carapace meets the top of his head. Don't put your hook in the black spot (his brain) just behind that. It will kill him.
- Other ways to hook live Shrimp: 1) break off his tail fin, hook into the tip of the tail, and

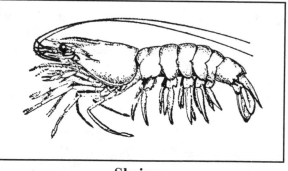
Shrimp

rotate point out the bottom; 2) bigger shrimp - just like #1, but after you've rotated out the bottom, push the hook on through a ways and rotate point back forward and bury it and the barb into the bottom of the tail - - you're now weedless; and 3) pin him up through the head on a jig head.
- My experience suggests fresh dead Shrimp, cut in appropriately sized pieces, is every bit as good for Pompano as Sandfleas.
- Sweeten your jigs and soft plastics with bits of dead Shrimp.

- For what it's worth, when you are using live Shrimp in the wintertime, don't be surprised to see them lying on their sides in your bait bucket. That's a normal reaction to cold. They'll straighten up when you put them on a hook.

You catch Scaled Sardines with gold hook or Sabaki rigs or chum them to you and get 'em with a cast net. Tough to keep alive so don't overcrowd.

- A great bait for almost everyone - - and a fine chum when "injured."
- Hook through the bridge of the nose if you're going to be slow trolling or casting and retrieving.
- If you're bottom fishing at anchor, and there's little or no current, try hooking where the pelvic fin joins the body. This will make your bait spin on the bottom, causing someone to eat it.
- Freeze any bait that dies and reuse later as chum.

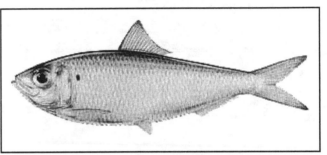

Scaled Sardine ("White Bait")

Catch Silver Trout over Inshore sandy bottoms on bottom rigs, small hooks and bits of cut bait. Heaviest concentrations around during winter months. Max size is around 10 inches.

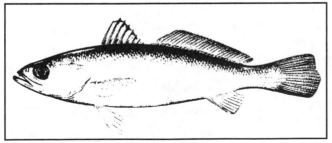

Silver Trout

- Great bait for both top water and bottom feeders.
- Particular favorite of Cobia, Grouper, Amberjack, King Mackerel and Barracuda.
- Red Snapper find Silver Trout irresistible!

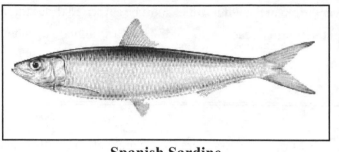

Spanish Sardine

Catch your own with a gold hook rig or with a cast net in shallow water. They often hang out over reefs or around piers.

- Another all-time area favorite - - that's making a good comeback after extensive and indiscriminate commercial netting.
- Can be used effectively live or dead, whole or cut.
- They work well Inshore or Offshore, in bays, off piers, casting, bottom fishing, or top water - - everyone likes Sardines.

Many bait shops carry live Bulls most of the year.

- A Flounder's favorite food. Fish him on a slip rig or sweeten a jig or grub with a small one.
- Specs, Reds, and Mangrove Snapper - - and small Grouper like Bulls, too.

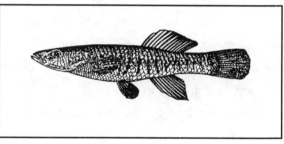

Striped Killifish ("Bull Minnow")

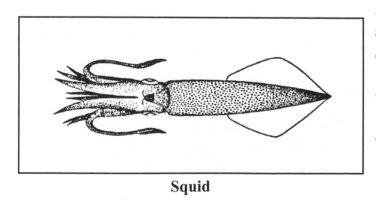

Squid

Although it is possible to catch your own at times, it's a lot easier to buy them - - either fresh or frozen.

- Rigged whole, it's a great bait for Tunas, Marlin, Swordfish, et al.
- Chunks or strips are durable and work well for Flounder, big Pompano, Triggerfish, Black Sea Bass, and Whiting.

You catch 'em with a cast net or gold hook rig. They usually are in tight schools that are visible on the surface. Don't overcrowd, and provide plenty of oxygen.

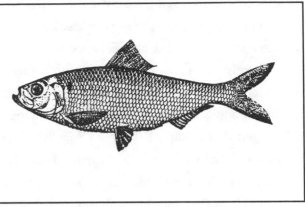

Threadfin Herring ("Greenback," "Greenie")

- A silver-sided, green-backed, five to ten inch cousin of the Menhaden.
- Will consistently catch everything from Snook to smoker Kings.
- Mr. Greenback can be hooked either through the eye socket or up through the lips.

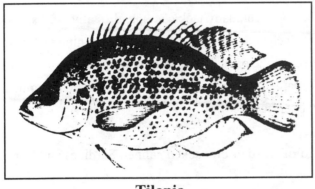

Tilapia

A few bait shops offer these guys live in sizes that are perfect for bait.

- Tilapia is a very clever adaptation by West Coast live bait fishermen.
- Tilapia originated in freshwater on the African continent - - but is now a great saltwater bait for Snook and Tarpon in particular.
- Hook and fish him as you would a Pinfish or Grunt.

MISCELLANEOUS BAIT BITES - Here are some final random thoughts about things in the bait department. They're presented in no particular order.

- Swimming Crabs - They're usually tan in color, 4" maximum in width, and inhabit floating debris. Permit, Cobia, and Grouper love them.
- Pass Crabs - Member of the swimming crab family. They apparently live in area bays most of the year. In late spring/early summer, they migrate out through area passes to spawn in the Gulf. Catch them with a dip net. Tarpon go nuts when these guys go through.
- Shiners - A generic term that, in a saltwater context, may include Pilchards, Mojarra, Scaled Sardines, and/or Greenbacks.

- Cured Shiners - Wild, freshwater baitfish that are caught and put in tanks of saltwater brine for "toughening." They can be purchased from a few area bait shops and are deadly for winter Snook. Slow troll them along channel edges.
- Squirrelfish - A tropical reef fish with big eyes, alternating red and white stripes on his body, and a bit of orange there, too. You catch them on bits of cut Squid in water up to 50 feet, over rocky or coral bottom. A Squirrelfish is a gourmet treat for Blackfin, AJ's, Grouper, Snapper, and Wahoo.
- Rigged Bait Recap - Big whole Squid for Marlin, Wahoo, and Tuna; small whole Squid for bull Dolphin; Ballyhoo for Sails, Dolphin, Tuna, Kings, and Wahoo; and small Mullet for Tarpon, Snook, Jack Cravalle, Barracuda, AJ's, Dolphin, Sails, Blue Marlin, and Tuna.
- Gold Hook Rig - About a 4 foot piece of mono with up to six #8 or 10 gold hooks equally spaced on it. There's a snap swivel on one end and a barrel swivel on the other. It's a buy or make item.
- Sabaki (Bait Chaser) Rig - Similar to a gold hook rig except each small hook has a bit of bright plastic, yarn, quill, etc., on it. You can buy them in different hook sizes and line strengths - - light small hook rigs for Sardines, Cigar Minnows, etc., and heavier rigs for Blue Runners, Goggle Eyes, etc.
- Alewife Rig - This goofy looking thing can be bought at many tackle shops. It really works. The rig consists of a 2 foot piece of red yarn with a 4 inch wide piece of mono netting running its length. A small sinker is on one end and a barrel swivel on the other. To operate the rig, you just lower it into the water and that's it. The Alewife are apparently curious about the yarn, come to examine it, and get their heads caught in the net. Stupid, but effective.
- Chum/Chumming
  - For bait: Canned Jack Mackerel and a loaf of bread or oil packed canned Sardines and brown bread. Fish based cat food is an alternative.
  - Store bought: Many bait shops sell blocks of frozen chum for reasonable prices (i.e., seven pounders for $5).
  - Do It Yourself: 1) Pound of whole wheat flour, pound of yellow cornmeal, 10 ounce box of cracker meal, and a jar of anise seed. Mix Menhaden Oil into this stuff till damp; 2) Menhaden Oil which you buy for about $14 a gallon and dispense with a squirt bottle; 3) Grind up any kind of bait fish you catch and/or carcasses from oily gamefish (Kings, Spanish) - - freeze mix in cardboard milk cartons; and 4) Menhaden Oil mixed with sinking catfish food in pellet form (buy at a feed store).
  - For Trout: On the flats, use "crippled" live White Bait.
  - Sandballs: Use for Yellowtail Snapper. Mix thawed frozen ground chum with masonry sand, oats, canned corn, and cooked macaroni. Tie a #1 hook on the end of your line with a small egg sinker running free above it. Put a piece of Ballyhoo, fresh Bonito, Squid, Cigar Minnow, or whatever on your hook. Make a fish sized "sandball" around your bait and wrap the bottom few inches of your line around it. Lower the whole mess to the bottom.

- Crushed oysters/barnacles: Sheepshead, Permit, Pompano, Black Drum, and Redfish.
- Tactics: 1) When anchored on a reef, hang chum bags at different levels (i.e., bottom for reef dwellers, 10 feet below the surface for pelagic; 2) When you've had a bag on the bottom, try raising it slowly to the surface - - fish will often follow it up; and 3) try chunking bait fish while drifting. After a bit, put your hook in one of the chunks. This works great for Blackfins, among others.
- Tube Worms: Another name for Blood Worms. These are imported from the Northeast US coast and work great for Sheepshead and other bottom dwellers.
- Neat Idea: Use food coloring to add color to your live and dead baits. Green and red colors seem to work well in clear water, yellow in murky water. For live baits like Menhaden, add a few drops of food coloring to saltwater in a gallon bag and drop in a few baits. Take them out 15 seconds later and put them on your hooks. Five minutes is a good soak time for whole or cut dead baits.

So much for natural baits. We'll now close out this section with an admittedly cursory overview of artificials that have been proven performers on Florida's West Coast. As in other parts of Florida, and the world for that matter, imagination and experimentation are the keys to success in selection of lures. The guys who consistently catch the most and biggest fish on artificials are usually the guys who aggressively pursue new and better ways to convince their target that it really does want to eat a piece of plastic, lead or Mylar.

ARTIFICIAL BAITS

At the outset, a couple of observations are probably appropriate to introduce the subject of artificial lures. First, a reasonably competent and knowledgeable fisherman can probably catch about 80 percent of available gamefish species using about four or five basic types of lure. My vote would go to bucktail jigs, spoons, top water plugs, diving plugs and, perhaps, feathers for Offshore work. Having said that however, the second observation has to be that fishermen believe they must stay on the leading edge of lure technology to have any chance at success. Are these observations contradictory? Perhaps. But they do provide a reasonably accurate explanation for the incredible proliferation of lure styles, sizes, colors, smells, features, and alleged/demonstrated performance characteristics.

One way to deal with the ambiguity inherent in these observations is to adopt a simple principle. The principle says that if a particular lure has or does work for you or you believe it has for others - - then use it. With that in mind, let's take a look at some representative families of currently popular artificials that have proven, credible, performance records. Following the pictures, we'll close out this section with an incredibly busy, but hopefully useful, matrix - - highlighting West Coast favorites in the lure department. Just remember as we fish through this subject, it is more than likely that everything in your freshwater tackle box will work just fine for saltwater gamefish.

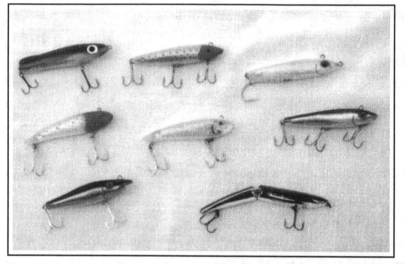

Twitch Baits

Targets - Specs, Reds, Snook, Tarpon, Bluefish.
Popular Brands - Mirrolure, Bagley, Bomber, Mann's, Kalin's Rapala, and Rebel.

Most twitch baits are effective when retrieved with short twitches or long sweeps of the rod. Quick, short twitches produce a frantic action that imitates a wounded baitfish, while long deliberate sweeps create sonic vibrations and action that call in predatory gamefish. This is a versatile type lure that allows you to vary retrieval rates and action to adjust to various water conditions.

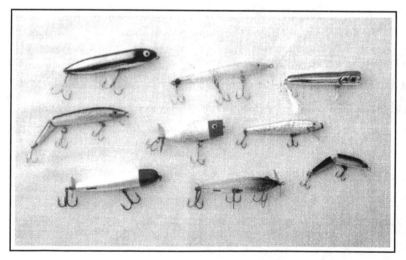

Top Water

Targets - Specs, Bluefish, Spanish Mackerel, Snook, Reds, Tarpon.
Popular Brands - Heddon, Mirrolure, Sosin, ZZ Top, Rebel, Rapala, Creek Chub, and Storm.

There are a number of types of good top water lures available. Stick baits can be made to walk along the surface with an erratic, darting action that makes them ideally suited for the shallows. Prop baits use counter - rotating spinner blades to create a surface commotion that imitates injured baitfish. Poppers deliver a special action, surface gurgle, splash, and ring-like ripple that provoke strikes when fished with a twitch - and - stop retrieve.

Spoons

Targets - Specs, Reds, Bluefish, Flounder, Spanish, Cero Mackerel, Snook, and all kinds of Jacks.

Popular Brands - Clark, Gator, Mann's, Johnson, Krocodile, Hopkins, Big Fish, Tony Accetta, Kastmaster, Cotee, and Love Lures.

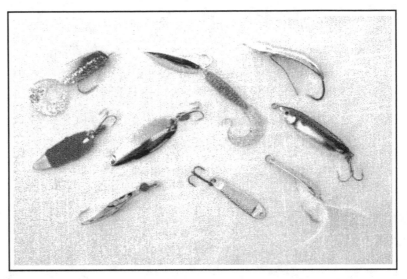

As one of the oldest and most versatile artificials, a spoon is simplicity itself. There are basically two types, fixed single hook and free swinging treble hook. Until recently, about the only additional feature available was a weed-guard on some single hook models. Today, there are several new versions to choose from. One offers a way to "screw on" a twister tail or other kind of soft plastic grub. A second provides a way to thread the same kind of grub on the spoon's primary hook. Another new variant uses a snap-on conformal plastic rattler that can be moved from spoon to spoon. A variety of feathers have always been an option on many traditional spoon models.

Crank Baits

Targets - Specs, Redfish, Jack Cravalle, Spanish, Cero Mackerel, Bluefish.

Popular Brands - Rat-L-Trap, Mirrolure, Rebel, Rapala, Bagley, Bomber, and Cordell.

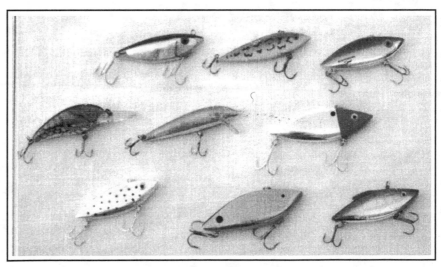

There are fundamentally two kinds of crankbaits. One relies on some sort of a lip to dive and wiggle from side to side. The other relies only on hydrodynamic shape as its dive and wiggle mechanism. Both work well in appropriate conditions and suitable applications.

Soft Plastics

Targets - Flounder, Specs, Reds, Snook, Tarpon, Pompano, Permit.
Popular Brands - Culprit, Kalin's, Berkley, DOA, Bass Assassin, Cotee, Mann's, and Bass Pro Shop.

Mind boggling is the only appropriate adjective for this family of fish catchers. The word "overwhelming" also comes to mind when considering the number of shapes, sizes, colors, tastes, smells, and combinations that are available. And the soft plastic part is only half the story. The jig heads that attach to many offer great variety too - - in terms of weight, color, shape, and noise making ability. Probably the best suggestions in the soft plastics area are blinding glimpses of the obvious. Keep your ears and eyes open for combinations that work - - and don't hesitate to experiment.

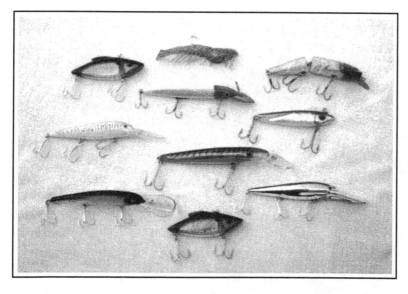

Miscellaneous Inshore/Offshore

Targets - King Mackerel, Tarpon, Dolphin, Cobia, Barracuda, Blackfin Tuna, Wahoo, Grouper, and Jack Cravalle.
Popular Brands - Creek Chub, Cordell, Mirrolure, Bomber, Rebel, Rapala, Bagley, Williamson, Boone Cairns, Tony Accetta, and Storm.

As you can tell from this photo, size is the single biggest difference between deep water and shallow water hardware. The examples in the photo tell the story. Classic shapes and styles work regardless of where you're fishing or what you intend to catch.

Figure 6.0 wraps up this section with an overview of proven West Coast artificials.

West Coast Gamefish	Proven Artificials
Amberjack	Very large plastic grubs/twister tails, hair/feather jigs, large jointed plugs.
Barracuda	Imitation minnow plugs, orange and chartreuse tube lures, spoons, chuggers.
Black Drum	Clark and other small spoons, plastic grubs, and jigs (occasionally).
Black Sea Bass	Small grubs, twister tails, or grubs of any color, silver spoons, small plastic worms.
Blackfin Tuna	No-Alibi and California feathers, bubble making softheads, erratic swimming HALCO Tremblers, Tuna Tango's, Clark spoons, rubber squid skirts, small hexheads, Tuna Clones and Zukers, any plug that resembles a Ballyhoo.
Bluefish	Tony Accetta Pet Spoons, yellow Ragmops, tube lures, surface and diving plugs, jigs.
Blue Marlin	Softheads, C&H, Snider (large), Reto's Rigs, Boone's Airheads R&S small Teardrops, rubber squid, #1400 Sevenstrand Konaheads, Kona Klones, The Spooler (Moldcraft), Island Black Hole and Sea Star, Fat Boy family.
Bonito	Almost anything in your tackle box. Chrome jigs with squid skirts are deadly.
Cobia	1 - 3 oz hair jigs, soft plastic eels, other swimming soft plastics, large swimming plugs, jig/plastic worm combos, DOA plastic crabs.
Dolphin	Baby Dusters, small feathers, Moldcraft Hookers, Dolphin Jr's and Sr's, Jelly Bellies, Boone Sea Minnows, bucktail jigs, most of the small and medium size Marlin lures, Magnum Rapalas, Mann's Stretch 25+, Bagley DB0 10.
Flounder	Small jigs, soft plastic grubs and twister tails, small gold spoons, small deep running imitation minnow plugs, 1/4 oz Bubba jig with 3" glitter twister tail and similar combos.
Grouper —	One oz jig heads with clear silver metalflake and rootbeer twister tails, jigs, big spoons (Accetta, Capt. Action), DOA Bait Buster Mullet in gold glitter, Big Mirrolures (111, 113MR, 116), Rapalas, and Bombers, 1/3 and 3/4 oz Rat-L-Traps in blue chrome and black shad. Yo Ho Ho and Sea Strike metal jigs in mackerel colors, 103 and 113 series Mirrolures.
Jack Cravalle	Top water chugger plugs, bucktail jigs, spoons, Cordell Spots, 85 M Mirrolures, Zara Spooks.
King Mackerel	17 series Bombers, metal King Getters, Accetta spoons, Cordell Spots, dusters, Cisco Kids, Rapala CC-18, Depth Raiders, Clark spoons, all kinds of jigs with plastic worm sweeteners.
Permit	White jig head and half a white plastic grub tail (sweetened with a live shrimp), DOA Crab, a number of flies, skimmer jigs in white, yellow, and pearl.
Pompano	1/4 and 3/8 oz beige jig heads with yellow, white, hot pink, and orange skirts, dark green and red and yellow Cotee jigs (all work better with a small flea or bit of shrimp as a sweetener).
Redfish —	Soft plastic jerk baits (Berkley Sand Worms, 6" Slug-Go, Bass Assassin Shad, Cotee, Reel Magic) gold weedless spoons 5M, 7M, and 28M Mirrolures, 12-Fathom Phantom, plastic grubs/twister tails, Cordell Spots, crank baits (fire tiger), Dorky Mullet.
Sailfish	Moldcraft Softhead Hookers and Birds, Tony Accetta Jelly Bellies, Arbogast Reto's Rigs, Boone Airheads, rubber squids.
Sheepshead	Small jigs and flies (occasionally).
Snapper —	(Mangrove) crappie jigs, 7M Mirrolures, small 4" floating Rebels and Rapalas.

West Coast Gamefish	Proven Artificials
Snook	5M, 7M, and 97MR Mirrolures, Bomber Long A, Ratl Stick, Goldeneyes, Snook Stomper, black and silver Magnum Rapala, Boone Castana, all kinds of jerk baits, Cisco Kid, DOA Shrimp, Dalton Special, Hellraiser, Jerkin Sam, all kinds of plastic grubs/shad twister tails.
Spanish Mackerel	Clark spoons, Floreo jigs, Mackerel Trees, Straw Rigs, Gator Spoons, Rat-L-Traps, Rebels, and Rapalas.
Swordfish	Unknown.
Tarpon	DOA Jumbo Shrimp, 4 inch twister tail grubs, 12-fathom Tarpon Taker, Culprit Shrimp, Coon Pop breakaway, Zara Spooks, soft plastic jerk baits, 82MR12 and 72M22 Mirrolures, Bomber Finger Mullet, bucktails, DOA Terror Eyz, bucktail jigs, Storm Threadfin Minnow.
Triggerfish	Small jigs tipped with squid or shrimp (occasionally).
Tripletail	Small jigs with plastic twister tail sweeteners, bucktails (hot pink is a good color).
Trout	Rapala, Rebel, Bomber Long-A, floating Rat-L-Traps, 28M and 5M Mirrolures, Bang-O-Lure SP-5, Devil Horse, Zara Spooks, Rebel Pop-R, Kalin's Dorky Mullet, Bagley Finger Mullet, plastic grubs and twister tails, Berkley Power Popper, Boone needlefish, gold spoons.
Wahoo	Deep trolled terminator black and red No-Alibi with Ballyhoo, Magnum Rapala, Mann's Stretch 25+, Rebel Jawbreaker, Bagley DBO 10, R&S Tuna Dart, Mini Dart, C&H Wahoo Whacker.
White Marlin	Hoochie skirt with Ballyhoo, Sevenstrand or No. 1220 Flying Fish Clone, Rito's Rigs, Boone Airhead, R&S small Teardrops.
Whiting	Jigs
Yellowfin Tuna	Spreader bars with 9-11 plastic squid or birds ahead of bright skirted plastics, Magnum Rapalas, feathers.

Figure 6.0 - Proven (and Popular) Artificials

TACKLE SUGGESTIONS

The tackle used effectively in the water along the West Coast is as diverse as the kinds of fish that can be caught. Some suggestions are presented below for each of the major types of fishing available to area fishermen.

For most species in the surf, light freshwater - type tackle works just fine. Rods from five to seven feet in length and either spinning, closed face, or bait casting reels are more than adequate for fishing the troughs. Eight to ten pound test line is about right for Pompano, Flounder, Sheepshead, and Whiting. The same kind of tackle works great in area bays for Trout, Mangrove Snapper, and Pompano.

Slightly heavier surf tackle may be in order if you intend to pursue Bluefish, Redfish, Spanish or Snook. For these, rods to nine or more feet, open faced spinning reels, and twelve to fifteen pound test line are about right. This kind of outfit will permit the longer casts necessary, while having the extra power to effectively fight these larger fish.

Regardless of the kind of fish you're after, a sand spike is almost a necessity in surf fishing. Most are nothing more than a piece of large diameter plastic pipe with a point on one end. They're cheap to buy or make and infinitely useful to hold your rod and reel while you're baiting up, changing lures, or waiting for a bite.

For pier fishing, and depending on the kinds of fish you're after, two different kinds of tackle are required. If you intend to fish in the surf close to the beach (Pompano, Whiting, Flounder, etc.), think light. Bait casting and fresh water spinning gear with six to ten pound test line is ideal. If you intend to fish farther out (King Mackerel, Cobia, etc.), heavier equipment is in order. A medium action, seven to nine foot spinning rod and a large dependable spinning reel, loaded with at least three to four hundred yards of fresh fifteen to twenty five pound test line, are essential. Many bait shops and piers in the area have this kind of tackle available at reasonable rental rates.

Light tackle with eight to twelve pound test line is about right for catching Trout, Reds, Flounder, Snapper, Sheepshead, etc., in the area's bays, rivers and sounds. Ultra light tackle with four to six pound test line is also a lot of fun for catching these guys. If you intend to go for bigger game (Cobia, Kings, Jack Cravalle, etc.), you'll want to use much stouter equipment. For these guys, two different setups are required. To successfully land a Jack, for example, you'll want to use a six to seven foot, medium action spinning rod matched with an open faced spinning reel sufficiently large to hold two hundred to three hundred yards of twenty to forty pound test line. Your reel must have a smooth, fully functional drag. For the giant Black Drum that inhabit the area, an Inshore bottom fishing setup is about right. A five to six foot medium action rod paired with a well maintained 4/0 reel with at least two hundred yards of thirty pound test line will give both you and the fish a chance.

Tackle for Tarpon, regardless of where you find them, varies considerably between fishermen. Much of the diversity is a function of how the fish are being pursued. Here are a few of the combinations in common usage:

- Rods in the 6 to 8 foot range with roller or ceramic guides. Reels like the 3/0 or 4/0 Penn, filled with 50 or 80 pound test Dacron line (Boca Grande Guides Association).
- Seven foot spinning rod and reel holding 300 yards of 12 pound test mono (bottom fishing dead bait in protected water).
- Six to eight foot rod and revolving spool reel filled with 250 to 300 yards of 30-50# mono (bridge, pier, boat in close quarters).

- A variation of the previous combination substitutes 36 or 45 pound test braided squidding line for the monofilament (traditional beach rig).

Regardless of where and how you intend to go after Mr. Tarpon, your reel must have a drag that is absolutely smooth and fully functional. You'll lose every time if it isn't.

If you're going to try all the kinds of fishing available Inshore and you want to maximize your sport in the process, you will need up to four rod and reel combinations. These are summarized below:

- King Mackerel, Bonito, Blackfin Tuna, and perhaps a stray Wahoo. Effective trolling for these fish requires a five to six and a half foot glass, fiberglass or graphite boat rod. It should have a medium or heavy action, since you may be pulling planers or large diving plugs from time to time. Roller rod guides are a good feature but not critical to success. The rod should be rated for somewhere between twenty and fifty pound test line. Your reel should be a well lubricated 6/0, loaded with at least two hundred fifty to three hundred yards of fresh, quality, line. The reel's drag must be fully functional and absolutely smooth during operation. For this kind of trolling, successful fishermen usually set their strike drag tension at approximately one-quarter of the rated strength of their line.

- Inshore bottom fishing - A five to six foot, medium action, rod, rated for fifteen to thirty pound test line is about right for this kind of fishing. It should be paired with a well maintained 4/0 reel with at least a two hundred yard line capacity. As an aside, many successful bottom fishermen prefer medium weight spinning tackle for this kind of fishing. That's because this kind of tackle is usually a lot lighter and has a much more rapid retrieve.

- Casting for Cobia - Distance and precision are the name of this game. Accordingly, a six to seven foot medium action (1-3 oz lures) spinning rod works well. It should be matched with an open faced spinning reel sufficiently large to hold two hundred to three hundred yards of twenty to forty pound test line. Use of line in the lower end of this range absolutely requires a smooth, fully functional drag.

- Casting for Dolphin - At various times, tide lines, and weed lines, form Inshore. Schoolie Dolphin take up residence and the fun begins. Break out your light spinning gear, with six to twelve pound test line and have the thrill of a lifetime.

- Offshore - Although tackle requirements for Offshore trolling are almost open ended, they don't have to be. Unless you're independently wealthy, requirements can be constrained by focusing on the area you plan to fish. Many local area fishermen, for example, specialize in mid-range trolling. Lighter tackle can be used in this area, with thirty pound class gear quite adequate for all but the biggest fish. Targets of interest would include Dolphin, Wahoo, White Marlin, Sailfish, and Blackfin Tuna. For bottom fishing, your tackle should be relatively heavy. A popular combination includes a seven to seven and a half foot solid glass rod, a 6/0 reel loaded with one hundred pound test line (either mono or Dacron). Because up to twenty oz sinkers are often required, some fishermen use electric motors on their reels. And then, there's Blue Marlin tackle . . . for a mere $1,500 or so, you, too, can own a nice seven foot Murry Brothers "Master" series big game trolling rod and a Penn International 130ST two speed reel. The price does not include the cost of 950 yards of 130# test line required to fill the reel. Oh well . . .

CONCLUSION

That just about wraps up our extended fishing trip down Florida's West Coast. Geographically, we only covered about 240 air miles between Cedar Key and Naples. But, from a fisherman's perspective, we did much more. In one way or another, we fished our way down several thousand square miles of the best saltwater sportfishing water in the world. That's not an exaggeration. Florida's West Coast is a fishy place indeed. Every bay, pass, stretch of surf, oyster bar, river channel and tributary creek more than likely holds fish. The real problem in fishing the West Coast is simply choosing which of an almost unlimited number of alternatives to pursue on any given day. I sincerely hope this book will help you in your selection process because - - the big ones are out there waiting . . . for you! Good luck.

-- PERSONAL NOTES --

FLORIDA SALTWATER
RULES AND REGULATIONS

The following information has been tailored to fishing and related activities on Florida's West Coast. State waters in this area extend nine miles out into the Gulf of Mexico and State rules and regulations apply. Beyond nine miles, federal regulations are in effect. A table of applicable federal size and bag limits is provided at the end of this appendix.

Before beginning this summary, a word of caution to the reader is important. Florida saltwater fishing rules and regulations have been and continue to be dynamic in nature. Sometimes, the rules change with almost no advance warning. Therefore, although the material contained in this appendix is current now, that may not be true a week or month from now. Smart fishermen monitor the rules closely over time - - and avoid nasty surprises from our friendly Florida Marine Patrol!

Who needs a saltwater fishing license? Almost everybody who wants to catch saltwater fish. But there are exceptions. The following citizens do not need a license.

- Anyone under 16 years of age (both resident and non resident).
- Any Florida resident fishing from land or a structure fixed to the land (pier, bridge, dock, floating dock, jetty, or similar structure).
- Anyone fishing from a boat that has a recreational vessel saltwater fishing license (West Coast party, charter, and guide boats almost always have one).
- Any Florida resident 65 years old or older.
- Anyone fishing from a pier that has been issued a pier saltwater fishing license (West Coast area piers that charge an entrance fee have the required license).
- Any Florida resident who is a member of the Armed Forces, not stationed in Florida, and home on leave for 30 days or less (your leave paper is required proof).

Who is considered a Florida Resident?

- Anyone who has continuously resided in the state for six months (owning, paying taxes on, and/or periodically occupying a second/vacation home or rental property does not satisfy the requirement).

- Anyone who has established a domicile in Florida and who has met the requirements of such law.
- Anyone enrolled in a college or university in the state.

Where can I buy a license? How much do they cost?

- Any county tax collector's office and almost all bait and tackle stores sell licenses.
- Resident licenses: 10 day for $10, one year for $12, and five years for $60.
- Non-resident licenses: Three day for $5, seven day for $15, and one year for $30.
- A tax collector's office adds a service charge of $1.50 to all licenses, commercial establishments add $1.

ADDITIONAL IMPORTANT POINTS

Are there any saltwater fish I can't catch and keep?

- It is against the law to harvest, possess, land, purchase, sell or exchange the following fish: Jewfish, Sawfish, Sawshark, Basking Shark, Whale Shark, Spotted Eagle Ray and Sturgeon.

Are there rules about tackle and fishing line?

- Yes. To help avoid entangling and injury of people as well as marine and shore life, hook-and-line gear must be tended at all times. It is against the law to intentionally discard any monofilament netting or line into or onto the waters of the State of Florida. Monofilament line can and does entangle birds, marine mammals, marine turtles, and other marine life, killing or injuring them.

Is it OK to use some kinds of traps?

- Yes. Traps may be used for recreational purposes for Stone Crab, Blue Crab, Shrimp, Pinfish and Black Sea Bass, pursuant to the appropriate regulations.

What's the penalty for fishing without a license?

- Fifty dollars plus the cost of the applicable license or stamp.

Speaking of licenses, are there any special requirements associated with Tarpon or Snook fishing?

- Yes. A $50 special tag is required to kill or possess a Tarpon. "Harvesting" Snook requires a $2 Snook Permit.

What's the law on displaying a "Diver Down" flag?

- Absolutely mandatory whenever you (or your kids regardless of age) are diving or snorkeling. For all kinds of very valid reasons, the Marine Patrol aggressively enforces this rule.

Are treble hooks still legal for catching gamefish?

- Yes and No. Yes for all fish except Redfish, Black Drum, Pompano, and Trout. Treble hooks cannot be used with any kind of live or dead bait to catch these four species.

What are Florida size and bag limits?

- They're summarized in Figure A-1. Only species that have restrictions associated with them are shown in the figure.

Fish	Min. Size (fork)	Min. Size (overall)	Max. Size (overall)	Daily Bag Limit
Amberjack	28 in.			1
Black Drum (1)		14 in.	24 in.	5
Black Sea Bass		8 in.		
Bluefish	12 in.			10
Blue Marlin (3)	86 in.			
Cobia	33 in.			2
Dolphin				
Flounder	12 in.			10
Grouper (4)		20 in.		5
King Mackerel	20 in.			2
Permit (2)	10-20 in.			10 aggregate of Permit and Pompano
Pompano (2)	10-20 in.			10 aggregate of Permit and Pompano
Redfish		18 in.	27 in.	1
Sailfish (3)	57 in.			
Sheepshead	12 in.			15
Snapper (Lane) (5)		8 in.		
Snapper (Gray, Black, Mangrove) (5)		10 in.		5
Snapper (Mutton) (5)		16 in.		10

Fish	Min. Size (fork)	Min. Size (overall)	Max. Size (overall)	Daily Bag Limit
Snapper (Vermillion Mingo)(5)		10 in.		
Snapper (Queen, Blackfin, Dog, Mahogany, Silk, Yellowtail) (5)		12 in.		10
Snapper (Red) (5)		16 in.		5
Snapper (Schoolmaster) (5)		10 in.		10
Snook (6)	24 - 34 in.			2
Spanish Mackerel	12 in.			10
Tarpon				2
Triggerfish (Gray)		12 in.		
Tripletail	15 in.			2
Trout (Speckled) (7) Pasco County North Pinellas County South		15 in. 15 in.	24 in. 20 in.	7 5
White Marlin (3)	62 in.			

Figure A-1 State Size and Bag Limits

Notes

Blanks in the figure indicate no applicable specific limit. The numerical coding in the figure is explained below.

(1)   One fish in the bag may be over 24 inches.

(2)   Ten fish aggregate limit between 10 and 20 inches. One may be over 20 inches.

(3)   Possession limit is one billfish (Blue Marlin, White Marlin, Sailfish or Spearfish). Length is measured from tip of lower jaw to fork of tail. It is illegal to buy or sell billfish.

(4)   Minimum size applies to Black, Red, Gag, Scamp, Yellowmouth and Yellowfin Grouper; bag and possession to all Groupers in the aggregate, except one Warsaw Grouper and one Speckled Hind per boat may be taken in addition to the aggregate limit. Nassau Grouper and Jewfish are closed to harvesting.

(5)   Aggregate limits on Snapper are 10/day. However, not more than 5/day may be Gray/Black/Mangrove. Not more than 5/day and 4 in the aggregate may be Red. Lane and Vermillion (Mingo) Snappers are exempt from bag limits.

(6)   One fish may be over 34 inches. Snook season is closed Dec 15 - Jan 31 and the months of June, July, and August. A $2 Snook stamp is required to harvest fish in open season.

(7) One fish may be over the maximum size. Spec season is closed from Pasco County north in February and from Pinellas County south in November and December.

(8) A $50 tag is required to kill or possess a Tarpon.

FEDERAL

There are significantly fewer restrictions imposed in Federal rather than State waters. Those relevant to Florida's West Coast are summarized in the following figure.

Fish	Min. Size (fork)	Min. Size (overall)	Bag Limit
Amberjack	28 in.		1
Cobia	33 in.		2
Grouper (1)		20 in.	5
King Mackerel	20 in.		2
Spanish Mackerel	12 in.		10
Blue Marlin (2)	86 in.		
White Marlin (2)	62 in.		
Sailfish (2)	57 in.		
Sea Bass (Black)		8 in.	
Snapper (Lane and Vermillion)		8 in.	
Snapper (Red)		16 in.	5
Snapper (other) (3)		12 in.	10
Swordfish (4)	20 in. or 33#s	41 lbs.	
Yellowfin Tuna	27 in.		

Figure A-2 - Federal Size and Bag Limits

<u>Notes</u>

(1) Minimum size applies to Black, Gag, Red, Yellowfin and Nassau Groupers; bag limit to all Groupers in the aggregate.

(2) Blue and White Marlin, Sailfish and Spearfish may not be sold.

(3) Minimum size applies to Gray, Mutton and Yellowtail Snappers; bag limit to all Snappers in the aggregate, excluding Red, Lane and Vermillion.

(4) Swordfish minimum weight is measured with the fish dressed and head and tail removed.

DON'T MISS ...

the rest of the CATCH FISH NOW! series

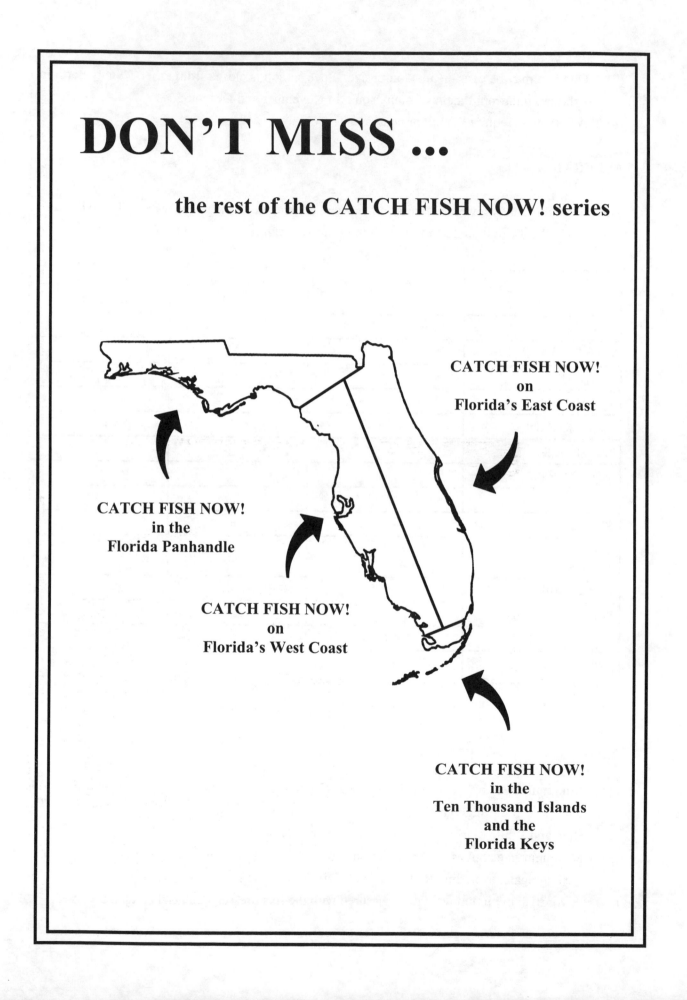

CATCH FISH NOW!
on
Florida's East Coast

CATCH FISH NOW!
in the
Florida Panhandle

CATCH FISH NOW!
on
Florida's West Coast

CATCH FISH NOW!
in the
Ten Thousand Islands
and the
Florida Keys

ABOUT THE AUTHOR. . .

Mike Babbidge is a former Air Force Officer, aerospace industry executive, and independent consultant to the defense community. He has also been a life-long saltwater fishing fanatic. This has led to hands-on fishing experience in the central and south Atlantic, Caribbean Sea, Gulf of Mexico, Gulf of California, U.S. and Mexican Pacific coastal and Offshore waters, Hawaii, and the South China Sea. In recent years, Mike has published numerous articles on Florida saltwater fishing. He is also the author of the best-selling **CATCH FISH NOW!** *in the Destin Area*, and **CATCH FISH NOW!** *in the Florida Panhandle*.

ABOUT THE AUTHOR'S WIFE. . .

Sherry Babbidge is a licensed Realtor with over twelve years' experience and a multi-million dollar sales record. She specializes in waterfront/gulf-front properties, including single family residences and condominiums. The Gulf coast and waterfront communities of Destin, Ft. Walton Beach, South Walton County, and Niceville are particular specialities. For coastal properties throughout the rest of Florida, just call and she can refer you to a Realtor in your area. Put her enthusiasm, experience and referral network to work for you! Please call 800-862-1662+1662.

-- PERSONAL NOTES --

DISCARD